Investigating Sociological Theory

'In this authoritative and strikingly original book, Charles Turner demonstrates that sociological theory far from being some dry, boring meta-discourse of society is an ethically engaged enterprise, intimately connected to the arts of living in the contemporary world. Accessible to both students and seasoned practitioners, this book is at once a terrific defenvce and itself an elegant example of the continuing relevance and intellectual vitality of sociological theory. Turner's brilliant discussion thoroughly deserves to resonate across the discipline of sociological theory in both its European and north American versions.'
Thomas Osborne, University of Bristol

Investigating Sociological Theory

Charles Turner

Los Angeles | London | New Delhi
Singapore | Washington DC

SAGE Publications Ltd
1 Oliver's Yard
55 City Road
London EC1Y 1SP

SAGE Publications Inc.
2455 Teller Road
Thousand Oaks, California 91320

SAGE Publications India Pvt Ltd
B 1/I 1 Mohan Cooperative Industrial Area
Mathura Road, Post Bag 7
New Delhi 110 044

SAGE Publications Asia-Pacific Pte Ltd
33 Pekin Street #02-01
Far East Square
Singapore 048763

Library of Congress Control Number: 2009930424

British Library Cataloguing in Publication data

A catalogue record for this book is available from the British Library

ISBN 978-1-84920-374-6
ISBN 978-1-84920-375-3 (pbk)

Typeset by C&M Digitals (P) Ltd, Chennai, India
Printed in India by Replika Press Pvt Ltd
Printed on paper from sustainable resources

Contents

Acknowledgements

This book has been a long time coming and even now its results feel provisional. Had it not been for several people they would be more so; firstly, life in today's university would be less rewarding were it not for students who either say things that surprise you or force you to think more clearly. Over the years there have been several who have contributed, often in ways of which they are not aware, to what I have written here. They are Jody Adams, Ian Ashbridge, Vivienne Boon, Simon Campbell, Luke Doggett, Katherine Ellett, Lucy Hewitt, Maarten Hillebrandt, Will Leggett, Andrew Nicholls, Minerva Ocolisan, Kevon Perry, Natalie Pitimson, Elisabeth Simbuerger, Angelica Thumala, Rolando Vazquez and Julie Walsh. I have benefited from conversations with and suggestions from friends and colleagues Ariadna Acevedo, Jim Beckford, Daniel Chernilo, Rachel Cohen, Tony Elger, Robert Fine, Mike Gane, Peter Lassman, Herminio Martins, and Jennifer Platt. For helping me sustain a long-running lament about the state of sociology and how it isn't like it was(n't) in our day a special mention should go to The Four Yorkshiremen: Mark Erickson, Paul du Gay, Graeme Gilloch and Tom Osborne.

The book is dedicated to the memory of Irving Velody, inspiring teacher and friend; while I am resigned to the thought that he might have rolled his eyes and guffawed in places, I would like to think that he would have been sympathetic to parts of it.

Finally, one more thing: thank you to my wife, Zeynep, without whom this book would have been finished earlier.

Figures 3.1, 3.2, 3.3 and 3.4 from Mary Douglas (2003) *Natural Symbols: Explorations of Cosmology*. Routledge (Routledge Classics), Diagram 4 ('Grid and Group') page 60. Reprinted with permission.

Figure 5.1 from John Scott (1995) *Sociological Theory*, Aldershot, Edward Elgar. Reprinted with permission.

Figure 5.2 from Richard Munch (1988) 'The dispositions of the personality system', *Understanding Modernity*, Figure 9, p. 140. Routledge. Reprinted with permission.

Figure 5.5 from BONNER, ANTHONY; SELECTED WORKS OF RAMON LLULL 1232-1316, VOLUMES 1 AND 2: © 1985 Princeton University Press Reprinted by permission of Princeton University Press.

Figures 5.8 and 5.9 from T. Parsons and N. Smelser (1958) *Economy and Society*. London: Routledge & Kegan Paul. Reprinted with permission from Neil Smelser.

Figure 5.10 from POWER AND PRIVILEGE: A THEORY OF SOCIAL STRATIFICATION by Gerhard Emmanuel Lenski, Jr. Copyright © 1984 by the University of North Carolina Press. Used by permission of the publisher. www.uncpress.unc.edu

Figure 5.13 from E. Gellner (1983) *Nations and Nationalism*. Oxford: Blackwell. Reprinted with permission.

Figure 5.14 from M.S. Archer (1982) 'Morphogenesis versus Structuration: on combining structure and action', *The British Journal of Sociology*, 33 (4): 445–83. Reprinted with permission.

Figure 5.15 from Mary Douglas (2003) *Natural Symbols: Explorations of Cosmology*. Routledge (Routledge Classics), Diagram 4 ('Grid and Group') page 60. Reprinted with permission.

Figure 5.16 from M. Douglas (1975) *Implict Meanings*, p. 224. London: Routledge & Kegan Paul. Reprinted with permission.

Figure 5.17 from E. Gellner 'Concepts and society', in B. Wilson (ed.), *Rationality*. Oxford: Blackwell. Reprinted with permission.

Figures 5.19, 5.20 and 5.22 from A. Giddens (1984) *The Constitution of Society*. Cambridge: Polity Press. Reprinted with permission.

Figure 5.21 from C.G. Jung ([1948] 1970) 'A psychological approach to the dogma of the trinity' in *Collected Works*, Vol. 11, p. 125. London: Routledge & Kegan Paul. Reprinted with permission.

Introduction

This book is not an encyclopaedic survey of the most influential or important sociological theories of the 20th century; nor is it an institutional history of sociological theory. It is not a textbook, a distillation of the accumulated knowledge of a particular discipline; nor is it a crib, a set of ready-made and easily-remembered answers to imagined examination questions. It is more of a reader's guide, a series of hints and suggestions for those who, whether students or teachers, believe that sociology is a profession and a discipline but also something more.

Sociology will be understood here as a mode of encounter with the social world and a mode of orientation within that world, and sociological theory as the articulation of the moves, problems and themes that arise in connection with this encounter. Orientation in the social world is a problem for actors as much as it is for professional sociologists, and so the moves, problems, and themes identified here as central to sociological theory will not be thought of as wholly distinct from those germane to living a life and being a competent social animal. Sociology will be understood as a discipline but also as a certain sort of sensibility, a mode of response to the world, a way of seeing. Whether sociological theory can equip anyone for the broader task of living a life will remain an open question, but hints about an answer will be offered towards the end.

Although sociologists are perhaps the last people one should turn to for advice in this direction, and while the personal lives of many of the great sociological theorists could hardly be described as a model for anyone, the life's work of each is its own sort of instruction, being a sustained attempt to construe, constitute, frame, and interpret the social world. In this respect, however eccentric they might have been, they were no different from each one of us, for our social life would not be our social life were it not for our need and ability to frame our experience, to place it 'under a description'. This does not mean that sociological theory is no more than an elaborate and more explicit version of what each of us has to do in order to live a life. If matters were so simple then much of the more baroque sort of sociological theory would be pointless (though some of it may well be), and we could say with Wittgenstein, in a maxim he did not always follow himself, that whatever can be said can be said clearly.

On the contrary, the task of the sociological theorist is always to create a distance towards those phenomena that others routinely treat as self-evident; and it is then to encourage us to see the world a little differently. In this sense the sociological theorist's task is analogous to that of the artist or the novelist who, in establishing a distance towards the world, is bound to introduce a measure of perspective, or one-sidedness, an angle, a particular emphasis at some remove from those that define our implicit or everyday understandings. No sustained effort to understanding the social world is worthwhile if it thinks that it can dispense with new and even puzzling criteria of significance. As the philosopher and sociologist Helmuth Plessner put it:

> ... in any artistic representation which penetrates to the spirit of things through appearances, there must be some distortion about the work, some partiality, selectivity, emphasis – in a word, some distancing mechanism – in order to bring the object to light. With different materials and with different means of expression, the good writer and even the historical scholar will obey the same law. In composing his material he must fashion it with a good dose of selectivity and partiality, but in such a way that this hand can be seen to work selectively if the material is to come alive, as the portrait does, and communicate to us in pictorial terms. The forcefulness of even Hegel, or Marx or Spengler, owes its heightened value to this. It brings things to light; it stimulates the inner eye; it gives us different eyes. Exaggerations, figures of speech, bold constructions too, fulfil the same function of perceptual counterfoil to understanding. (Plessner, 1978: 32)

Here we may want to say that there is a difference between the artist or novelist and the sociological theorist, namely that the former addresses our vision more directly that the latter, or that the sense of wonderment or dislocation produced by Goya or Dostoyevsky is greater than that produced by Talcott Parsons or Jürgen Habermas; it is hard to imagine a sane person saying '*The Social System* changed my life', or 'I read Giddens and the scales fell from my eyes'; it is made harder by the apparent lack of interest among many sociological theorists in serious art or literature either as topic or as model. Sporadic appeals for sociology to be considered an art form have largely fallen on deaf ears (Nisbet, 1976; Brown, 1977). This is not because sociology has moved closer to the natural sciences and embraced their standards of rigour; the picture, rather, is one in which research methods have become increasingly elaborate and sophisticated but at the cost of any capacity to say something significant about society, while theory has become split between the rigorous and systematic work of Niklas Luhmann or Jon Elster and the more nebulous but influential work of Zygmunt Bauman or Ulrich Beck.

The result of this split between what we might call rigour and wisdom is that the problems associated with conceptualising the social for the purposes of a science of society can seem to be distinct from the problems that confront modern people in their efforts to make sense of and live their lives. While such a distinction is important, and while the task of the more rigorous sociological theorists might be said to be the preservation of the discipline's identity, the distinctiveness of sociological theory also consists in something more than the capacity to manipulate concepts: it is an attitude of mind. In order to convey something of this I have organised the book in terms of theoretical tools and devices that sociological theorists use and the problems and difficulties that can be involved when they try to use them; this is not, then, a normative exercise in the elaboration of theoretical principles.

Nor for that matter is it organised around the substantive problems of our time, interesting though these are. Clearly it is important to know what Weber thought about the future of rationalised societies, how Durkheim saw the prospects for socialism or how Adorno saw contemporary culture; it is interesting to reflect on whether democracies are made more robust by reducing the proportion of the population working in agriculture, on the apparent reversal in the relationship between the dynamics of work and family life in post-industrial economies, or on the role played by the relationship between glob-alisation and risk in the formation of modern or postmodern conceptions of individuality. But knowing what particular sociologists say 'about' these things will not tell you about the kinds of sociologist they are, about their intellectual style. And intellectual style is what matters here. There may be substantive differences between Marx and Parsons over private property or the direction in which they thought modern western societies were heading, but more important here is that it may also be true that both make use of clear concep-tual hierarchies. Parsons may not have been a Marxist yet his conceptualisation of power owes much to the way in which he conceptualises money; his con-clusions about power are also remarkably similar to those reached by Michel Foucault, a very different sort of thinker. Functionalism and Marxism have tra-ditionally been seen as different ways of thinking, yet functionalism, premised unquestionably on conservative assumptions, has proved remarkably fruitful for many versions of Marxism and neo-Marxism in the 20th century; indeed, many of the more colourful and exotic efforts at theorising that one encounters in sociology today are frequently accompanied by a ritual invocation of indepen-dent variables such as class, gender, ethnicity, and age that are drawn straight from a functionalist lexicon.

It is in the spirit of such observations that apparently unrelated thinkers will be placed in some proximity to one another rather than being separated into schools or traditions. They will be compared with one another, though there will be no suggestion of an independent standard against which they might all be measured; neither will there be the remotest prospect of amalgamating them into a grand synthesis. The approach adopted here is perhaps best described as 'theoretical liberalism', a term that sounds woolly but which is inspired by something that the political theorist Isaiah Berlin used to say. Berlin thought that even if we could arrive at a definitive theory of justice, or freedom, or equality, or beauty, or democracy, or truth, these liberal values, worthy though they may be in themselves, perhaps even transcending all human prejudices, are irreducible to one another; therefore, any attempt to organise society in such a way as to realise them all at the same time was utopian, and likely to end in tyranny. The task of a liberal society was to find ways of negotiating the con-flicts between these equally valid principles (Berlin, 1997). Now our problem is the relationship between sociological theories rather than between liberal values and, as such, a less consequential enterprise. But its history may also be written as one in which one theorist produces a brilliant theory of one aspect or dimension of social life – the state, religion, emotions, gender, science – while another theorist does the same in another field, or one theorist writes an abstract theory of society that makes sense of an aspect of social experience while failing to say much about others. And it is also marked by attempts by some theorists to synthesise these major breakthroughs in particular fields into

3

a single science of society. Indeed, few sociological theorists have entirely lacked this kind of utopian, theoretically illiberal ambition. Plessner's idea, then, that the good writer or social thinker fashions his material with partiality or selectivity, needs to be qualified by the observation that many of our heroes believe that they are doing more than this, that they are seeking and, so they believe, finding, definitive answers to basic questions, bringing to an end a search that was begun by their predecessors. Many have sought to show, for instance, how their work addresses both broad questions of social structure and the role of human agency, the large and the small scale, conflict and consensus, history and order, and so on. Yet they all failed; the light they cast on one thing was bound not to fall on something else, and the work of all of them can be read, and will be read here, as a story about the limits of inquiry, limits run up against and limits overstepped.

In order to convey a sense of these limits I have organised the book in a way that may strike some readers as peculiar. For instance, I have chosen not to have chapters on 'ontology', 'epistemology', 'methodology', 'agency and structure', 'conflict and consensus' and so on; similarly, the different schools or national traditions of theory have been discussed so many times before that nothing new could come of doing so here; there are also many good collections of essays about individual thinkers. All of these approaches have their virtues: there *are* basic principles of theorising, there *have* been schools of theory, and most theorists *have* been men and women sitting alone at their desks thinking ... or at least writing. Here I try something different and offer 'classics and canons', 'description', 'categories', 'metaphors', 'diagrams', 'cynicism and scepticism', and finally 'sociological theory and the art of living'. The point of this will be to allow us to compare the ways in which different thinkers use or misuse the same tools, to keep returning to themes addressed in previous chapters, and to discuss the same thinker in more than one chapter. Each chapter will address only a few theorists but, hopefully, the points made about each will be general enough to provide the reader with a way of seeing the work of many others. In any case, the idea is to deepen our acquaintance with sociological theory by a process of re-reading, the result of which ought to be that our sense of how a particular theorist thinks will be different at the end from what it was at the beginning.

It will also hopefully have the virtue of allowing us to see with different eyes a standard question in the philosophy of social science, namely that of whether sociology is a science or an art; for it seems to me the normative question that is usually asked here, namely whether sociology should be a science or an art, is less interesting than that of whether a theorist's actual use of a device pushes his or her inquiry in the direction of science or in the direction of art or literature.

The book is devoted almost entirely to the work of familiar figures, and many names that some readers may think important are left out. Hopefully, the points I make about the selected few will be clear enough for those readers to have them in mind when reading the work of their own favourites. On the other hand, I do think that as university teachers we are the custodians of a tradition of inquiry, and so the book begins with the idea of a sociological classic, albeit one in which 'classic' will mean something a little broader than usual; there are classic statements of problems and classic mistakes as well as classic examples of inspiration. Indeed, a confrontation with intellectual failure can be as instructive as a confrontation with greatness, so that the term 'classic' is retained but as part of a discussion that goes beyond the question of tradition or debates between those who love old books and those who lament the baleful influence of dead white men. There are, incidentally, some things to say about the practice of directing criticism at people on the basis of ascriptive categories, especially when they are no longer there to defend themselves, but beyond this the criterion governing the selection of material here is intellectual stimulation, with the proviso that such stimulation will have to be as much a product of what can be read into the material as of the assumed effect that it has on the inexperienced reader; just as the attraction of classic texts is that they might help us to see with different eyes, so the task of a reader's guide like this is to make it easier for them to have that effect.

Nevertheless, there is a sense in which any discussion of the sociological classics is the product of a traditional attitude, and has to be motivated by the thought that when he or she is not being encouraged to do 'group projects' as preparation for the world of team working, the student of sociology is, as much as the student of literature, a lone reader sitting at a desk with a book, engaging in a dialogue with other minds as well as with himself or herself.

The student is also a social actor and the second chapter, on description, attempts to do justice to this by addressing the most general task that social actors confront, namely the need to see the social world from one point of view rather than another, as having significance. 'Description' here will not refer to something we do before doing something more serious, such as explaining, but is a general term for the way in which we order our world and find our way about in it. In exploring some of the difficulties encountered by the sociologist in his or her efforts to describe – levels of abstraction, amount of detail, formality of presentation, completeness, use of terminology, translatability into another idiom – the chapter on description points up dilemmas we all face as actors for whom language is the primary means of getting about. The problem it addresses is actually an ancient one, reaching back to the time when our ancestors constructed myths as a means of dealing with a dangerous or troubling reality. Hans Blumenberg's formulation of this, while it appears to mock the terms on which it is understood in this book, is worth quoting:

The 'art of living' – that primary skill, which has become obsolete even as a phrase, of dealing with and husbanding oneself – had to be acquired as a faculty for dealing with the fact that man does not have an environment that is arranged in categories and that can be perceived exclusively in its 'relevances' for him. To have a world is always the result of an art, even if it cannot be in any sense a universal artwork. (Blumenberg, 1985: 7)

If the problem of description, seeing the social world as significant, as having contours, is the most general one we know, the rest of the book consists of variations on it.

The following chapter examines the role of categories, as devices we use to create significance for ourselves. As we have been taught by writers from Jorge Luis Borges to Oliver Sacks, an inability to classify appropriately, be it through over-attention to detail or an inability to perceive anything other than abstract forms, is the mark of a cognitive and also a social failure. Borges' stories are full of the problems of this sort, and the intuitions behind them are shared by philosophers from Aristotle to Kant and by sociologists and anthropologists from Durkheim and Mauss to Mary Douglas, who thought that you could understand much of how a society worked by understanding its dominant systems of classification. The problem of finding our way about, however, is not exhausted by the problem of classification; as theorists in the phenomenological tradition have shown, the lineaments of a shared culture are sustained not only by the capacity of classificatory systems to transcend time and place and acquire a measure of permanence; there is also an art of typification, in which the attribution to individuals of certain categories of social membership is a live performance.

If categorisation is central to social competence, it is also central to sociology. No version of sociology can operate without categories, a banal enough statement until you realise that from its inception sociology has been beset by a division between radically distinct approaches to categorisation; three of these will be discussed: classificatory, dialectical and ideal typical; their chief representatives will be Talcott Parsons, Theodor Adorno and Max Weber. After giving Parsons more of a run for his money than he usually gets these days we will see how, for the latter two, 'merely classificatory' reason restricted the scope of inquiry, and how both saw the need to overcome classification and develop more dynamic and flexible ways of theorising.

If Parsons' work is a site on which to demonstrate the shortcomings of a classificatory approach to sociology, it is also in its later form a surprisingly fine illustration of the role of metaphor in sociology. His conceptualisation of society 'as' a system is just one case in which metaphor is used in sociology not just as a decorative device but also as something on which the entire course of an inquiry is dependent. Other metaphors of this sort – what Paul Ricoeur calls metaphor at the level of discourse – include drama, text, game, network and so on. Metaphor may also operate at the level of words, in individual sentences, as a means of dramatising an observation rather than structuring an entire argument. In either case metaphor reminds us of the extent to which theorising – the use of concepts – depends upon what is pre-conceptual. Our focus in this chapter will be both the pervasiveness and seeming unavoidability of metaphor and also the ways in which metaphor can both open up new horizons for inquiry but also close them off; or if you prefer a different image, some theories take flight as a result of their deployment of metaphor and others become trapped by them.

Part of the discussion of metaphors will be about the relationship between metaphors, models and imagery, and this will lead into a chapter on the role of diagrams in sociological theory. At first sight this may appear a marginal issue, but it becomes less so when we realise the extent to which theorists have had to resort to diagrams. Students in particular can be puzzled by these: what are these boxes and arrows and strange shapes trying to tell us? Do they provide the theorist with what Mike Lynch has called a 'pictorial work space' (Lynch, 1991) in which the theorist achieves something he or she cannot achieve through words alone? Or are they merely a didactic tool, a means of simplifying a theory for the reader's benefit? In so far as they are more then mere decoration or illustration, we can ask about the work they do, about whether they, like categories and metaphors, are an aid or a hindrance to inquiry.

Although attending to the differences between the ways in which theorists make use of categories, metaphors and diagrams does not tell the whole story, it can take us some way towards an appreciation of their intellectual sensibilities. Nevertheless, a sixth chapter brings together themes introduced earlier and tries to refocus the discussion in terms of more basic attitudes to inquiry. Although no sociological approach to the world has taken anything at face value or accepted self-evidence where the chance to propose new ways of seeing has offered itself, there are different ways of destroying self-evidence. I focus on two of these, and call them 'cynicism' and 'scepticism', though in a way that owes little to the venerable philosophical traditions that bear these names. The difference between them becomes apparent when we observe their effects on the study of culture. The difficulty both face is that, while sociological analysis can destroy culture's self-evidence and propose new ways of seeing, culture — novels, plays, poetry, music — is itself a destroyer of self-evidence, already an achieved distance, a new way of seeing in its own right. Indeed, this is what makes some novelists better literary critics than the professionals (Kundera, 1995, 2007; Grossman, 2006). The sceptical sociologist will be defined as one who, while suspicious of culture's purity or autonomy vis-à-vis other aspects of social life, knows that sociology's claims to know better than a novel or a poem or a painting rest on shaky ground; the cynic will be defined as one who, whether or not he or she believes that sociology is a science — and some cynics do believe this — believes that the point of inquiry is to get behind or beneath appearances to the 'real' forces at work in the social world, to see the artistic achievement of distance as the erection of a further piece of self-evidence that itself needs to be dismantled.

The ambition of the cynic and the restraint of the sceptic raise questions about the relationship between scientific and non-scientific reasoning and about the limits of sociology itself. Some cynics harbour the belief that sociology might not only go beyond its own analytical limits but also provide answers to the question of how to live. Against this stands Weber's dictum that science cannot and should not do this. Weber's account of what science can and cannot achieve, however, and his invitation to his students to 'find the demon who holds the very fibres of your life', continues to fascinate us today, even if the context of his remarks has been lost or forgotten. Although Weber raises the question of how to live numerous times in remarks scattered all over his work, he also leaves it hanging in the air. A final chapter, then, explores ways in which sociological theory does or does not imply distinct attitudes to conduct. I call these individual utopias. The work of most theorists does contain a sense, however vague, of how life should be lived;

it is there in Weber or Simmel or Schutz or Adorno or Douglas. But it is also there in literature, often more overtly so. The cynic who wants not only to destroy self-evidence but also to debunk culture is unlikely to be open to the claims of literature here. That position may be contrasted with the more sceptical attitude of Weber, in whose household scarcely a week passed by without Tolstoy or Dostoyevsky being mentioned. In this sceptical spirit I will draw extensively on a novelist who was both an admirer of these artists and a trained scientist, but who also provided us with extended and incomparable accounts of what certain 'individual utopias' might look like. We will see that the three utopias discussed in Robert Musil's *The Man without Qualities* – the utopias of what he calls exactitude, essayism and everyday life – are defined in terms of the sort of attitudes that we will see cropping up repeatedly in our discussions of the differences between sociological theorists.

Musil was also one of the great modernists for whom the nuances of world-making and of our perceptions of reality were as important as particular substantive belief systems or ideologies. This problem of reality, and the way in which the tools employed by sociological theorists make it possible to address it, is also the central concern of this book.

1

Classic and Canon

The sociological theorists who appear in this book can all be described as classic figures. The fact that they are referred to as 'sociological theorists' rather than as 'social theorists' is no accident: there is a connection between attitudes to the classics and attitudes to disciplinary boundaries; belief in the continuing relevance of the classics often goes hand-in-hand with belief in the firmness of the boundaries of the discipline of which they are a part. By the same token, doubts about the relevance of the classics are often to be found among those who believe in an interdisciplinary approach to the human sciences.

Here two debates run more or less parallel to one another, the first normative, the second growing out of the history of ideas. In the first debate, arguments in favour of the classics, their status as a source of ideas, categories and vocabulary, what Gianfranco Poggi calls 'intellectual muscle' (Poggi, 1996: 43), confronts a series of anti-classical attitudes, ranging from the belief that these works are fatally compromised by the assumptions and working methods peculiar to their context, to the claim that the original object of sociology, society, has 'disappeared' (Wagner, 1999; Outhwaite, 2006). In the second debate, it is pointed out that even if we wished to invoke the work of those writing between 1880 and 1920, the period that we regard as the period of classical sociology in continental Europe, we would have to recognise that most of the major sociological statements from that time – with the exception of Durkheim – were made outside the confines of institutionalised sociology; Weber, Simmel, Tönnies and others spoke to a far more wide-ranging audience, and are better thought of as intellectuals whose sociological sensibility co-existed with a daunting erudition in neighbouring fields such as economics, history or law (Andreski, 1972). According to this view, when sociology did become institutionalised it did so in the form of empirical, applied research projects that were tied to various forms of social engineering, and jettisoned the political–philosophical traditions of thought that had defined classical sociology across Europe (Bloom, 1987; Wagner, 1991). Seen in the light of institutional disciplinary history, then, an appeal to the sociological classics looks like a form of nostalgia or antiquarianism, a quest for a glorious but unrecoverable past.

If that was not enough, consider Johan Heilbron's remark that 'with the unprecedented expansion of universities after World War II, disciplinary frameworks began to lose much of their function. As of 1960 research increasingly called for approaches that were interdisciplinary, multidisciplinary or transdisciplinary' (Heilbron, 1995: 4). Just who was doing the calling is a question in itself. By 1976 Wilhelm Baldamus was commenting acerbically on 'the contrast between the administrators' simple-minded trust in interdisciplinary studies and the social scientists' experience of the incommensurability of diverse methods' (Baldamus 1976: 118).

Since Baldamus issued that implicit warning, those seeking to carve out a new domain of inquiry for themselves free of traditional disciplinary constraint have been remarkably successful. Since the advent of area studies in the 1950s and cultural studies in the 1960s, we have witnessed the birth of, among others, women's studies, Victorian studies, Canadian studies, media studies, and post-colonial studies; there is now even something called mobilities research. The characteristic move of each of these is to take a particular substantive area, or problem, and then employ a more or less eclectic set of methods from different disciplines in order to study it. As if in acknowledgement of the tensions and ambiguities at work in such a procedure, there are now university departments that have removed a specific area from their name entirely and called themselves simply 'Interdisciplinary Studies'.

Seen in this light, one reason why discussion of the classics often appears early on in books about sociological theory is that the writer feels the need to reassure the student reader, a reader who is assumed to be resistant to anything written more than ten years ago. The writer making this assumption is often a man in his 40s who is old enough to fear the effects of the generation gap between himself and his students, yet not old enough to be absolved of the responsibility to keep up with the times. Beset by fears about whether his students will find these old books as interesting or important as he does, he feels the need for self-legitimation. Yet the writer should not despair; nor should students be so sure of themselves. The passions of our youth are fleeting, and with age and intellectual experience we come to realise that what we once thought was new and exciting was as tedious as whatever it appeared to have surpassed. Being a student is not simply about negotiating the relationship between one's finger-on-the-pulse attitude to life and the burdensome tasks imposed by one's out-of-touch lecturers; it is about an interplay between one's own sense of what is new and old, what can be discarded and what is worth retaining, and that proposed by others. In any case, no matter when it was written, a book you have not read before is new to thee. So lecturers who are watching films by Lars von Trier or Abbas Kiarostami, or reading Javier Marías while their students are reading Zadie Smith and watching Bruce Willis, should not feel old and tired; and students who are reading Jane Austen while their lecturers are reading the latest Murakami should not be so sure of themselves.

The reader is about to discover that the sympathies of this author are broadly with anyone who would rather read Emile Durkheim than Ulrich Beck, Weber rather than Giddens, Gellner rather than Urry. Curiously enough, though, one reason for this is that it is precisely through these older thinkers that one might meet the demand for interdisciplinarity half way; for the classical sociology that some say has been lost and some say should be forgotten was itself forged out of older, already-existing disciplines: Weber is unthinkable without political science, law, economics and history, Durkheim without political philosophy and law, Marx without political economy and philosophy, Simmel without aesthetics and moral philosophy. Apart from Durkheim, all were at the very least ambivalent about 'society' generations before people started prophesying the 'post-social' (Urry, 1999); perhaps this is what gives their work its range, its massive erudition and a power that far surpasses that of today's stars of the conference circuit (Van Gennep, 1967; Andreski, 1972).

Sociology Between Literature and Science

The status of the classics in any field is defined by the relationship between them and the works that precede and succeed them. A piece of work is classic if at least some of the ideas it contains transcend the circumstances in which it was produced. Now the way in which the sociological classics live on is peculiar, something we can appreciate if we compare the sociological classics with those in literature, philosophy and the natural sciences. Sociology has been haunted since its inception by all three, so much so that one might even say that the founding sociological classics display a combination of the qualities one is entitled to expect from each: they have the conceptual rigour of philosophy; the sensitivity to human fate and circumstance of the novel; and the natural scientist's insatiable curiosity. Precisely because of this it is not easy to treat the history of sociology in the same way in which we treat the history of literature or art or natural science.

Consider how mechanisms of reception and influence work in literature. Although much work has been done by postmodern literary critics on the ways in which the western canon is the product of continual reinterpretation, the status of Homer or Shakespeare or Dante derives from the fact that, regardless of the extent to which we can contextualise their work and talk about the ways in which it mobilises 'assumptions' about gender or race or sexuality current at the time of its production, the work lives on and speaks to today's reader as directly as it might have done fifty or a hundred years ago. Just what it is that still speaks to us may not be the same today as it was fifty or two hundred years ago, even though the words are the same – a theme brilliantly explored in Borges' story 'Pierre Menard, Author of the Quixote' (Borges, 1964a).

The idea that a text might be capable of appealing directly to our vision is not one we immediately associate with the classics of sociology; they seem too closely tied to the times as well as too opaque. Indeed, the gaze of the greatest sociological theorists has always been directed as much at their own times as at eternal verities. This is perhaps the main distinguishing characteristic of the sociological theorist as compared with the poet or philosopher. It would be a second-rank poet or philosopher whose work was primarily rooted in his or her time. Not so the sociologist. Most poets, like most sociologists, are forgotten in the end, but it is more likely that the poet is forgotten because he or she was simply not up to the mark. A sociologist, even one of the first rank, may be forgotten by future generations simply because, while he or she brilliantly delineated the times, those times are no more. This has been the fate of American sociologists in particular.

If we confine ourselves to the relationship between a writer and his successors, then, the difference between poets and sociologists is clear. It is less clear when one thinks about the relationship between the writer and his predecessors. Whether a writer is a poet or a sociological theorist, they cannot avoid the poetic or intellectual tradition which precedes them. Harold Bloom once argued that the relationship between the poet and his or her past was subject to 'the anxiety of influence' (Bloom, 1973). By this he meant that without the poet's fear that everything he writes might have already been written, nothing genuinely new would be created artistically. Poetic history on this account is made by 'strong poets' whose strength consists in the fact that they are not complete originals – which would after all make them incomprehensible – but who create through a misreading of the work of other strong poets. The effort to distinguish oneself as a poet ends in a kind of failure, but a failure which is heroic to the extent that its effect is the maintenance as well as the modification of a tradition. In a similar vein, Sheldon Wolin wrote of the 'epic theorising' of social and political thinkers who have sought to reassemble the world by an act of thought. Such epic theorising is like strong poetry in that it defines itself in relation to previous claims to legitimate knowledge. Nevertheless, such theorising is a political act in a way in which the writing of strong poetry is not, in that the referent of the theory is neither nature nor God nor the human condition but the theorist's own society. If we accept Bloom's account there is no progress in literature, in that the sources for the answers to the questions which literature raises are unlikely to be confined to any one historical period. As Hans Blumenberg puts it:

> Homer and Hesiod are our first and, at the same time, most lasting authors of fundamental mythical patterns. Homer is this, if for no other reason than because our literary tradition begins with him. But because he is also one of the greatest members, if not the greatest member, of that tradition, the scandal of the fact that we have to accept something so imposingly mature as its very first item remains concealed from us. (Blumenberg, 1985: 151)

The same may be said of the classics of philosophy. Although philosophy has undergone what philosophers have taken to be fundamental changes of direction, and philosophers have periodically claimed to have brought philosophy itself to an end, as an activity philosophy feeds off an implicit belief that the problems it addresses transcend time. Plato's doctrine of ideas or Aristotle's ethics can be discussed with profit in total disregard for the circumstances in which they were set down; it makes little sense to say that they are outdated. Machiavelli has given us an unforgettable image of the worth, the sheer pleasure, of reading the philosophical classics:

> In the evening I return to my house, and go into my study. At the door I take off the clothes I have worn all day, mud spotted and dirty, and put on regal and courtly garments. Thus appropriately clothed, I enter into the ancient courts of ancient men, where, being lovingly received, I feed on the food which alone is mine, and which I

was born for; I am not ashamed to speak with them and ask the reasons for their actions, and they courteously answer me. For four hours I feel no boredom and forget every worry; I do not fear poverty, and death does not terrify me. I give myself over completely to the ancients. (Machiavelli, quoted in Wolin, 2004: 22)

In the natural sciences there is an entirely different relationship between classic figures and their predecessors and successors: their achievements are as imposing as their work is neglected. The work of Newton or Copernicus or Darwin was revolutionary in a way in which the work of no poet or philosopher could be; it both called into question everything that had gone before and achieved such broad acceptance that entire epochs were named after them: we speak readily of a Newtonian universe or the Copernican world or the Darwinian age (unless, of course, we live in some parts of the USA). At the same time, neither the books they wrote nor their basic ideas can be said to hang over or haunt the subsequent development of science. As Thomas Kuhn wrote, everyday science has a routine, non-revolutionary character that consists in problem-solving within a paradigm which, once established, is not easily shaken off. While such a view of the history of science is not without its critics, in the natural sciences there are no classic texts, nothing which, while revered, is likely to be reread, reinterpreted and puzzled over. Even a revolutionary scientific achievement will be the product of repeatable experimental or observational procedures and/or theoretical innovation. The original text which made it all possible can be forgotten or ignored. No natural scientist reads Galileo or Newton or Einstein in order to reinterpret them; that is a task for historians of science.

What, then, of the classics of sociology? When Talcott Parsons famously opened *The Structure of Social Action* (Parsons, 1937), with the question 'who now reads Spencer?', it had an entirely different resonance from 'who now reads Newton?'. In asking it Parsons did not mean to imply that nobody needed to read the originator of an established method, but that Herbert Spencer's thought was so deeply rooted in the 19th century that it had been rendered obsolete by the passage of time and by the need for an emergence of new approaches to theorising, a need to be met by Parsons himself. Despite the fact that his own work depended on the work of selected previous thinkers – Marshall, Pareto, Durkheim and Weber – even they were appealed to as mere predecessors. If, as Weber said, science is chained to the course of progress, so that every scientist, natural or social, hopes that his work will be surpassed, then Parsons might have claimed to be fulfilling Weber's hope. The irony was that, in opening Anglo-American sociology to Durkheim and Weber, Parsons made us aware of how much more interesting their work was than his own; and despite his opening line about Spencer's obsolescence, in 1968 we find Theodor Adorno, the most distinguished representative of the neo-Marxist Frankfurt School, repeatedly recommending Spencer to a radical generation of German students (Adorno, 2000: 40, 97). All of which suggests that the classics of social science are neither timeless (in the sense of literary classics) nor tied to any discernible course of progress (in the case of the natural sciences), but that they come and go. An awkward and not very satisfying conclusion, and one that calls for a more refined terminology through which to make sense of their place and significance.

In an important survey Peter Baehr and Mike O'Brien have provided one (Baehr and O'Brien, 1994; Baehr, 2002). Before discussing it we should enter one caveat. While an account of the classics in any field is bound to say that a work is 'classic' if it begins something, establishes a vocabulary or a framework of understanding, makes possible what was not possible before, in short, provides a founding act, I will suggest later that we can expand the criteria of classicalness to include 'exemplary', and can include under that heading examples of failure as well as success; in other words, there may be, so to speak, 'stand-alone classics', writers who are more admired and loved than influential.

Borrowing from the work of Michel Foucault (Foucault, 1970), Baehr and O'Brien distinguish between three kinds of founders:

— founders of *transdiscursivity*, the status of whose work appears to be beyond question
— founders of *science*, who may establish something definitive and lasting
— founders of *discursivity*, who are constantly returned to for a sense of a particular discipline's primary coordinates.

Now discursivity, transdiscursivity and science are useful categories because they cut across the boundaries between disciplines, allowing both for the possibility that different kinds of founders can be located within the same discipline and for disagreements about what kind of founder a particular thinker is.

For example, while Aristotle is a good example of a founder of transdiscursivity, Marx and Freud have been regarded as founders of both discursivity and science. The range of Aristotle scholarship notwithstanding, Aristotelians do share a broad understanding of Aristotle's ideas about ethics and politics, even if they disagree about the prospects for an Aristotelian understanding of human action in the modern world. Marxists and Freudians by contrast may well disagree with one another about Marx's or Freud's basic message, so that their scholarship will be directed as much towards Marx's or Freud's own founding texts as towards the prospects for communism or an improvement in psychic health. The interesting point here is that the parties to the disagreement may both believe that the point of this discursivity is to bring it to an end and to show that Marx or Freud was the founder of a science.

Tensions arise, too, over the status of Durkheim and Weber. Both have been puzzled over by subsequent thinkers, Weber unquestionably more than Durkheim. Though Weber and Marx also appeal to a rhetoric of science, Durkheim saw himself as a founder of a science which might one day possess the dignity of physics, and he is unquestionably less of a founder of discursivity than the other two; there are far more books about Weber's life and work than about Durkheim's, far more efforts to fathom out what he is talking about. Weber manages to appear as a founder of science and a founder of discursivity at the same time, with the paradoxes to which this gives rise built into his work from the start. This is partly why he can sound both outdated and indispensable within the course of a few paragraphs. When he is at his clearest he reads like the founder of a science, and scholars continue to go to *Economy and Society* for definitions of basic terms; but read the two lectures on science and politics as a vocation and the sense of puzzlement can overwhelm you – suddenly he is a founder of discursivity. As a scientist he is, he says, chained to the course of progress, but this means not only that he wants to go beyond his predecessors but also that he wants his work to be surpassed by those who come after him. He says this in 1917, yet we today continue to be fascinated by it; Weber himself thought that he was setting problems for the social sciences that would take a hundred years to address, yet in saying so he knew that he was merely quoting a remark made by Kant more than a century before. Robert Merton has given us an incomparable account of such paradoxes (Merton, 1993).

All of this suggests that to refer to Marx, Durkheim and Weber as the founders of sociology is meaningless in the absence of any sense of the different ways in which they are founders. Writers of textbooks continue to refer to the different traditions which bear their names (Collins, 1994), but the difference is not only one between world views or basic beliefs about society and how it should be studied, but also one between types of relationship between founder and successors. This is important because it affects the degree of immediacy with which the classics can speak to us and the way in which they are taught and read, so much so that there are different, often conflicting, reasons for doing so. At one end of the spectrum, the point of reading the classics is to debunk them, to show the ways in which they have been agents of or complicit with a system of social or political power or oppression of which we, in the present, do not approve. Some feminist readings of the classics have this flavour (Marshall and Witz, 2004). At the other end, the classics are thought of as a beacon of excellence, the best that we have.

This has generated an unproductive debate that should probably be avoided; to do so we can adopt a broader definition of classic. Allowing for a looseness of terminology you could call it 'deconstructive'; we will see that some of the most important works of sociological theory are indeed exemplary, not only because they show us how sociology, or sociological theorising, should be done, but also because they are examples of heroic striving and failure. Jacques Derrida, often referred to with all seriousness and without a trace of irony as the founder of deconstruction, didn't quite put matters like this, but in his readings of other thinkers he demonstrated repeatedly how their efforts to write something meaningful, complete, clear and definitive constantly ran up against limits, limits beyond which lay the unacknowledged conditions of possibility of such an enterprise, conditions which, once the author begins to write, he cannot be in a position to take into account. This does not mean that Rousseau or Nietzsche did not know what they were doing, but it does mean that they could never succeed. Derrida at his best demonstrates that, far from being a sign that we should not read them, these shortcomings of even the greatest thinkers represent something deeply human and moving (Derrida, 1997).

The spectacle of failure in itself is not immediately inspiring; what is is the enormity of the tasks taken on. Working out the dynamics and direction of world history or the structure of the psyche or the origins of religion or the roots of the modern world, comparing entire civilisations and belief systems, delineating the lineaments of everyday interaction as they apply to every member of society, constructing a system of categories for the use of all social scientists; all require prodigious feats of learning even from teams of researchers let alone individual scholars. Yet this is what those individuals we call the sociological classics attempted. None of them succeeded and, we may say, the idea that they could have done so makes little sense. How could a single human lifetime be enough to arrive at the answers? The belief that it could is almost a definition of madness (Blumenberg, 1982). All of our heroes were forced to recognise this even as they did not see themselves quite as mere cogs in a machine, or as medieval stonemasons building cathedrals might have seen themselves, contributing to an enterprise they knew would take generations to complete but which would be completed. Their nobility derives from the fact that in refusing the mundane, in placing themselves foursquare before the most difficult questions social science can ask, they avoided egotism and instead devoted themselves to something greater than themselves, and did so with passion and a quest for knowledge, even while having to accept the endlessness of the task. It is this passion without egotism that might make them exemplary for us, both as students and as teachers.

For this reason, the following definition of a classic, from one of their staunchest defenders, is instructive for what it leaves out:

> Classics are earlier works of human exploration which are given a privileged status *vis-a-vis* contemporary explorations in the same field. The concept of privileged status means that contemporary practitioners of the discipline in question believe that they can learn as much about their field through understanding this earlier work as they can from the work of their contemporaries. (Alexander, 1989: 9)

Alexander goes on to say that the classic author 'has established fundamental criteria in his particular field'; yet what may be important about such an author is the failed attempt to make sociology the type of science it can never be, the false claim to have rendered previous endeavours obsolete, the forlorn struggle to provide the sort of definitive conceptual language it can never have, to establish a clear boundary between the language of social science and that of everyday speech. If you want to understand the spirit of this book, you need to set the fine sentiments of Alexander against the more jaundiced view of Reger, the musicologist in Thomas Bernhard's novel *Old Masters*:

> Only when, time and again, we have discovered that there is no such thing as the whole or the perfect are we able to live on. We cannot endure the whole or the perfect. We have to travel to Rome to discover that Saint Peter's is a tasteless concoction, that Bernini's altar is an architectural nonsense. We have to see the Pope face to face and personally discover that all in all he is just as helpless and grotesque a person as anyone else in order to bear it. We have to listen to Bach and hear how he fails, listen to Beethoven and hear how he fails, even listen to Mozart and hear how he fails. And we have to deal in the same way with the so-called great philosophers, even if they are our favourite spiritual artists, he said. After all, we do not love Pascal because he is so perfect but because he is fundamentally so helpless, just as we love

Montaigne for his helplessness in lifelong searching and failing to find, and Voltaire for his helplessness. We only love philosophy and the humanities generally because they are absolutely helpless ... One's mind has to be a searching mind, a mind searching for mistakes, for the mistakes of humanity, a mind searching for failure. The human mind is a human mind only when it searches for the mistakes of humanity. (Bernhard, 1989: 19–20)

The classics may well give us much of the grammar without which we would be unable to speak sociologically, unable to take our speech beyond banality, without which we would be like a child or a tourist, able to point at things in the world but unable to say why those things matter. But we need also to appreciate their richness, which means their inconsistencies, paradoxical conclusions and tensions, and their failures, qualities which make them and their authors human.

How to Recognise a Classic

According to what criteria, then, should a work be counted as a classic? Does a writer have to satisfy all these criteria or only some of them? Baehr and O'Brien suggest three criteria, but I will suggest two more.

The first and most obvious is *intellectual authority*, something implied by the passage from Alexander referred to earlier. Now intellectual authority doesn't come from nowhere, any more than political authority does; we could have a long discussion of how it is established, how certain texts come to be seen to have authority by being surrounded by an apparatus of commentary, and so on. In political theory authority signals a point at which discussion stops, some-thing beyond which there is no appeal. As long as there is authority in politics there is a framework within which struggles for power and position can take place. In this sense, there is an intellectual authority to Durkheim's chapters on solidarity, *conscience collective* and the law in *The Division of Labour in Society*; or in the opening chapters of Marx's *Capital*; or Weber's *Economy and Society*. The conceptual apparatus set down by each of them remained at the heart of soci-ological theory for decades afterwards, providing a framework, or at least a vocabulary, within which the investigation of more specific or local matters could take place. Of course, questions of sociological theory are not questions of life or death, whereas the collapse of political authority can mean anarchy or civil war. For this reason, if we speak of the founding figures of sociology as having intellectual authority, we can do so in a way that accepts that this authority can be questioned without the discipline collapsing.

The second criterion, suggested by Baehr and O'Brien, is *aesthetic power* (Baehr and O'Brien, 1994: 65). Given the complexity of the social world, one of the requirements of a theory with pretensions to classic status is that it reduce that complexity, render it manageable and provide the intellectual tools with which this can be done. As Plessner says in the passage we referred to in the introduction, simplification via theory takes many forms, which may not be readily reconcilable with one another. As we will see, despite the differences between them, Georg Simmel and Theodor Adorno both achieve it by means of the essay, a short, pithy account of a phenomenon considered from more than one angle, and marked by the absence of footnotes or bibliography. Durkheim does it in *Suicide* by reducing the multifaceted phenomenon of suicide to four types, themselves derived entirely from a theory of social order which Durkheim developed independent of the data on which the book was purportedly based; if social order is theorised in terms of social integration and social regulation, considered as sliding scales, then a society can be over-integrated (increased likelihood of altruistic suicide) or under-integrated (increased likelihood of egoistic suicide), over-regulated (increased likelihood of fatalistic suicide) or under-regulated (increased likelihood of anomic suicide) (Durkheim, 1952). Chapter 1 of Weber's *Economy and Society* begins with a simple, fourfold classification of types of action, establishes definitions of a social relationship, and works from there towards progressively more elaborate and large-scale forms of human connection, ending with the state. Baehr and O'Brien refer to the 'austere, sparse beauty' of that chapter (Baehr and O'Brien, 1994: 66), which sounds generous even to Weber's admirers; but if one can be allowed to stretch the meaning of terms a little then there is a sense in which every sociological theorist is a kind of artist, facing a blank canvas and needing to give shape to his perceptions and ours.

The third criterion for a work being considered a classic is obviously, and despite what we have already said, *foundationality*. The philosopher Richard Rorty introduced the term 'foundationalism' into intellectual discourse three decades ago, and since then it has been fashionable to dismiss the search for firm foundations for knowledge as a doomed enterprise, on the grounds that any such attempt is bound to owe much to previous attempts and that the search for new knowledge or the need to improve upon existing knowledge is the lifeblood of inquiry. But in saying this Rorty was also forced to acknowledge that his own intellectual heroes – Heidegger and Wittgenstein in particular – had themselves claimed to have brought philosophy to an end. They didn't want to end it by providing it with foundations which would support all subsequent philosophical activity, but they did want people to stop questing for knowledge in the way they had been doing hitherto (Rorty, 1982).

Marx, Durkheim or Talcott Parsons are all attempting to place social inquiry on firm foundations, but we need to be clear about what we mean by this. Somebody once told me, praising Durkheim's clarity, that he was 'the Descartes of sociology'. But Durkheim's efforts to place sociology on a firm footing bear little resemblance to Descartes' to do the same for philosophy. This is even less true for Marx or Parsons. Their work is better thought of as an example of Wolin's epic theorising (Baehr and O'Brien, 1994: 19), an attempt to rebuild the world in thought using the results of previous attempts as a basis. So Marx is not simply unthinkable without but actively depends on Hegel, he engages in a constant dialogue with him; Durkheim has a similar relationship with Saint-Simon and Comte, as does Parsons with the four theorists who feature in *The Structure of Social Action*. We will see later (Chapter 6) that we can make much of this metaphor of foundations and what is to be built upon them. But the most important point is that a work can only have pretensions to classic status if the foundations are the basis upon which others, and not only the one who laid them, can build. For instance, Wright Mills implies that Parsons not only never went beyond the foundation stage, but undermined the possibility of building anything by spending much of his career trying to sink the foundations ever deeper and dragging his followers down there with him. The most damning criticism of Parsons is that, for all the voluminous writings, Parsonian social inquiry never begins.

The three criteria mentioned so far — authority, aesthetic power and foundational ambition — are, perhaps, obvious ones to invoke when discussing the capacity of a classic text to make a claim on us. But the spirit in which I will discuss these classic authors demands that we add two further criteria, because the three considered so far provide more of a framework for discussing each classic author separately than a means of confronting them with one another.

We can borrow more terminology from Richard Rorty here. Rorty distinguishes between what he calls metaphysical and ironic approaches to the history of ideas (Rorty, 1989). The metaphysician sees the history of philosophy as the history of a series of attempts to grasp the same truth. The assumption here is that if the work of very different thinkers is linked in some way, it is by a common reference point independent of all of them. The ironist, by contrast, believes that there is no truth out there to be grasped, and hence no common project of which these writings can all be said to be a part. They are related to one another, but the relationship is the one they have with each other, not one between each of them and something else beyond them all, like 'reality'. The history of philosophy for Rorty is best seen as a conversation between these philosophers, one in which, rather than struggling in lonely isolation from one another on the same problems, they 'feed each other lines' (Rorty, 1989: 39). The moral of the story for Rorty is that this conversation never stops, even when someone seems to want to bring it to an end; it is also conducted independent of the historical context, so that we can imagine a conversation in which one writer's contribution is met with a reply from someone writing earlier. What I called 'theoretical liberalism' might be called 'theoretical liberal irony'.

The point of this distinction between the ironic and the metaphysical becomes clear when we consider our fourth criterion. In his essay 'Why read the classics?', Italo Calvino offers as many as 14 criteria for identifying a work of literature as a classic. However, most of them are variations on a single theme: *inexhaustibility*. He writes: 'classics are books of which we usually hear people say, "I am rereading", and never "I am reading", and every rereading of a classic is as much a voyage of discovery as the first reading' (Calvino, 2000: 127–8). This means that, while there are many books which are read only once, there are others which contain such richness and depth that they can be returned to repeatedly in the course of a reading life. It may happen that a book we thought wonderful when we were 20 says nothing to us at 30, and the reverse is also true, the book we were forced to read at school becoming a pleasure in adult life; the point is that a text may be called a classic if it seems to contain something new and interesting even though we know we have read it before. We are never finished with a classic because it is so rich in possibilities that it does not offer itself to us completely on the first occasion, or on any occasion.

Compare this with what happens when you read Brian Tomkins' article on old people and healthcare in Nuneaton, or Diane Ridley's chapter on social relations in a sex change clinic in Brighton in a collection specially commissioned by East Sussex county council. The chances are that, once you have read it and taken your notes, there will be no need to read it again. Ten years later it will seem no more or less interesting and important than it once was. The same things that struck you as significant then will strike you as significant now, and if you were masochistic enough to take another set of notes they would look pretty much the same as they did before. Although Calvino is talking about literature, the point he is making applies to sociology too. *The Communist Manifesto* or Durkheim's *Suicide* or Weber's 'Science as a Vocation' are classics because of the sense of newness and surprise experienced even by a seasoned reader. The newness arises not from our having forgotten what was in them, but because they are able to modify or in some cases confound the image we had already built up of them. The act of rereading them entails, then, a small act of personal transformation, and it is not pushing the point too far to say that in this it is not unlike certain works of art, or that the feeling of newness may be compared to that induced during the act of love when the lover, who one has known for years, appears to one as though for the first time.

In an age of cribs and commentaries this leads to an interesting paradox. The idea of secondary texts, beginners' guides and so on is that they give the student not only a mediated but also a manageable way in to what are often fiendishly difficult works. Yet the more dependent our understanding of a writer is on such commentaries, the more these second-hand versions of their contents can appear insipid or superficial compared with the original. As long as the commentaries do induce us to go and read the original – and it is an open question today as to whether they can – we may well find ourselves saying: 'Durkheim is far more interesting than I realised'. For today's student, often without the peace of mind to study for its own sake, pressured into passing exams and therefore fearful of risk-taking, the idea that Durkheim might have postmodern tendencies, or that one of the virtues of the classics is to be disorienting as well as comforting, is not easy to accept. The student of today may feel the pressure to want straight answers, some easy formulas, and if the classics refuse to provide them then they may not be doing their job; but we would do well to take note of a remark by Harold Bloom:'... successful literary works are achieved anxieties, not releases from anxieties' (Bloom, 1995: 38). Because of their scientific pretensions the sociological classics can never be as openended as great works of literature and perhaps it is not quite their task to induce anxiety in the sense Bloom intends. Nevertheless, they do not and should not yield themselves easily; as long as they do not, the reading of them will remain a challenging and rewarding experience.

Here it should be admitted that whether they do so yield themselves or induce anxiety may depend upon the circumstances of their reception. Twenty years ago now, Allan Bloom lamented the way in which the work of serious, brooding and difficult philosophers from the German tradition had been transformed into something safer and altogether more digestible after their importation into America:

> A few years ago I chatted with a taxi driver in Atlanta who told me he had just gotten out of prison ... Happily he had undergone 'therapy'. I asked him what kind. He responded: 'All kinds – depth-psychology, transactional analysis, but what I liked best was *Gestalt*' ... What an extraordinary thing it is that high-class talk from what was the peak of Western intellectual life, in Germany, has become as natural as chewing gum on American streets. It indeed had its effect on this taxi driver. He said that he had found his identity and learned to like himself. A generation earlier he would have found god and learned to despise himself as a sinner. (Bloom, 1987: 147)

Textbooks and cribs and other shortcuts to understanding increase the likelihood of this sort of thing and as such represent a threat to the classic status of the classics precisely through the way in which they make their content more widely available. To warn of the dangers of this is not to treat the classics as books to be read by members of an exclusive club, but to point to another criterion for identifying a classic.

Rereading

Classics are works that do not yield themselves on first reading but ask to be reread, on the basis that what they have to say to us in the future may be different from what they can say now. This raises the question of the lenses through which this rereading takes place. Are these lenses formed solely by the commentaries that we have read since the last time we read the originals, by everything that has happened to us in the meantime, or by everything that we have read in the meantime? Will the simple process of getting older and presumably having more experience make us better able to extract new significances from texts, see things that we were previously blind to? And is seeing more, finding more variety, likely to lessen or heighten the anxiety?

This is not a textbook, or at least not an attempt to dispel anxiety by providing you with a shortcut to significance. As long as there is no truth about society, or the social world, or history, or the self, or power, as long as the various approaches to sociology both believe that they are getting closer to the truth and know more or less secretly that that truth is unattainable, there can be no definitive reading of the classics. In the face of this, the best we can do is not to provide a grand overview (if such a project was intellectually worthwhile, those with far more talent than the authors of textbooks would have done it) but to play off different classic authors against one another, one set of anxieties against the other, and to try to allow significance to emerge that way. The classics should be reread, then, in the light of other classics; which means that this book is less a textbook than a prod in the back for the student facing towards the library. If this appears to be an esoteric way of going about things, it shouldn't – it is what we all do all the time, as we negotiate the heights and depths of our everyday life.

We know that the truth about how to live will forever elude us, and that nobody's idea of what is significant can definitively triumph over everybody else's. We know this, in our society, even if we have religious convictions; but it does not prevent our leading a life. Nor should the knowledge that no sociological theorist got it right prevent us from identifying ourselves with the intellectual enterprise in which each plays a part.

The Sociological Canon

Do these writings, taken together, add up to something more than the sum of their parts? Is there a body of works which, if you read them, will turn you into a sociologist? Is there, in other words, a sociological canon?

Most sociologists today, even those who believe that there are books you should read and those you can live without, are suspicious about the idea of a sociological canon. One reason for this is that the idea of the canon has been associated traditionally with Christian apologetics and with the idea of a set of texts held together by a clear doctrinal coherence, each of them as necessary as the next. In sociology, by contrast, the obvious and indeed welcome disparity of world-views, which is already a threat to the idea of a sociological canon, is unlikely to be compensated for by a unity of method or procedure. This means that we cannot simply compile for ourselves a list of sociology's essential texts, sit down and read them all and at the end claim to have mastered the discipline. Sociology's criteria of truth and knowledge are more exacting than Christianity's; the truth about society is in many ways far more elusive than the truth about God, so the history of the discipline is not cumulative. It is, instead, a history of problems and questions and recalcitrant difficulty, so much so that there is a fifth criterion for a work being considered a classic in sociology: *a work of sociology may be considered a classic if it presents to us in an exemplary manner one of the important and enduring problems which sociology faces in its battle to make sense of and conceptualise the social.* For all Alexander's claims that an author becomes a classic by establishing 'fundamental criteria in his particular field', no author can control the emergence of new criteria on the part of other classic authors, criteria which then act as standards against which to judge the work of the already established classic. The result of this proliferation of criteria is neither the uncontrolled accumulation of criteria nor progress, in which new criteria simply replace older ones. It is, rather, a process of universal mutual criticism with neither an end nor beginning, a perpetual departure from and return to things in which the work of the better thinkers may be examined for their blind spots, inconsistency and one-dimensionality as well as for their integrity, intellectual authority and inspiration. It is a process in which chronology is a minor inconvenience; why not treat Weber as a critic of Adorno or Simmel as a critic of Goffman?

There is another factor which militates against our seeing classic texts as canonical. Sociology, like any other intellectual endeavour, perhaps even like the act of writing itself, is prey to the problems which arise in the course of any attempt to say something meaningful, to turn an idea into a finished product, a vague set of imaginings into a conceptual apparatus. It is one concerted effort to interpret the world, an effort that, Marx's eleventh thesis on Feuerbach notwithstanding, is not to be sniffed at. It can be broken down into a series of smaller efforts, and that is what we will do here. The point is that in making these efforts, people make moves, formulate propositions, picture the world, use metaphors, make assumptions about the difference between humans and nonhumans, draw diagrams, use two thousand words instead of the three or four that are needed, and use a hundred words where we need twenty thousand. Attending to what happens when they do these things, we may hope to understand something of what we may call the grammar of inquiry. This grammar is perhaps a less sturdy thing than the grammar of a language. But without it, we would not be able to speak. Robert Nisbet once wrote: 'strip from the present-day sociology the perspectives and frameworks provided by men like Weber and Durkheim, and little would be left but lifeless heaps of data and stray hypotheses' (Nisbet, 1967: 5).

There are, then, sociological classics but there is no sociological canon because there is no sociological dogma or sociological faith, even if many of the writers discussed in this book appeared to be in search of something like this. They failed, but this does not mean that their work taken together amounts to nothing more than a few stray hypotheses or a hill of beans; or a pile of bricks waiting to be turned into an edifice. Without them, and the conversation and argument between them, we would be nowhere. It is time that we turned to them.

2

Description

Introduction

What difference does theorising make to the sociologist's capacity to make the reader see with different eyes? How does it help the sociologist make a world (Goodman, 1978)? In the philosophy of the social sciences a common response is that, since explanation is the most elevated activity known to science, sociology can only make us see differently if it can explain social phenomena; some have doubted whether it can do this but continued to believe that it might; some have argued that sociology does seek explanations but explanations of a different type from those pursued in the natural sciences; some claim that sociology's objective is a different kind of knowledge altogether, one in which the role of explanation is marginal.

I have called this chapter 'description' for two reasons: firstly, because the aim here is to emphasise the sense in which the tasks of sociological theory may be continuous as well as discontinuous with the task of finding our way about as social actors, actors for whom a world is made and sustained insofar as it exists 'under a description'; secondly, because the difference between sociological theories that make us see with different eyes and those that do not cuts across the distinction between explanation and description – there may be convincing explanations that leave us cold, just as there may be descriptions that change the way we think about or see something. Some examples of classic pieces of sociological description will be given here.

At the same time, we will only gain a sense of the relationship between the problems of theorising and the art of living if we are able to distinguish sociological concepts from everyday talk, and take seriously the aim of every sociological theorist to provide or operate with a language that has a measure of rigour and precision. Although rigour and precision may be unattainable, the search for these is part of the very human story of striving and failure that is the history of sociology.

The activity of describing generally receives short shrift from those who believe that the social sciences should be modelled on the natural sciences. At best, description is a preliminary activity, something on the way to explanation but no more. For all those who believe that sociology should be an explanatory enterprise, the phrase 'too descriptive' is definitive criticism. Even where description is treated as a serious objective, its position may be highly circumscribed. A good example is found in Runciman's *A Treatise of Social Theory*, which began to appear in the early eighties. The social sciences, writes Runciman, have for too long occupied themselves with whether they can explain or predict anything. In fact, he argues, 'there is no special problem of explanation in the social sciences, but only a special problem of description' (Runciman, 1983: 1). He makes the point by saying that the most general task of the social sciences is 'understanding', and that this understanding has a primary, secondary and tertiary character. Primary understanding is the task of 'reportage', the act of conveying 'what happened'; secondary understanding is the task of explanation, the act of saying 'why it happened'; and the task of tertiary understanding falls to 'description'. The point of this distinction is not to say that the social sciences are wholly different in character from the natural sciences, but that their task is to do what the natural sciences do – report and explain – but then to do something more, describe. The expression: 'there is no problem of explanation in the social sciences' is meant to be taken seriously: there is no problem because the social sciences can adequately report 'what happened' and can provide adequate and plausible explanations for it. They must, however, describe as well as report and explain because, unlike electrons or planets or bacteria, the objects of inquiry have a subjective sense of what is happening to them. In the social sciences we try to say 'what it was like' for the participants in those events and processes that have been adequately reported and explained; we want to know what it was like for soldiers in World War I or for minor officials in the Austro-Hungarian Empire or for freed serfs in Russia or janissaries in the Ottoman Empire. Indeed, 'the test of descriptive sociology … is whether honest and self-aware informants agree with the sociologist describing the structure and culture of their society that that is what it is or was like for "them"' (Runciman, 1998: 134).

Now this appears to give description an unusually prominent role in the social sciences. But for Runciman, apart from the description of subjective states of mind, everything else in the social sciences is to be carried out along lines set down by the natural sciences. It just happens that the social sciences can and should perform an additional operation, the description of actors' experiences.

In order to say this Runciman has to be confident that the sociologist can keep these three modes of understanding distinct. For Wilhelm Baldamus such confidence is misplaced. In *The Structure of Sociological Inference* he seeks to show that the relationship between explanation and description is more fluid than Runciman suggests. Baldamus was one of the few sociologists to be seriously interested in what he called 'theoretical methods', in how theorising gets done. After claiming that 'literally nothing is known of such methods' (Baldamus, 1976: 49), he advises us that this does not mean that the history of theory is 'nothing more than a discontinuous sequence of ad hoc inventions thrown up by the intuitive inspirations of prominent scholars'. In fact, he says:

… despite the large number and the diversity of topics that are covered by courses entitled 'Sociological Theories and Methods', there is only one single method.

I know this sounds incredible ... This is Weber's celebrated method of constructing ideal types ... The professional theorist will readily agree. (Baldamus, 1976: 9)

We will see in the next chapter that this claim is far-fetched. Nevertheless, Baldamus's point is that all sociological theorists, whether they know it or not, are constructing typologies of one sort or another. The consequence of this is that, in contrast to the story told by Runciman, who separates the explanation of social phenomena from the description of 'what it is like' for social actors, often in sociology an inquiry that begins with the admirable intention of explaining ends up as nothing more than a description of states of mind. Sometimes this happens because the investigation almost wilfully does this. Goldthorpe et al.'s famous book, *The Affluent Worker in the Class Structure* (Goldthorpe et al., 1969), for instance, begins as a study of social structure, power, class, inequality between worker and owner, but ends, according to Baldamus, as an account of workers' perceptions of these matters; this means that an inquiry of large explanatory scope is 'attenuated' (or 'trivialised') in so far as description replaces explanation. Sometimes it happens because, despite the theorist's best efforts to construct rigorous, genuinely constructed types, the 'source material' asserts itself, so that theorists' constructs are no different from those that already serve to structure the social world:

a great deal of what theoreticians do, whether they are aware of it or not, really amounts to an essentially empirical enterprise of recapturing a reality that happens to be already prestructured. Under that assumption the existence, indeed the indispensability, of unsystematic techniques of theorising, would hardly be surprising. (Baldamus, 1976: 89)

Even a theorist like Talcott Parsons (of whom more later), who was more self-conscious about his use of typologies than anyone else, never achieved anything resembling an explanatory model. He strove for a kind of exactitude, but it turned out to be an exactitude of definition alone (Baldamus, 1976: 99).

We have, then, three perspectives on description: an old school philosophy of social science, which sees description as a preliminary adjunct to science proper; Runciman's defence of description as something that sociology can and must do in addition to something else, explaining; and Baldamus's claim that often in sociology what begins as an attempt to explain is attenuated into the non-scientific activity of description, a process that occurs because sociological concepts are unavoidably vague and because the theoretical methods that sociologists deploy in order to combat this vagueness are destined to fail.

Now the perspective of this book is different from all of these, being directed partly at the student who may have no desire to become a professional sociologist. According to this perspective, the social world we have to get about in is one that demands of us that we make sense of it, and sense-making – world-making – consists in the simultaneous carrying out of all the modes of understanding Runciman outlines. 'What it is like' for us is not a separate question from the way in which we carry out our *own* tasks of reporting, explaining and evaluating. Social life is not quasi-natural processes plus the subjective experience of individuals. Rather, social life is meaningful in so far as it exists 'under a description', in so far as it is constituted by the devices through which we make sense of it. Whether or not we can explain what is happening to us by getting behind the surface of things, whether or not we develop a coherent evaluative position towards the world, we are never not faced with the task, to borrow a phrase from Wittgenstein, of finding our way about.

Wittgenstein also said that philosophers mistakenly believed that the relationship between philosophy and ordinary life was a competitive one, so that, instead of exploring the different ways in which human beings do find their way about, they themselves went about looking for some kind of permanent calculus against which to measure the efforts of everybody else:

> We are under the illusion that what is peculiar, profound, essential, in our investigation, resides in its trying to grasp the incomparable essence of language. That is, the order existing between the concepts of proposition, word, proof, truth, experience, and so on. This order is a super-order between – so to speak – super-concepts. Whereas, of course, if the words 'language', 'experience', 'world', have a use, it must be as humble a one as that of the words 'table', 'lamp', 'door'. (Wittgenstein, 1994: §97)

Taking this plea for humility seriously would mean the end of philosophy; sociological theorists too can harbour the illusion that they are grasping the incomparable essence of society or history. But rather than dismiss these as illusory, or pointless because they are doomed to inevitable failure, as some followers of Wittgenstein might, we can see them as deeply human, an example of a kind of striving which we may admire even if we are not capable of it ourselves. When Wittgenstein says that our use of the big, magic words must be just as humble as our use of the ordinary ones, we can take him to mean that the magic words are as important as the humble ones.

Nor, if we put the matter like this, do we have to propose a simple division of labour in which there are sociological theorists who try to grasp the essence of society and other people who simply know their way about, or that there are people whose vocabulary consists of phrases like 'organic solidarity', 'pastoral power', 'bureaucratic individualism', 'lifeworld', or 'Weltanschauung', while that of others consists of more prosaic terms. The first set of words appears daunting, a specialist language; yet on closer examination, it is less specialised than it appears. The sociologist, try as he or she might, will never be an expert in the sense that the natural scientist is an expert. It turns out that Allan Bloom's lament – cited in the last chapter – about the trivialisation of German ideas by their importation into America is misplaced, for however hard they try, sociological theorists' terminology can never be resolutely 'technical', being vague in the way that all sociological concepts are vague. Perhaps for that reason they are translatable into the idioms of everyday speech.

To say this is, perhaps, not to say very much. Translatability aside, are the everyday actor and the sociologist arriving at fewer and more systematic accounts of the same reality, or is there a competitive relationship between the two types of account? Consider the following passages from Alfred Schutz:

The thought objects constructed by the social scientists refer to and are founded upon the thought objects constructed by the common-sense thought of man living his everyday life among his fellow-men. Thus, the constructs used by the social scientist are, so to speak, constructs of the second degree, namely constructs of the constructs made by the actors on the social scene, whose behaviour the scientist observes and tries to explain in accordance with the procedural rules of his science. (Schutz, 1962: 6)

... these models are not human beings living within their biographical situation in the social world of everyday life. Strictly speaking they do not have any biography or any history, and the situation into which they are placed is not a situation defined by them but defined by their creator, the social scientist. (Schutz, 1962: 41)

Schutz seems to imply both that the sociological theorist is humbly articulating what is already there and that sociological concepts belong to an independent universe of discourse woven out of the language the theorist happens to find congenial. There is unavoidably an element of this, just as in the natural sciences such as physics a moment arrives when conjectures about the natural world arising from observation are placed before the court of mathematics. In the social sciences too the theorist has in his head a vision of what the world must be like as well as what it is like. The difference is that in the social sciences observation has a less disciplining effect on the sociologist because his or her theorising is less subject to the discipline of an agreed theoretical apparatus or experimental procedure. The simple fact is that there is not and never will be a means of overcoming the apparent arbitrariness of sociological reasoning and the vagueness of its concepts. And as Baldamus observes: '... one only has to glance at the alphabetical author index of an introductory textbook, make a list of the most frequently quoted sociologists and then ask oneself: what did they ever discover?' (Baldamus, 1976: 25).

The theorist's fate as well as his/her task is to make a world through language, and as we said, language makes some things prominent and others irrelevant, creates a landscape of meaning with contours, and therefore with points from which some things can be seen clearly and others obscured. The most that we can hope for, therefore, is that, since theorising has a transformative character, it may make new things visible in a manner that amounts to more than an arbitrary coining of new words and phrases.

Discovery versus invention aside, the difficulty is that it is not easy to distinguish between theorising that generates genuinely new descriptions and theorising that does not. As we are about to see, C. Wright Mills thought that he could do so, and saw the work of Talcott Parsons as an example of theorising the grandiosity of whose ambition was matched only by the paucity of its findings. Yet he was also ready to admit that Parsons had followers and that this must have had something to do with his capacity to make them at least see with different eyes. I am tempted to say that little has changed since then; Parsons is long gone, but new intellectual heroes have taken his place, heroes whose writings are as baffling to the non-specialist as Parsons' were; and now as then, for every few readers who find the writings of Bourdieu or Luhmann overblown and banal, there is one for whom they possess the power of revelation (Gumbrecht, 2006).

In order to make some progress here we need to refer again to Schutz's distinction between first- and second-order constructs. This is an unavoidable distinction, one without which sociology's claims to be a distinct enterprise are bound to appear hollow. Once we have made it, we can make a further distinction that will take us closer to the heart of what theorising is about and closer to a sense of the kind of description that it is capable of generating. It is a distinction between types of second order constructs.

Formal and Substantive Theorising

In *Sociological Theory: What Went Wrong?*, Nicos Mouzelis distinguishes between two types of second order constructs which, following the philosopher Louis Althusser, he calls Generalities II and Generalities III. The difference between them, he says, is 'absolutely essential' (Mouzelis, 1995: 2). Generalities II are theoretical constructs which act as tools or conceptual devices on the basis of which further investigation may take place. Generalities III are theoretical constructs which take the form of organised statements purporting to tell us something new about the social world. A rough translation is that there is formal theory and there is substantive theory, theory designed to provide direction and coherence to a discipline, and theory which directs our attention to substantive matters – class, power, inequality and so on – in such a way that our empirical data amount to more than a disorganised heap of random discoveries or facts. Examples of Generalities II would be Parsons' pattern variables (of which more in Chapter 3), or his four-fold distinction between societal subsystems (of which more in Chapter 4), or Marx's statements about dialectical and historical materialism, or Weber's statements of method in his essays on objectivity and ethical neutrality and in parts of *Economy and Society*; examples of Generalities III would be Marx's distinction between the different modes of production in history – feudalism, capitalism and so on – and the mechanism of historical change which leads from one to the other, or Weber's accounts of the various relationships that are possible between religious ethics and the world in *Economy and Society* and in his essays on the world religions.

Incidentally, the generation of readers brought up on Hollywood films is probably wondering what happened to Generalities I. Here is Althusser himself:

> In ... the process of the production of knowledge, Generalities I are the abstract, part-ideological, part-scientific generalities that are the raw material of the science, Generalities III are the concrete, scientific generalities that are produced, while Generalities II are the theory of the science at a given moment, the means of production of knowledge. (Althusser, 1969: 183)

Althusser's virtue was to have drawn our attention to different types and levels of abstraction with a care and rigour that many working today in the social sciences ignore; his vice was to have assumed, once he had made these distinctions, that Generalities I were defective in relation to those produced by science, and that it was the task of science in the form of Generalities II to 'work on'

Generalities I and transform them from an 'ideological myth' into something else. We will discuss the shortcomings of this attitude in Chapter 6.

The distinction between Generalities II and III allows us to add another criterion for identifying someone as a classic theorist: they should have contributed to sociology's available stock of both Generalities II and Generalities III, should have given us a set of tools that would stand the test of time long enough to be taken up by future generations (Generalities II) and produced generalisations about the nature of social processes or mechanisms of social change that would inspire future theorists to challenge them (Generalities III). It must be said here that part of the reason that the classics were able to do this was that, despite what Mouzelis says, Generalities II and Generalities III were never allowed to drift entirely apart.

When we put it like that, we may suggest a reason for sociology's failure to produce many classics to compare with its founding figures: the expansion of sociology in the 20th century brought with it an increasing specialisation focused primarily on individual substantive problem areas, each of which developed its attendant body of localised theory. The proliferation of this kind of theory has outstripped that of formal theory; sociology today is home to a rich body of work that provides a 'theory of', say, education, or religion, or nationalism, or violence, or the family, or science, or modernity, but has less to show for its efforts at the level of the kind of formal theorising that defines the discipline's basic intellectual procedures. Indeed, formal theory seems to have become ever more esoteric; rational choice theory, neo-functionalism, critical realism, the more obscure versions of analytical Marxism, and even mathematical sociology now lead a life of uneasy co-existence.

The history of, say, the sociology of nationalism or the sociology of religion might be written as one in which an initial competition between Marxist, Durkheimian and Weberian approaches to nationalism or religion – which were also Marxist, Durkheimian and Weberian approaches to anything else – has gradually given way to internal debates about nationalism or religion among specialists in those areas and the development of in-house 'theories of' nationalism or religion. From there it has sometimes been a short step to the jettisoning of the formal theoretical apparatuses altogether and a readiness to embrace increasingly interdisciplinary inquiries into the phenomenon of nationalism or religion. Indeed, it is now possible to devote an entire career to one specialist area without worrying too much about the integrity of the tools one deploys to study it. This sequence – sociological inquiry into X on the basis of established disciplinary procedures, expansion of the discipline by means of the increasing proliferation of specialist areas, development of localised substantive theories within those areas, abandonment of formal theory altogether, an embrace of interdisciplinary methods and the establishment of departments or centres of 'X studies' – was what the German sociologist Friedrich Tenbruck had in mind in his essay on 'the law of trivialisation' (Tenbruck, 1975; see also Baldamus, 1976; Geertz, 1973).

Seen in this light, it is not surprising that the distinction which Mouzelis regards as 'absolutely essential' is not always respected. A prominent example of work that ignores it entirely is that of of Ulrich Beck. Beck has risen to prominence as a diagnostician of 'late modernity', but more recently, flushed with his success, has come to consider himself as a theorist, in which role he has claimed that today's social and political problems have given rise to the need for new modes of theorising. In his writings on globalisation and now on 'cosmopolitanism', the founders of sociology are accused of 'methodological nationalism', an approach at the core of which is the nation-state as the basic unit of sociological inquiry. Methodological nationalism is incapable of making sense of today's globalised world. The point for us is that in order to say this Beck has to neglect the fact that there is nothing in the concept of, say, the ideal type (Generalities II) that implies that the nation-state should be the primary unit of social analysis. After all, while Weber may have been politically a nationalist of sorts, the sociology of religion to which he devoted much of his career focuses on entities considerably larger than this, such as civilisational wholes. Nor is it obvious that Durkheim's injunction to 'consider social facts as things' has anything to do with a belief that 'society' implies 'the nation-state'. It is true that Durkheim's substantive writings on, say, professional ethics and civic morals do seem to see the state as the highest form of human organisation; but this assumption has nothing to do with *The Rules of Sociological Method*. Beck can only use the term 'methodological nationalism' because he ignores the difference between formal and substantive theory; there is no place at all in his work for the former.

The recent work of John Urry makes a similar move, claiming that the globalised world that we live in is increasingly 'complex' and that therefore sociologists need to engage with theories of complexity – theories that were first developed by people with no interest in sociology – in order to understand it.

> Racing across the world are complex mobile connections that are more or less intense, more or less social, more or less 'networked' and more or less occurring 'at a distance'. There is a complex world, unpredictable yet irreversible, fearful and violent, disorderly but not simply anarchic. Small events in such systems are not forgotten but can reappear at different and highly unexpected points in time and space. I suggest that the way to think these notions through is via the concept of global complexity. (Urry, 2003: x)

In order to appreciate the conflation of Generalities II and III here one only has to remind oneself of something that was written by Baldamus ... in 1976:

> To the trained sociologist the mere suggestion that the complexity of society might be as real as the structure of atoms is unthinkable. Yet the idea of complexity is today among the most emphatically emphasised characteristics of the sociological discourse. (Baldamus, 1976: 55)

As well as involving a false appeal to topicality, Urry's invocation of complexity theory is undermined by the fact that this theory has also been embraced by those who have no interest whatsoever in the large-scale problems facing a world of 'spaces of global flows' and 'interconnected global networks', but claim to find it just as useful in the study of familiar areas such

Description

31

as education or housing (Byrne, 1998). To be sure, as Weber says, the light of cultural problems moves on and new problems suggest themselves, so that changes in society are bound to suggest new ideas about institutional structures and mechanisms of order and change and so lead to the development of new substantive theories; but the point here is that the development of formal theories – always supposing that 'development' is the right word – tends to obey its own rhythms, which are not those of social change and, more importantly, do not have to be.

Even among theorists who maintain the distinction between the two, the relationship between formal and substantive theorising varies. Some theorists write as though claims about the social world can be made directly on the basis of formal theoretical moves; Talcott Parsons, for instance, often wrote as though his framework for understanding was itself an understanding. For other theorists, the formal theory may well be the product of a basic philosophy – materialism, idealism, positivism, neo–Kantianism, and so on – but the generalisations that make up the substantive theory – Generalities III – will be grounded just as much in the results of an empirical research programme. This is true, I think, of the work of Marx, Durkheim, Weber, De Tocqueville, Freud, Elias, Foucault, Bourdieu and Goffman.

Figure 2.1 summarises these distinctions.

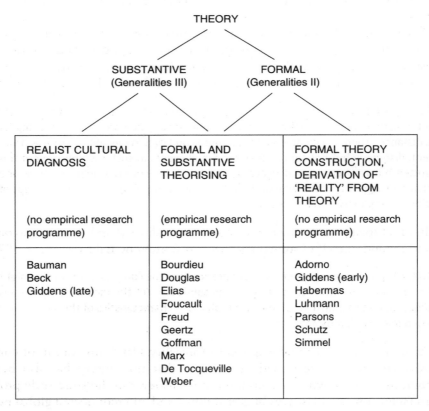

THEORY

SUBSTANTIVE (Generalities III)   FORMAL (Generalities II)

REALIST CULTURAL DIAGNOSIS	FORMAL AND SUBSTANTIVE THEORISING	FORMAL THEORY CONSTRUCTION, DERIVATION OF 'REALITY' FROM THEORY
(no empirical research programme)	(empirical research programme)	(no empirical research programme)
Bauman Beck Giddens (late)	Bourdieu Douglas Elias Foucault Freud Geertz Goffman Marx De Tocqueville Weber	Adorno Giddens (early) Habermas Luhmann Parsons Schutz Simmel

Figure 2.1

The theorists who stand in the middle column never believed that the reality of the social world might be woven solely from the thread of concepts; there was always something for them to discover, even as they made contributions to the development of theory's conceptual arsenal. Theirs is, to be sure, a language of indirectness, their conceptual apparatus is artificial, but it is not so artificial that it becomes the basis for a self-sufficient claim about social reality. By contrast, those in the right-hand column make substantive claims about the social world solely on the basis of a conceptual apparatus; Karl Mannheim called this 'logicism'. Those in the left-hand column make such claims often without the use of any distinct conceptual apparatus at all, appealing instead directly to the reader's vision; Mannheim called this 'intuitionism' (Mannheim, 1982). While it would perhaps be inaccurate to describe them as intuitionists, none has written extensively on the problems of concept formation or theoretical language, or at least not for some time; Beck's concept of 'risk society' for instance, while an unquestionably successful verbal innovation, is not a contribution to sociology's formal conceptual apparatus; Bauman's use of metaphor – 'liquid fear' or 'liquid modernity' or 'the gardening state' – is certainly striking, and has contributed to his prestige, but it seems difficult to convert these hunches into a research programme.

This does not mean that there is anything wrong with cultural diagnosis and commentary; after all, Marx and Weber filled hundreds of pages of newsprint with it. The difference is that nobody at the time would have described their newspaper articles as sociological or social theory; their descriptions of historical events and processes did owe a great deal to the theories they had developed elsewhere, but those theories themselves were grounded in some basic principles of theoretical method as well as in a feel for historical reality.

This is one respect in which, although I consider his work to be scandalously neglected, I differ from Baldamus. Baldamus believed that sociology *may* be capable of cumulative knowledge and of making discoveries, but that if we want to know whether there are any lasting achievements in sociology – and 'we must always remember that there may not be any at all' (Baldamus, 1976: 119) – then we need to examine its most robust theoretical statements and its most impressive empirical research for long-term trends, but not work that lies somewhere in between, since this contains neither great theoretical sophistication nor rigorous standards of empirical inquiry. While I have some sympathy for this position, Baldamus's refusal to discuss any middle-range theorising at all is a serious shortcoming in a work purporting to address what sociologists actually do.

A good example of a middle-range piece of writing is Marx's 'The Eighteenth Brumaire of Louis Bonaparte', his account of French politics between 1848 and 1851. Here there is a constant interplay between parliamentary factions, events in Paris, class interest, and the overall character and direction of events, but all of it is interspersed with statements of Marx's basic theoretical principles. These principles, however, are never simply stated at the beginning of the piece and then 'applied'; the concrete events and processes are not there simply as illustrations of self-sufficient arguments, as might be the case in a piece of analytical philosophy. For instance, in one paragraph he writes:

> Just as the Bourbons were the dynasty of the big landed property and just as the Orleans were the dynasty of monarchy, so the Bonapartes are the dynasty of the peasants, that is the mass of the French people. Not the Bonaparte who submitted to the bourgeois parliament, the Bonaparte who dispersed the bourgeois parliament is the chosen of the peasantry. (Marx, 1978: 105)

In the next sentence he invokes, in the light of observations about the conditions of the French peasantry, his famous distinction between *class-in-itself* and *class-for-itself*, between the objective condition of an identifiable group, and the capacity – or lack of capacity – of that group to identify its shared interests, to develop a common outlook or consciousness and to organise itself accordingly. The point here is that Marx is not doing applied philosophy: although he took the distinction between in–itself and for–itself from the philosophy of Hegel, he did not seek to impose it upon reality or force reality into ready–made categories. Rather, he did theoretically informed historical sociological analysis.

> A smallholding, a peasant and his family; alongside them another smallholding, another peasant and another family. A few score make up a village, and a few score of villages make up a Department. In this way, the great mass of the French nation is formed by simple addition of homologous magnitudes, much as potatoes in a sack form a sack of potatoes. In so far as millions of families live under economic conditions of existence that separate their mode of life, their interests and their culture from those of the other classes, they form a class. In so far as there is merely a local interconnection among these small-holding peasants, and their identity and their interests beget no community, no national bond, they do not form a class ... They cannot represent themselves, they must be represented. Their representative must at the same time appear as their master, as an authority over them ... The political influence of the small-holding peasants, therefore, finds its final expression in the executive power subordinating society to itself. (Marx, 1978: 106)

This is a fine example of sociological description from the classical tradition. It is neither bogged down in detail nor neglectful of the concrete social relations it is trying to depict, and as a result it is able to make connections between economic conditions, the state of communications and type of political regime, retaining throughout a sense of the difference between what is significant and what is not.

Max Weber too, for all the complaints that have been made about the length of his sentences, wrote magnificent pieces of sociological description informed by both substantive and formal theory. Here he is describing Confucianism in the conclusion to *The Religion of China*:

> A true prophecy creates and systematically orients conduct toward one internal measure of value. In the face of this the world is viewed as material to be fashioned ethically according to the norm. Confucianism in contrast meant adjustment to the outside, to the conditions of the 'world'. A well-adjusted man, rationalising his conduct only to the degree requisite for adjustment, does not constitute a systematic unity but rather a complex of useful and particular traits ... not reaching beyond this world, the individual necessarily lacked an autonomous counterweight in confronting this world. Confucianism facilitated the taming of the masses as well as the

dignified bearing of the gentleman, but the style of life thus achieved must necessarily be characterised by essentially negative traits. Such a way of life could not allow man an inward aspiration toward a unified 'personality', a striving which we associate with the idea of personality. Life remained a series of occurrences. It did not become a whole placed methodically under a transcendent goal. (Weber, 1951: 235)

Here we see that terms from Weber's substantive theorising – 'rationalisation', 'personality', 'world', 'prophecy', 'inwardness' – are combined with elements of his formal theorising – a concern with value, and with a comparative approach to the study of civilisations, a comparative approach that manifests itself here as elsewhere in Weber's work in a constant series of comparative references and asides, all of them made from the point of view of their significance 'for us'. Although Confucianism is of interest in itself, as one example of how the shaping of a human life is made possible on the basis of ideas about conduct, it is also of interest as an example of such shaping that contrasts with that in which life is 'placed methodically under a transcendent goal'. By setting up contrasts of this sort and expressing them at the level of individual paragraphs and sentences, Weber was able to dramatise and make more urgent the questions that he had been wrestling with in *The Protestant Ethic and the Spirit of Capitalism* about the causes and the consequences of the emergence of Protestant asceticism in the West. Even in the more detailed descriptions of Chinese history that occur in the main body of the book, the big questions that Weber was wrestling with all his life were never far away.

Now Marx was writing at a time when, although the rhetoric of science provided powerful support for the emerging social sciences, even the natural sciences had not yet developed a language that was specialised enough to appear esoteric to a lay readership. Two generations later, Weber and Durkheim were still producing texts that are for the most part models of lucidity.

Since then, however, as formal theorising and substantive theorising have grown apart, neither allowing itself to be fed or inspired by the other, the language of sociology along with other social sciences has grown more specialised. While formal theorising sometimes seems to have been striving for a kind of *perfection*, substantive theorising has been oriented towards a kind of utilitarian concern simply with theory that is of *utility* for a substantive problem. In the next section, then, we examine some illustrations of this trend.

Perfection Versus Utility

Here is the whole of a story by Borges called 'Of Exactitude in Science':

In that empire, the craft of cartography attained such perfection that the map of a single province covered the space of an entire city, and the map of the empire itself an entire province. In the course of time these extensive maps were found somehow wanting, and so the College of Cartographers evolved a map of the empire that was of the same scale as the empire and coincided with it point for point. Less attentive to the study of cartography, succeeding generations came to judge a map of such magnitude cumbersome, and, not without irreverence, they abandoned it to the rigours of sun and rain. In the western deserts, tattered fragments of the map are still to be found, sheltering an occasional beast or beggar; in the whole nation, no other relic is left of the discipline of geography.

From *Travels of Praiseworthy Men* (1658)
by J. A. Suarez Miranda. (Borges, 1975)

The point of this tale is apparently obvious: the function of a map is not to represent or reproduce every detail of a landscape or a city; it is to provide us with a means of orientation, of finding our way about. This involves a reduction of scale, where the difference between large-scale and small-scale is not one between accurate and inaccurate, but between useful and useless. The maps on the screens in transcontinental airliners are of little use for walking in the mountains, but nor is one which reproduces every feature of the landscape point for point. In the first chapter of *The Savage Mind*, Claude Lévi-Strauss discusses the general function of reductions of scale, saying that they serve to domesticate the object they represent (Lévi-Strauss, 1972). Works of art are an obvious example, a vast and potentially incomprehensible object – God, love – becoming more manageable. Another effect of reduction is intellectual: as well as being a specific analysis of the object represented it is an invitation to consider alternative representations of it. We can extend Lévi-Strauss's observation and say that sociological theory, too, reduces an incomprehensible object, 'society', to what can be contained in the pages of a theory book; and in Chapter 5 we will see that the contents of a daunting and incomprehensible theory may themselves be made more manageable – though not necessarily more comprehensible – by reducing them to a diagram.

For now, consider the word 'perfection' as it appears in the title of Borges' story. It has been suggested that the earliest sociologists, such as Auguste Comte, were driven by an idea akin to the one that motivated Borges' cartographers: to produce a 'perfect copy' of society, a comprehensive and all-embracing account of its workings, sources of order and change, and so on (Bryson, 1983; Velody, 1989). The complication here is that sociology is largely a verbal rather than a visual enterprise, so that a quest for perfection in the depiction of society may involve less the search for the most perfect short sentence or paragraph than an endless spinning out of words, so much so that the quest for the perfect map may appear modest by comparison. The possibility of such endlessness is nicely illustrated by another Borges story, 'An Evening with Ramón Bonavena'; here the narrator travels to meet a writer who has just published a book of six volumes, and asks him how he came to fasten on his subject. The writer explains that he began with the idea of writing about his native city, realised that he knew too little of it, and lowered his ambitions to a book about his family; this in turn proved to be too daunting a topic, and he decided upon an autobiographical novel; yet even here his knowledge of himself was too slight, and so, obeying the maxim that you should only write about what you know, he settled on a corner of his writing desk. The punchline has the narrator praising him for the economy of a style in which the relationship between the pencil sharpener and the stapler is described in a mere 26 pages (Borges and Biog-Casares, 1982).

These two Borges tales remind us that sociological theory, whose task it is to structure, organise and perhaps change our perception of social reality, faces a number of dangers. It can become, for instance, an object of pure aesthetic contemplation, like the old maps stored in the British Library, beautiful but no longer of any use. Clifford Geertz, who may or may not have known Borges' story, put it like this:

> Cultural analysis is (or should be) guessing at meanings, assessing the guesses, and drawing conclusions from the better guesses, not discovering the Continent of Meaning and mapping out its bodiless landscape. (Geertz, 1973: 20)

In a second scenario reminiscent of the second Borges story, a project that begins with the ambition of 'getting at' social reality turns into the expansion and elaboration of a series of initial insights and categorical constructions to the point where the theorist believes that in adding more and more detail to the system he has devised he is making empirical discoveries.

This question of detail is at the heart of C. Wright Mills' famous discussion of Talcott Parsons in *The Sociological Imagination*. Parsons was the most ambitious sociological theorist of them all, believing that the conceptual scheme that he developed during the war years – the scheme of what he called 'pattern variables' – would make possible 'a complete description of a functioning social system' (Parsons, 1949: 144). Eventually he developed this initial statement of intent into his second proper book, *The Social System*, the 550 pages of which Mills claimed to be able to 'translate' into 150 pages of plain English without a loss of content, and ultimately reduce to four paragraphs. In an apparent concession to Parsons, Wright Mills accepts that anything can be expressed in one sentence or 20 volumes. Indeed, he offers a one-sentence summary of one of his own books. This is an unfortunate move because it suggests that what he has done to Parsons can be done to him, and misses the point that there are some ideas that can be reduced to a single sentence or expanded to 20 volumes without a loss of content and some for which a change of length would mean a change of identity. Supporters of Parsons might point out that what Mills edited out is not verbiage at all, but a process of argumentation and reasoning, in which the great theorist lays bare the processes through which he arrives at his results and opens himself up to scrutiny by other members of a scientific community. By reducing this reasoning to something briefer, and removing much of the important 'argumentative' detail, Mills has presented Parsons in a manner akin to the famous image of Einstein, tongue sticking out, with '$E = mc^2$' written on the blackboard behind him, the isolated product of a process of reasoning that can now be forgotten.

Wright Mills in turn would have made short work of such a comparison, as he effectively did in his most famous statement about Parsons:

> Grand theory is drunk on syntax, blind to semantics. Its practitioners do not understand that when we define a word we are merely inviting others to use it as we would like it to be used; that the purpose of good definition is to focus argument on fact, and that the proper result of good definition is to transform argument over terms into disagreement about fact, and thus open arguments to further inquiry. (Mills, 1960: 42–3)

Wright Mills may be right about Parsons. But his own list of the categories we need in order to discuss matters of fact – capitalism, class, etc. – is rooted in a concern with the immediate problems of his own time and society. To be sure, Parsons may have failed to descend from 'a very general level of thinking' to observation. He does not simply tell us, for instance, that industrial society is marked by a substantial service sector alongside manufacturing, or a workforce a significant proportion of which is made up of professionals or that respect for the rule of law has become an important part of the self-understanding of people in liberal democracies. He describes industrial society as 'a system of universalistic, specific, affectively-neutral, achievement-oriented roles' (Parsons, 1951: 177). We will have more to say about this in the next chapter, but for now note that Wright Mills' own definitions were not always ones that other members of a scientific community might draw upon, precisely because they were rooted in his own sense of the urgency of the problems he was addressing. They were what Baldamus called 'verbal innovations of a very fast rate of obsolescence' (Baldamus, 1976: 37).

The differences between Wright Mills and Parsons, then, hang on more than a taste or disdain for abstruse language. Parsons inherited an almost Newtonian belief in sociology as a science, Wright Mills the belief that sociology should address the urgent problems of its day. The difference is reflected in the fact that Wright Mills remains a fascinating figure, witnessed by his *Letters and Autobiographical Writings* (Mills, 2000), but one whose influence on sociology's central concepts and procedures has been limited. Parsons, by contrast, though an unworldly individual whose grasp of social reality was alarmingly slight for one of such eminence, sought to map out the bodiless landscape of meaning and to provide sociologists with workable definitions of terms, as a result of which he was enormously influential. 'Functionalism', for instance, is not the name of a school so much as a description of an intellectual sensibility that few sociological theorists since Parsons have been entirely free from.

Or to put it another way: Wright Mills' generalities were primarily Generalities III, while Parsons' were primarily Generalities II. If the distinction between them is 'absolutely essential', as Mouzelis says it is, it is hardly surprising that the two men did not see eye-to-eye.

Parsons appears in the right-hand column not only because none of his second-order constructs, his conceptual schemas, seem to owe anything to empirical research or historical inquiry, but also because at numerous points he writes as though these constructs are empirical descriptions of the social world. He does not say, 'if you want to study the relationship between doctor and patient empirically you need to have available to you such and such a set of categories', he says, effectively, 'this *is* the relationship between doctor and patient, this is what, in our society, it is like. It is, shaped by a particular combination of pattern variable choices which are made, implicitly, by doctors and their patients, just as it is made by teachers and their pupils or lawyers and their clients.' Without having done any social psychological work or recorded consultations or spent time in a surgery, Parsons thinks that he has grasped something about the way in which people in our kind of society define their social involvements. Without saying so in so many words, he writes as though his conceptual schemes are formalised or reconstructed versions of those used by us in our efforts to make sense of our surroundings and 'define the situation'.

This means that, although Parsons is frequently drunk on syntax, there are numerous cases where he attempts to deploy his conceptual scheme in the description of empirical social processes. The example here is offered with caution, because it concerns a topic that commentators on Parsons generally avoid: love. A universal human experience, subject to endless variations, and described and depicted in myriad ways in poetry, literature, and art, perhaps it is not wholly surprising that love did not escape the roving eye of the grand theorist intent on a complete description of society. The quotation below shows how Parsons described love using the conceptual dichotomy universalism–particularism. The meaning of these terms will be discussed in the next chapter, but for now what matters is the way in which Parsons generates – or seeks to generate – a sense of social reality by conceptual manipulation, with a dose of common knowledge thrown in for good measure. Bear in mind, too, that in the article in which this passage appears – and one whose title, 'Pattern Variables Revisited', must qualify as the dullest in the history of sociological theory – Parsons was responding to criticisms and attempting to clarify his approach:

> Particularism in this context means that from the point of view of the action system, the most significant aspect of an object is its relationality to the actor: as compared with other objects which can 'intrinsically' be classified as similar to it, the significance of *this* object to the actor lies in its *inclusion* in the same inter-active system. In the contrasting case of universalistic modalities, the basis of an object's meaning lies in its universalistically defined properties, hence its inclu-sion in classes which transcend that particular relational system. For example, when a man falls in love, it is this *particular* woman with whom he falls in love, it is this particular woman with whom the love relationship exists. He may, like some other gentlemen, prefer blondes, but he is not in love with the category, but with one particular blonde. Thus the same kind of dilemma exists here as for the two pattern variables described above – it is impossible to maximize the particu-laristic meaning of objects and their universalistic meaning at the same time. A man sufficiently in love with blondeness as such, who therefore pursues any blonde, cannot establish a very stable love relationship with a particular woman. That there is an important 'matching' between consummatory bases of interest and particularistic meaning of objects is clear; its significance is discussed below. (Parsons, 1960: 472)

There are various terms for what has happened here: 'the fallacy of misplaced concreteness', 'concept fetishism', or following Parsons himself, 'falling in love with the category'. At any rate, here is a process in which a formal analytical device designed to aid description – the distinction between universalism and particularism – becomes the only tool of description, so that description becomes nothing more than definition. It is characteristic of much of what Parsons wrote.

Perfection, Utility and the Concept of Society

In Figure 2.1, Parsons has some strange bedfellows. One of them is Georg Simmel. Although Simmel did no more empirical research than Parsons, there is a widespread perception that he could not be more different in sensibility. While Parsons was committed to a version of science pursued relentlessly in his office at Harvard, Simmel is the urban aesthete in Berlin at the turn of the 20th century, the friend of Rodin and Rilke, a man who wrote a two-volume work on social differentiation and a major treatise on money, but also essays on Goethe, Rembrandt, and sexuality. Parsons claims to be able to offer a complete description of society; Simmel writes essays on specific and varied topics. You do not have to read very far into Simmel's work before you feel that what is being conveyed is something different from that offered by Parsons. Nevertheless, Simmel shares with Parsons a willingness to weave sociological description from a single theoretical thread, though the thread is silk where Parsons' is wool; Simmel has left us some of the finest passages of sociological description we have, but also some of the most elusive.

Simmel's major theoretical statement, *Soziologie*, was published in 1908 and partly it was an attempt to give sociology an intellectual foundation when it still lacked any institutional status in German universities. The first chapter is called 'The Problem of Sociology', central to which is the question 'what is society?'. He says that there is a danger either of dismissing the concept of society or of claiming too much for it: we dismiss it if we say that there are only individuals, that only they are 'real'; we claim too much for it if we say that the results gleaned from other disciplines like history, law, psychology, economics, and politics can be synthesised by sociology as 'society'. Neither of these views – society is nothing because there are only individuals, society is everything – is very helpful. Against the first, it should be observed that social actors as well as social scientists readily treat as real phenomena that clearly go beyond, are more abstract than, the individual: we speak routinely of large entities like 'Catholicism' or 'social democracy' or 'cities' or 'Gothic art'. Against the second, to say that other disciplines offer only partial perspectives on society is to turn sociology into a master social science.

The trouble is that the third possibility, namely that 'society' is sociology's particular object domain, to be placed alongside those of law, history, and so on, hardly makes sense either. Something in us wants, quite rightly, to say that all of these, too, are society.

Simmel's solution to this problem is deceptively simple:

> In so far as sociology is based on the notions that man must be understood as a social animal and that society is the medium of all historical events, sociology contains no subject matter that is not already treated in one of the extant sciences. It only opens up a new avenue for them. It supplies them with a scientific method which, precisely because of its applicability to all problems, is not a science with its own content. (Simmel, 1950: 13–14)

How can a new science not have a distinctive content of its own? Simmel explains this in two stages.

In the first he refers to what he calls *general sociology*. Every science, whatever it studies, involves abstraction, looking at something from a particular point of view under the guidance of a particular set of concepts. For example, we could study the history of art or law or anything else under the category of *objectivity*, isolating for analysis only the internal aspects of the art work; or we could study art history under the category of *subjectivity* and examine the work of art from the point of view of the psychology of individual artists. Sociology gives another point of view on the same material, a *social* point of view. A sociologically-oriented art history might study patronage networks in the Renaissance, attitudes to the production of images in the reformation, or the growth of art markets in the 20th century. It might be interested in the power of different social groups in so far as they are affected by the phenomenon of art. And it may even be the case that, having conducted a series of such large-scale inquiries, a socially-oriented history comes to the conclusion that history has a law-like character or at least that we can distil, from the mass of material that history throws up, some generalisations about how history happens which cut across the differences between individual episodes.

This is what Hegel, Marx and Comte do when they say that history can be divided into stages which display the workings of a single mechanism; it is what Durkheim does when he identifies an evolutionary trend from mechanical to organic solidarity; it is what Max Weber does when he identifies an historical tendency for charismatic eruptions to be followed by processes of routinisation. As we will see in Chapter 6, most of Pierre Bourdieu's work is like this. What Simmel calls general sociology makes use of and also generates Generalities III, second-order constructs or abstractions that have a substantive reference and are based upon observations of specific empirical processes.

The reason that Simmel has been placed in the right hand column of Figure 2.1 is that his account of the kind of abstractions which sociology operates with does not stop here. 'The first problem area of sociology … consisted of the whole of historical life insofar as it is formed societally. Its societal character was conceived as an undifferentiated whole. The second problem area now under consideration, consists of the societal forms themselves' (Simmel, 1950: 22). So there is general sociology – putting things in their 'social context', doing 'the sociology of' nationalism, education, art, or sport – and there is *formal sociology*. What are societal forms?

A collection of human beings does not become a society because each of them has an objectively determined life-content. It becomes a society only when the vitality of these contents attains the form of reciprocal influence … If, therefore, there is to be a science whose subject matter is society and nothing else, it must exclusively investigate these interactions, these kinds and forms of association. (Simmel, 1959: 315)

By 'life-content' Simmel means drives, interests, desires, beliefs, sources of motivations that may be economic or political or religious or sexual. But as such, before any interaction has occurred with other human beings, these contents are not yet social, and cannot be the object of sociological inquiry or description.

That there is nothing social about them may be illustrated by the phenomenon of religion. A formal sociological approach to religious phenomena might well note that the content of certain religious beliefs has an influence on the maintenance of a religious community and its devotion to its God or gods. But reference to those beliefs is not the only way in which to make sense of what occurs at a religious ceremony or of the relationship between religious officialdom and a religious congregation. The key point here is that very different life contents may give rise to similar social forms and that the same life content may give rise to different social forms. Thus a trade union or a political party may exhibit an intensity of devotion or type of social hierarchy analogous to those which arise in religious communities, based upon an entirely different set of contents. Neither a religious ceremony nor a political ritual are wholly religious or political: they are both 'social', in so far as they are governed by a relationship between 'forms of sociation'. By the same token, a belief in salvation may be expressed in the form of a church or a sect; or economic interest may be expressed in the form of a free market or central planning. Social forms, then, give stability and permanence to what might otherwise be nothing more than an incoherent strip of social action.

Whereas general sociology studies 'large social formations' – institutional structures, politics, economics, religion, classes, political parties – formal sociology addresses itself to social interaction as such – or sociation, as Simmel calls it. Whereas general sociology is like the 'older science of anatomy' which studies the 'major, definitely circumscribed organs such as heart, liver, lungs, and stomach', formal sociology will address 'the innumerable, popularly unnamed or unknown tissues', because 'on the basis of the major social formations … it would be … impossible to piece together the real life of society as we encounter it in our experience. Without the interspersed effects of countless syntheses, society would break up into a multitude of discontinuous systems' (Simmel, 1950: 9). Simmel calls it formal sociology because he wants to isolate social forms for sociological analysis. One only has to glance at the chapter titles in his major sociological statements to see the distinctiveness of his approach: 'Quantitative Aspects of the Group', 'Superordination and Subordination', 'The Secret and the Secret Society', 'The Stranger', 'Faithfulness and Gratitude', 'The Adventure', 'Flirtation', 'The Metropolis and Mental Life'. Each is an attempt to describe the quality of a form of sociation regardless of when and where it may occur.

Simmel appeals to anatomy for an image of what he is doing, but his approach has also been called sociological aesthetics, on the grounds that the relationship between the form of social life and its content is akin to that between art and social reality. The key concept here is that of 'distance'. Art, by virtue of its being a representation of reality, creates a distance between the representation and the object; all social forms entail a particular distance between the individual and other individuals. Just as a painting reveals the world to us close up and in detail, or far away and in general, a social form like conflict, for instance, may bring strangers closer to one another, while a social form like secrecy may place those who know one another well at a distance from one another. There are vertical distances, such as those involved in subordination, or horizontal distances, such as those involved in fashion. In short, there is not an arena of social life which cannot be understood in terms of the degree of involvement or detachment that it demands from its participants. The upshot of this approach is that, instead of looking at, say, marriage and its place in modern society (old anatomy), formal sociology will observe that any marriage contains secrecy, subordination, reciprocity, gratitude, flirtation, dyadic relationships, triadic relationships and so on, just as human conduct in any other large-scale institutional sector of society will. These are all social forms. It will then isolate these forms for analysis. Thus in the long section on 'The Secret and the Secret Society', the same point about the relationships of proximity and distance that secrecy establishes may be illustrated by material taken from areas as diverse as marriage, card playing and state security. 'Social form' is Simmel's master concept.

Noteworthy here is that Simmel had less influence on the discipline than Parsons did. Why should this be? After all, if we compare the expressions 'general sociology' and 'formal sociology', we might think that formal sociology dealt with matters that were, so to speak, more general than those dealt with by general sociology, with the most basic building blocks of society or its basic tissue. If general sociology provides us with relatively general Generalities III that apply only for a limited time until the light of cultural problems moves on, isn't formal sociology's business Generalities II, the heart of the discipline's identity over time? Not quite. At one point Simmel flirts with the idea that the isolation of a complete set of social forms would be the sociological equivalent of geometry, which suggests that sociology might have available to it a basic mode of reasoning in much the same way that physics has mathematics. In the same passage, however, he writes that the isolation of the form of social life from its content is always a difficult task, so much so that it may not be possible to teach it; it turns out that being able to map out the bodiless landscape of meaning to the point at which you get drunk on syntax depends on the talent of the individual thinker. That is something one could never say of geometry, which is a teachable skill. Max Weber described Simmel as a genius, but his praise was double-edged, because Weber knew that Simmel was not providing sociology with a coherent body of concepts, but articulating a unique and inimitable vision. Weber meanwhile was writing his own treatise, *Economy and Society*, which was eventually to become the starting point for almost anyone working in political science or historical sociology.

Simmel does talk of 'abstracting' social forms from the content of social life but this does not mean that a concept is plucked from thin air and then 'applied' to or imposed upon reality. Social forms are, he says, not invented by the sociologist at all, but merely extricated by him from the social life in which they are embedded (Tenbruck, 1959: Outhwaite, 2006: 76–8). In so far as they are embedded, ordinary actors operating with their first order constructs are, most of the time, not orienting themselves towards them because any strip of interaction can entail more than one form; these forms are, then, never purely 'there' in the course of interaction because they mutually limit each other. The nearest that ordinary actors come to isolating them is in the phenomenon known as 'sociability', or as Simmel puts it, 'society without qualifying adjectives' (Simmel, 1971: 129). Sociability is, he says, the 'play' form of association, in which economic, political or religious aspects of our being are not simply channelled by means of social forms but are completely forgotten. The expression 'the art of conversation' refers to face-to-face interaction in which the content of what is said is irrelevant to the 'success' or pleasure which the interaction affords. So the abstractions Simmel performs, the creation of second-order constructs, are an attempt to articulate a process which is driven and maintained by the implicit understandings – though not the explicit descriptions – we bring to bear upon it.

It is time that we quoted a piece of Simmelian description. Earlier we quoted a passage from Marx's 18th Brumaire in which he describes barriers to class formation and solidarity among peasants and the way in which this lack of solidarity increases the likelihood of Bonapartist rule. Now in one passage of *Soziologie*, Simmel suggests the opposite conclusion to Marx, namely that it is precisely through subordination under one ruler that feelings of solidarity can be created:

> The unificatory consequences of subordination under one ruling power operate even when the group is in opposition to this power. The political group, the factory, the school class, the church congregation – all indicate how the culmination of an organisation in a head helps to effect the unity of the whole in the case of either harmony or discord. Discord, in fact perhaps even more stringently than harmony, forces the group to 'pull itself together'. In general, common enmity is one of the most powerful means for motivating a number of individuals or groups to cling together. This common enmity is intensified if the common adversary is at the same time the common ruler. In a latent, certainly not in an overt and effective form, this combination probably occurs everywhere. (Simmel, 1950: 192–3)

Note that, in contrast to Marx, there are no concrete examples here. Unification as a consequence of subordination to a single ruler is simply a basic form of sociation that Simmel has arrived at by deduction rather than on the basis of historical knowledge. Not that there are no examples of what Simmel is describing; on the contrary, examples can be found at all times and all places in history, and Simmel openly refers to them. But he presents them in the form of random lists of cases that suddenly appear after a bout of formal analysis such as the one just quoted. Take his fascinating account of the importance of numbers for social life. At one point he says that social groups may show certain characteristics only above or below a certain size, something that is made clear by the readiness of groups legally to specify a maximum or minimum number of members. This very general observation is then backed up like this:

> In the early Greek period, there were legal provisions according to which ships crews could not consist of more than five men, in order to prevent them from engaging in piracy. In 1436, the Rhenish cities, fearing the rise of associations among apprentices, prescribed that no more than three apprentices should go about in the same dress. In fact, political prohibitions are most common in this category generally. In 1305, Philip the Fair forbade meetings of more than five persons, regardless of their

rank or the form of the meetings. Under the *Ancien Régime*, twenty noblemen were not allowed without special concession from the King to assemble even for a conference. Napoleon III prohibited all organizations of more than twenty persons that were not specifically authorised. In England, the Conventicle Act under Charles II made all religious home assemblies of more than five persons subject to punishment. English reaction at the beginning of the nineteenth century prohibited all meetings of more than fifty persons that were not announced long in advance. (Simmel, 1950: 175–6)

What has happened here is that episodes or details from a variety of historical periods and contexts have been taken out of those periods and contexts and collected and displayed in a kind of thematic sociological antique shop. In one paragraph, one display cabinet, we are able to view materials from the ancient Greek world, 15th-century Northern Europe, pre–revolutionary France, 17th– and then 19th-century England, all of them helping to make the point about the significance of numbers for social life.

Such displays of erudition are also to be found in Weber's work, particularly in *Economy and Society*, where basic distinctions between 'church and sect' or 'asceticism and mysticism' are followed by a bewildering array of illustrations taken from any and every period in world history. Theodor Adorno thought that there was little to choose between Weber and Simmel in this respect, and indeed the difference between them is not always easy to discern. But it is there. For hovering over everything that Weber wrote, even in *Economy and Society*, which was intended as a kind of encyclopaedia for use by other social scientists, is the urgent question of why the modern world in particular is as it is. 'Church and sect' are not simply two forms of organisation that can be exemplified many times over; the emergence of the sectarian form of organisation is central to the emergence of a certain attitude to conduct that had profound consequences, and that is why the distinction between church and sect is of interest; asceticism and mysticism are not simply two forms of religiosity, but again, the former, in its inner-worldly form, was central to early modern Protestantism. This politico-historical dynamic is always there in Weber's discussion of ideal types, which are intended as devices or tools for further research; but it is largely absent from Simmel's account of social forms: secrecy, subordination, reciprocity, dyadic and triadic relationships, and so on, can contain any and every example, for any historical period. Simmel's generalisations, then, are far more general than Weber's, while his examples are much more individual and arbitrary.[1] The paradox is that while Simmel discusses social forms using far more robust generalisations, generalisations that often sound like social laws, it was Weber's lower level abstractions that proved the more influential.

This is not to say that there are no areas in which Simmel was able to break the shackles of his own formalism. It is true that Weber's sensitivity to political and economic history dwarfed that of his colleague, but the same might be said of Simmel's sensitivity towards aesthetic and erotic matters. Earlier we quoted Parsons struggling manfully to come to terms with love, so we will end this section with a passage in which Simmel discusses the same phenomenon. Love is not a social form, but for Simmel it can be described in terms of the dynamic of involvement and detachment, of social distance, that he deployed in order to understand many other things. Some elements of his descriptions, like those in the Parsons passage, also owe something to the prejudices of his day.

> Gretchen knows nothing of the uniqueness of Faust's personality. She probably does not even suspect it. In any case, she is not in love with it. When she speaks of Faust in her monologues, the language is remarkably lacking in individuality. For her, Faust is 'this sort of man'. However, that this general image is worthy of the entire intensity of her emotions and the commitment of her entire existence is based on the fact that for women as such, the general – sexual life as a whole, the relationship to children, the activities and emotions that define the sphere of home and family – easily becomes a thoroughly individual experience. Because of their ostensibly or actually more profound emotional depths they intensify what the man accepts as something general and typical, to the point that it becomes a matter of purely individual fact and the ultimate focus of the personality. (Simmel, 1984: 173–4)

Like the passage we quoted from Parsons, this owes a good deal to the formal apparatus and terminology with which Simmel might have described any number of social relationships. Nevertheless, we would not feel that Simmel is forcing a particular phenomenon into the terms laid down by his conceptual scheme even if we might feel that what he sees is based on particular substantive assumptions about women's erotic and emotional life. He is not simply mapping out the bodiless landscape of meaning or getting drunk on syntax; it cannot be read as a challenge or supplement to Parsons' statement about men and blondes because Parsons' account is never going to 'transform argument over terms into disagreement about fact, and thus open arguments to further inquiry' in the way that Wright Mills demanded. Simmel's description here, however elusive and allusive, is motivated by a concern for the dynamic of personality, emotion, the integrity of the self, and the forms of interaction pertinent to the phenomenon of love. His second-order constructs are, unlike Parsons', straining to find their way into the middle column of our diagram.

Parsons and Simmel are not alone in their ability to generate distinct approaches to description from a well worked out theoretical language and to have believed that no arena of social life could defeat their ambitions. Of the generation that followed Parsons perhaps Niklas Luhmann is the most notable, and if anything he was even more ambitious than Parsons in this respect; Parsons did at least believe, however deludedly, that the point of his theoretical work was to provide the tools for empirical research. Luhmann, too, wrote of love; or rather he wrote about it, as 'a symbolic mode of communication' (Luhmann, 1986).

For now, though, we turn briefly to a third example of description that arises out of a theorist's talent for formalisation. Erving Goffman is not always seen as a systematic social theorist; indeed, he had little ambition to see sociology as a science in the sense that Parsons intended it. While his second-order constructs are clearly distinct from first-order ones, sometimes to the point of wilful obscurity, he manipulates them with such skill that the reader rarely feels that he or she is being plunged into an impenetrable thicket of categories.

In fact, many readers on encountering him for the first time may feel that they are being told something they already know; only later do they discover that if they themselves try to imitate Goffman's style they flounder. There is, to be sure, a measure of linguistic alienation in Goffman as there is in all theorising, but in his case I am tempted to say that it is precisely the sort which is achieved by great art, allowing the reader to see his or her own social involvements through a new lens, with different eyes. As we will see in Chapter 4, there are numerous passages one might choose to illustrate this, but for the sake of comparison with Parsons and Simmel I have selected Goffman's analysis of hand-holding as a ritual idiom in western societies. The point here is that this bristles with an unfamiliar, formal and seemingly cold terminology – 'tie-signs', the 'ends' of a human relationship, 'main involvements', 'side involvements', 'pairings', 'withs' (Williams, 1983) – yet manages to be delightful and insightful; the distance achieved towards what, after all, is an intimate matter, does not devalue the activity whose description the distance is intended to facilitate. And it ends with a remark that Parsons' attitude to theorising makes impossible.

> But note that tie-signs involving physical acts of love, such as kissing and embracing, also tell us that two ends are engaged in their relationship and in a relationship quite like the one under consideration. The difference, however, should be apparent. Love-making is properly engrossing; it is not only a main involvement, but it can itself brook little by way of simultaneous side-involvements. Hand-holding, on the contrary, is in its very nature a side-involvement – an involvement subordinated to some other activity or sustainable along with other side-involvements, such as smoking and walking, without threat to itself. To elevate hand-holding into a main focus of attention would be to utterly spoil it. (Many men have travelled distances to make love, but few presumably to hold hands.) (Goffman, 1971: 273)

Good and Bad Utility

Despite the differences between them, Parsons, Simmel and Goffman might all be described as theorists in search of perfection, Parsons striving for the perfection of a complete description of society, Simmel doing so by distilling the whole history of social experience into a description of basic social forms, and Goffman by seeking a terminology that might capture the most basic dynamics of face-to-face interaction forever. Any discussion of the work of these thinkers is bound to address the question of whether sociology can be a science. However, we said that this striving for perfection may be contrasted with a search for utility, and that this search for utility is best exemplified by the emergence of localised theories whose purpose is to help us make sense of a particular substantive area: religion, the family, art, science, the state. Clifford Geertz drew attention to the way in which this utilitarian requirement could lead to a kind of theoretical atrophy, in which the phenomenon under consideration becomes more important than the integrity of the theoretical apparatus used to study it; he thought, too, that the 'stultifying aura of conceptual ambiguity' that results is not much reduced by the 'preferred remedy' of 'theoretical eclecticism'. Geertz wrote these words in 1963 and his target was the social scientific study of 'nationalism'; interestingly enough, since then, nationalism has been one of few substantive areas in which theoretical eclecticism has been balanced by the co-existence of theories that refuse to compromise with one another. One of the best examples of a theory of nationalism that maintains its theoretical integrity, and displays it in its descriptions of the nationalist phenomenon, is the work of Ernest Gellner.

Gellner's basic claim is that nations are not long-lasting, pre-existing entities that can be dated to before the industrial revolution; they are rather the product of that industrial revolution, of the rise of science and the decline of religion, and of the emergence of modern states in which the majority of the population is literate and undergoes a universal, homogeneous and general education. Only on the basis of this universal theory of the differences between agrarian and industrial society, Gellner argues, can we make sense of nations and nationalism. Here is a typical passage:

> In the agrarian order, to try to impose on all levels of society a universalised clerisy and a homogenised culture with centrally imposed norms, fortified by writing, would be an ideal dream. Even if such a programme is contained in some theological doctrines, it cannot be, and is not, implemented. It simply cannot be done. The resources are lacking.
>
> But what happens if the clerisy one day is universalised, becomes co-extensive with the entire society, not by its own efforts, not by some heroic or miraculous internal *Jihad*, but by a much more effective, deeply-rooted social force, by a total transformation of the productive and cognitive forces? The answer to this question, and the specification of the nature of that transformation, will turn out to be crucial to the understanding of nationalism.
>
> Note also that in the agrarian order only some elite strata in some societies were systematically gelded, by one or another of the specific techniques described above. Even when it is done, it is difficult, as Plato foresaw, to enforce the gelding indefinitely. The guardians, be they Mamluks or Janissaries, bureaucrats or prebend-holders, become corrupted, acquire interests and links and continuity, or are seduced by the pursuit of honour and wealth and the lure of self-perpetuation. Agrarian man seems to be made of a corruptible metal.
>
> His successor, industrial man, seems to be made of purer, though not totally pure, metal. What happens when a social order is accidentally brought about in which the clerisy does become, at long last, universal, when literacy is not a specialism but a precondition of all other specialisms, and when virtually all occupations cease to be hereditary? What happens when gelding at the same time also becomes near-universal and very effective, when every man Jack amongst us is a Mamluk *de Robe*, putting the obligations to his calling above the claims of kinship? In an age of universalised clerisy and Mamluk-dom, the relationship of culture and polity changes radically. A high culture pervades the whole of society, defines it, and needs to be sustained by the polity. *That* is the secret of nationalism. (Gellner, 1983: 77–8)

Gellner's 'theory of nationalism' owes much to philosophy, sociology, social anthropology and history, but insights from these different disciplines are held together within a coherent framework that seeks to do justice to the morphology of entire societies and historical periods, to objective material imperatives and to the motivations of social groups. What matters to Gellner is not that we accept his theory of industrial society but that this theory proves useful for an understanding of nationalism. But by the same token, the understanding of nationalism is only possible on the basis of perspectives, ways of seeing, opened up by theories of industrial society. Otherwise the study of nationalism becomes just another specialist area, with all the scope for narrowness and triviality that specialism – including specialism in theory! – brings with it.

Like Marx in his essay on the 18th Brumaire, Gellner allows utility – the need for a theory 'of' nationalism – to triumph over perfection without compromising theoretical integrity. Yet in an academic world in which there is an increasing readiness to carve out careers by proclaiming the existence of new substantive problem areas, this is likely to become rarer. Consider, for example, this passage from one of Britain's most prominent sociologists:

> If there are no longer any powerful societies then I try to establish what new rules of sociological method and theory are appropriate. In particular I elaborate some of the material transformations that are remaking the 'social', especially those diverse mobilities that, through multiple senses, imaginative travel, movements of images and information, virtuality and physical movement, are materially reconstructing the 'social as society' into 'the social as mobility'. (Urry, 2003: 2)

Note the way in which a claim about objective changes in society, a claim that may or may not be true, is used to justify the further claim that there exists a new domain of research – mobilities research – and that this necessitates a new set of conceptual tools that are 'appropriate' to the study of it. Here, the tensions between formal and substantive theorising, tensions that made it possible for Marx or Weber or Gellner to produce the memorable descriptions that they did, cannot get off the ground.

Theoretical Description as Compensation and Denial

Regardless of whether the sociological theorist is striving for perfection or utility, theorising is an act of distancing of the second order, the deployment of tools of sense-making that are not those that are deployed by ordinary actors. One way of putting this is to say that the spare and impersonal language of theory generates descriptions that fail to connect with the organic and pulsating character of social life 'itself'. But another is to say that the way of talking preferred by theory is just that, another way of talking. Here is the opening paragraph of Robert Musil's great novel, *The Man without Qualities*, about which there will be much more later:

> There was a depression over the Atlantic. It was travelling eastwards, towards an area of high pressure over Russia, and still showed no tendency to move northwards around it. The isotherms and isotheres were fulfilling their functions. The atmospheric temperature was in proper relation to the average annual temperature, the

temperature of the coldest as well as of the hottest month, and the a-periodic monthly variation in temperature. The rising and setting of the sun and of the moon, the phases of the moon, Venus and Saturn's rings, and many other important phenomena, were in accordance with the forecasts in the astronomical year-books. The vapour in the air was at its highest tension, and the moisture in the air was at its lowest. In short, to use an expression that describes the facts pretty satisfactorily, even though it is somewhat old-fashioned: it was a fine August day in the year 1913. (Musil, 1995: 3)

Both descriptions, the meteorological and the everyday, the scientific and the non–scientific, are valid, there is no competition between them, each can be used as the occasion demands; they will be used as required by the respective language games of which they are a part. A sociological theorist like Parsons might claim that the relationship between social scientific and everyday constructs is like this too, that the account of love we quoted earlier is just the sociological theorist's attempt to make sense of it and that as such it sits alongside those to be found in literature or in life itself.

This, though, is too agnostic, for as soon as we discuss the relationship between second–order and first–order constructs we establish some sort of relationship between them. On the one hand, the one may be a variation of the other: Baldamus thought that even the most abstract sociological concepts were beset by the kind of vagueness that pervades everyday speech; Wright Mills thought that the most abstract of all, Parsons', could be translated into that everyday speech. On the other hand, all theorising, even that which so to speak leaves everything as it is, may be seen as a challenge to those everyday modes of speech by virtue of the fact that it engages the reader in a transformative cognitive act. We will see that this is how some members of the Frankfurt School saw the task of theorising: fans of Adorno will tell you that after reading him things will never seem the same again.

There is, though, a curious third possibility. Later on in the first chapter of *The Man without Qualities*, an accident occurs in which a lorry – a rare and dangerous object in 1913 – knocks over and injures a pedestrian. A 'lady and her companion' witness the event:

The lady had a disagreeable sensation in the pit of her stomach, which she felt entitled to take for compassion; it was an irresolute, paralysing sensation. The gentleman, after some silence, said to her: 'These heavy lorries they use here have too long a braking distance'. Somehow the lady felt relieved at hearing this, and she thanked him with an attentive glance. Though she had doubtless heard the expression many times before, she did not know what a braking distance was, nor had she any wish to know; it was sufficient for her that by this means the horrible happening could be fitted into some sort of pattern, so becoming a technical problem that no longer concerned her. (Musil, 1995: 5)

Putting events into a pattern establishes the man's sense of control over events, a form of technical mastery, but it also establishes a distance or cushion between the events and his companion, reduces them to the talk of braking distances and thereby makes them manageable even if they are not technically comprehensible. It might be said that theoretically informed sociological description is capable of carrying out this dual function, in that it enables us to get a firmer grip on social life, enables us to master situations or see them from alternative viewpoints, to enlarge our vision and understanding and become aware of alternative ways of acting.

It also brings with it two dangers: the first danger is that we can learn to use a vocabulary without understanding what it means; this danger is never far from the surface of sociological theory, a few magic words giving one a sense of intellectual power; the second is that the vocabulary can become a means with which to deny a painful reality when there is a genuine need to confront it more directly. When, long ago, a friend who was 'into' theory expressed his frustration with his girlfriend by informing me that he was having difficulty 'gaining access to her database', or when another, clearly enraptured with the power of psychoanalytic terminology, told me on the point of tears that in order to get over her previous boyfriend she would have to 'decathect', one could not help feeling that something had gone awry.

Conclusion

In this chapter we have passed in review some notable pieces of sociological description inspired or based upon particular theoretical commitments. Had I been a literary theorist of a certain type I might have subjected the passages quoted here to a more extensive analysis, focusing on the minutiae of their language, the cadence of the sentences and so on. However, in the introduction I stressed that the process at work in this book is one of rereading, in which the differences between theorists' intellectual sensibilities will hopefully emerge gradually. Admittedly, phrases like 'intellectual sensibility', though tempting, can also be vague and unsatisfying, and so I introduced a distinction between formal and substantive theorising in order, hopefully, to get at differences in theorists' aims. In the next chapter we will turn our attention to the role played by categories, both in society and in sociological theory. We will see that you can get a sense of someone's intellectual style if you can get a sense of the way in which they deploy categories.

3

Categories

Categories: Classificatory, Dialectical, Ideal-Typical

All sociologists, whether they are theorists or not, make use of categories in the course of their efforts to make sense of the world; by the same token, so do all of us. One of the ways in which societies are rendered coherent and orderly is through the construction and maintenance of systems for the categorisation of persons and things. Categories are the most basic devices we have for making a world. Without categories, interpretive devices, frameworks, none of us would be able to get about, the world would be not so much a world as a chaos of random events and constant surprises. Within sociological theory there is little dispute about the need for such frameworks, although there is variation in the extent to which categories as such are seen as a problem worthy of discussion. The real disputes arise over the way this need is met, the *kind* of categories which are deployed and, as a consequence, the styles of thinking of which sociology is capable. In this chapter we will discuss three approaches to categories:

i)   classification/taxonomy: here natural or social phenomena are divided in order to establish more or less fixed relationships of resemblance and difference; there are distinctions between left and right, high and low, sacred and profane; 'vertical' distinctions between genus and species; or horizontal distinctions between subspecies; distinctions between different social groups – classes, status groups and so on.
ii) dialectics: here the neat and tidy oppositions beloved of taxonomists, in which each individual item can be located in one box rather than another, are called into question, on the basis that social phenomena are not so easily pigeon-holed, but rather are subject to change, transformation, mutation, development or decay.
iii) ideal-typical thinking: here the social world is ordered according to types but these are acknowledged as 'artificial' devices to be used in empirical inquiry. Crucially, a single phenomenon does not have to be placed once and for all in one category but may exhibit elements of more than one type, as when, in Weber's political sociology, a given regime displays elements of charismatic, legal-rational and traditional authority.

It is not an over-simplification to suggest that these three approaches to categorisation have arisen with the three dominant sociological traditions deriving from Durkheim, Marx and Weber. But it is important to realise that they also presuppose different ideas about what the relationship is between categories and the reality they are there to help us study. There is a difference, in other words, not only between types of category, but also between the epistemological presuppositions of those deploying them. Marxian dialectics, for instance, does not simply offer itself as an alternative way of 'thinking about' society, a particular theory or method, but is held by many of its proponents to reflect the 'real' movement of history. The world here is found, not made by the theorist. Durkheim and Weber, by contrast, were more self-conscious about the 'world-making' character of their theoretical apparatus. Weber's *Economy and Society* can of course be read as a series of substantive historical sociologies (Generalities III), but it was also conceived as a giant toolkit, an apparatus parts of which could be deployed by all members of the scientific community to investigate other socio-historical phenomena. Durkheim too, though he often claimed to be a world-finding realist investigating social facts 'as things', is often quite shameless in his use of interpretative devices for the 'creation' of a world. Nowhere is this more true than in *Suicide*, where the fourfold classification of suicide is not the product of empirical investigation at all but is derived from the twofold schema of regulation and integration which Durkheim had already developed theoretically.

Sociological interest in categories as a social phenomenon and an object of inquiry began in 1903 with Durkheim and his nephew, Marcel Mauss. In their essay 'Primitive Classification' they were interested in two types of category:

i) elementary categories – such as space, time, causality, number
ii) social categories – such as sacred and profane, public and private, those which define an individual as belonging to a gender, race, social class, or status group.

This looks like a distinction between philosophical and sociological categories, so that only the latter are of interest to us. Yet despite the fact that philosophers from Aristotle to Kant had claimed to set down the most basic categories without which no experience was possible, Durkheim and Mauss set out to show that even these categories had a social origin. While acknowledging that these categories are 'the solid frames that confine thought', or 'the skeleton of thought' (Durkheim, 1995: 9), Durkheim argued that Aristotle and Kant had only established their necessity, which is not the same as explaining where they had come from, which is what Durkheim and Marcel Mauss sought to do. For instance, in his essay on the category of the person Mauss writes:

> We have concentrated most especially on the social history of the categories of the human mind. We attempt to explain them one by one, using very simply, and as a temporary expedient, the list of Aristotelian categories as our point of departure. We describe particular forms of them in certain civilisations and, by means of comparison, try to discover in what consists their unstable nature, and their reasons for being as they are. It was in this way that, by developing the notion of *mana*, Hubert and I believed we had found not only the archaic basis for magic, but also the very general, and probably very primitive, form of the notion of cause. It was in this way that Hubert described certain features of the notion of time ... Likewise

also, my uncle and teacher, Durkheim, has dealt with the notion of the whole, after we had examined the notion of genus. I have been preparing for many years studies on the notion of substance. (Mauss, 1985: 1–2)

Even the most basic categories – space, time, causality, action, relation, the self – are derived from experience rather than being properties of the human mind. Durkheim and Mauss thought that by arguing this way they could achieve two things: they could say, as Kant did, that the categories were not a matter of arbitrary individual choice, but were the same for all who deployed them, but at the same time they could show that the source of the constraint was society rather than the mind. The categories, then:

> ... do indeed express the most general relationships that exist between things; having broader scope than all our ideas, they govern all the particulars of our intellectual life. If at every moment, men did not agree on these fundamental ideas, if they did not have a homogeneous conception of time, space, cause and number, and so on, all consensus among minds, and thus all common life, would become impossible. (Durkheim, 1995: 16)

This basic position became the foundation for many if not all later anthropological investigations of what makes a common life common, although anthropologists themselves have given different interpretations of it. Mauss claims in his remarks on the category of *mana* that it should be possible to discover in the operation of primitive belief systems not merely the origins of a particular idea of causality but the very idea of causality itself (a universalising ambition taken up by Claude Lévi-Strauss). Less ambitiously, it has been argued that the basic categories vary from society to society and are the product of investigable historical development. There is a common life within the same belief system which provides a society with its 'root paradigms', but that is all (Victor Turner, Clifford Geertz). Or finally, a common life may be held to depend less upon agreed upon basic categories than upon more concrete, social categories (Mary Douglas).

However, we said earlier that the point of this chapter is to show you that categories are not only a topic of sociological theory but also a resource for it. And if we take seriously Durkheim's idea of a common life being dependent upon agreed upon basic categories which have 'a broader scope than all our ideas', then we may be tempted to draw some alarming conclusions about sociology, the chief among these being that the much-lamented fragmentation of sociology, its absence of a distinct disciplinary identity, is due to the absence of such basic categories, and that this absence has been exacerbated by the very efforts of different thinkers to overcome it. The absence of a permanent calculus for sociology, which we have mentioned before, turns out to be the absence of a common set of categories of social space, social time, social relationships, social action and so on. In fact, the history of sociological theory is notable for the arbitrary way in which basic categories have been arrived at. The most notorious example, as we will see presently, is Parsons' pattern variables. As Wilhelm Baldamus acerbically noted, they were intended as the basic building blocks for a science of society, yet nobody knows where Parsons got them from.

A less extreme case is Weber. Weber's categories of sociology are less arbitrary, but the common life from which they do originate is a specifically German tradition of legal theory (Turner, 1994). The basic terms of Marxian dialectics, too, are hardly intended as a means of placing the entire sociological community on a common basis. So from a Durkheimian point of view, what I earlier called 'theoretical liberalism' might well be called mere arbitrariness, the failure of sociology to embody the very idea of the 'whole' that was supposed to be its lifeblood. But in the absence of a standard pre-existing calculus of how things ought to be done or how society looks or works, all we can do is read different theorists against one another. Our sense of what sociological theory is, and how it relates to our life, will not resemble a picture which emerges when a series of partial images or fragments are laid on top of one another to form, so to speak, the perfect image. It will consist in nothing more than the accumulated experience of making connections between perspectives.

Classification

In the last chapter, on description, Borges presented us with the idea of a map the same size as the territory it depicts. We could describe what went wrong as the triumph of accuracy over functionality, of representation over communication, of perfection over utility. Many Borges stories are like that. Another, 'Funes the Memorious', is about a man whose memory is, as he puts it, 'like a garbage heap'. He can remember the shape of the clouds at a particular time of day several months before or the form of ripples on the surface of a stream viewed at a precise instant, or the difference between both and the pattern of a crocodile's skin; he believes that there ought to be different names for each of these images and/or each separate occasion on which they are seen. 'Not only was it difficult for him to comprehend that the generic symbol dog embraces so many unlike individuals of diverse size and form; it bothered him that the dog at three fourteen (seen from the side) should have the same name as the dog at three fifteen (seen from the front)' (Borges, 1964a: 93). Funes has even devised his own way of counting, such that each integer has its own separate name: 'In place of seven thousand thirteen, he would say (for example) Maximo Perez; in place of seven thousand fourteen, The Railroad; other numbers were Luis Melian Lafinur, Olimar, sulphur, the reins, the whale, the gas, the cauldron, Napoleon, Augustin de Vedia' (Borges, 1964a: 93). As with the story of the map, so here the profusion of detail defines a task which is both interminable and useless. Funes is 'not very capable of thought. To think is to forget differences, generalize, make abstractions' (Borges, 1964a: 94).

The absurdity of Funes's world reminds us that without abstractions we are lost; but it is only a starting point before we confront the more basic questions. What degree of abstraction is required to make sense of what we want to make sense of? What kinds of categories do we need to share in order to know that we have a world in common? To what extent are the categories we deploy influenced by political or social power? Is there a difference of degree or of kind between everyday and sociological categories? What counts as a system of categories in the first place? Would this, for instance, be an improvement on Funes's teeming world of detail?

> animals are divided into: (a) belonging to the Emperor, (b) embalmed, (c) tame, (d) sucking pigs, (e) sirens, (f) fabulous, (g) stray dogs, (h) included in the present classification, (i) frenzied, (j) innumerable, (k) drawn with a very fine camel hair brush, (l) etcetera, (m) having just broken the water pitcher, (n) that from a long way off look like flies. (quoted in Foucault, 1970: xv)

This is another of Borges's jokes, the extract from a 'Chinese encyclopaedia' which Michel Foucault claimed moved him to write *The Order of Things*. The subtitle of Foucault's book is 'an archaeology of the human sciences'; our task is more modest, and so we need a more appropriate example, one that can give us some more direct purchase on classification as a problem for sociology.

In *The Man Who Mistook His Wife for a Hat* the neurologist Oliver Sacks relates the story of one of his patients, a Dr P., whose problem seems to be the opposite of Funes's. Like Funes, Dr P. finds it difficult to deploy abstract nouns like 'dog', but unlike Funes this is not because he is immersed in a chaos of details but because he can 'see' only abstract shapes. Handed a rose and asked to say what it is, he can only reply: 'About six inches in length … A convoluted red form with a linear green attachment'. What we might call a glove becomes 'a continuous surface … infolded on itself. It appears to have … five "out-pouchings", if this is the word' (Sacks, 1985: 13). Dr P's descriptions here are not wrong, but they are too analytical, the object being broken down into components which are themselves abstract shapes that might be deployed in the description of many other objects. His world is not private in the sense in which Funes's is, because whereas Funes employs a language which is arbitrary with respect to everyone else's, Dr P. deploys a familiar vocabulary. Nobody would dispute that the stem of a rose *could* be described as 'a linear green attachment'. But socially, he is just as much at sea as Funes, the categories with which he makes his way in the world being pitched at too high a level of abstraction to be of use in everyday talk. Imagine saying that 'my love is like a red red convoluted red form with a linear green attachment'.

The difference, however, between Dr P's social incompetence and Funes's is that while Funes provides us with the limit case which proves the necessity of some kind of abstraction, Dr P., who is capable of abstraction, raises the question of what kind it should be, what level of abstraction is appropriate in any specific situation. It was one of the many merits of Berger and Luckmann's *The Social Construction of Reality* to have pointed us to the ways in which the exigencies of social life make a variety of demands on us which have to be met by the deployment of appropriate categories. Berger and Luckmann called these typifications and argued that their level of abstraction varies with the occasion and setting, so that social competence, the successful performance of a strip of interaction, depends upon our having available a series of typificatory schemes that operate at different levels. Even if we do not utter any words, when we encounter another person we have to know whether to orient ourselves towards them by perceiving them as a man, a European, an Englishman, a jolly fellow, a student, or my friend Fritz. In fact, they argued, we are remarkably skilful in our deployment of categories, a point demonstrated by Harold Garfinkel in his famous breaching experiments, in which experimenters were able to cause considerable distress to their friends and family by the calculated adoption of the wrong level of abstraction in everyday talk (Garfinkel, 1967).

This does not mean that there may not be occasions on which the language of abstract geometrical shapes in Dr P's sense is entirely appropriate; when architects discuss plans or the drawings of a building, everyday vernacular terms like 'house', 'office block', 'museum' or 'library' are seldom heard, whereas terms like 'mass', 'volume', 'skin' and so on may be routine. Indeed, we may generalise and say that the eschewal of such vernacular terms – the refusal to call a spade a spade if you like – is a feature of scientific culture and expertise more generally, and that the more impersonal the topic, and the less there is at stake for the individual participants, the more likely is the resort to analytical terms of an abstract and generalising character.

Berger and Luckmann are making a point about categories as they are deployed in face-to-face performances in which a considerable amount of interactional 'work' has to be done. We now turn to categories that form a stable system for the classification of objects and people beyond the exigencies of interactional contexts. No theorist has contributed more here than Mary Douglas. Douglas does not share the ambitions of Durkheim's followers to establish the social origins of the most basic categories of thought, but rather to analyse the ways in which objects in the social environment, as well as other people, are classified, and the social dynamics through which systems of classification are maintained or undermined. Nevertheless, her work might well be seen as a response to the following remarks made by Durkheim and Mauss in the introduction to *Primitive Classification*:

> Even today a considerable part of our popular literature, our myths and our religions is based on a fundamental confusion of all images and ideas. They are not separated from one another ... with any clarity. Metamorphoses, the transmission of qualities, the substitution of persons, souls and bodies, beliefs about the materialisation of spirits, and the spiritualisation of material objects, are the elements of religious thought or folklore. Now the very idea of such transmutation could not arise if things were represented by delimited and classified concepts. The Christian dogma of transubstantiation is a consequence of this state of mind and may serve to prove its generality. (Durkheim and Mauss, 1967: 5)

The suggestion here is that a feature of the modern world is the absence of the kind of clear boundaries between phenomena characteristic of the societies studied in *Primitive Classification*: Australian aboriginal, Mexican and classical Chinese/Greek. Douglas's work is a counterweight to this, suggesting ways in which, even in rapidly changing societies like our own, there remain significant features of our social experience in which orderliness and predictability are sustained through classification. In Durkheim and Mauss's work the possibility of the collapse of clear classificatory boundaries was already hinted at, so that their most famous statement, 'the classification of things follows the classification of men', was only partially true. In fact, the book displays an evolutionary logic, so that while in Australia the classification of things arises from the classification of men, in Mexico there is an interaction between the two orders of classification, and China and ancient Greece are societies in which the classification of things has developed a life of its own, and is no longer rooted in social distinctions (Allen, 2000). The process in which classificatory or sense-making schemas are emancipated from their social roots culminates in modern science, and it has been suggested that Durkheim's work implies a development, from the systematic philosophy of nature characteristic of relatively unchanging primitive societies to the scientific classifications characteristic of our own, rapidly changing ones.

Douglas's work challenges this view in that it points us towards aspects of social phenomena in which those phenomena are interpreted in a way which is not scientific yet is perfectly systematic. Her most well-known contribution here has been in the area of pollution behaviour, encapsulated in the claim that 'dirt is matter out of place'. The paper in which this claim was first made was 'The Abominations of Leviticus', in which Douglas (1966) argues that all cultures make distinctions or sets of distinctions between clean and unclean, between what can and cannot be touched or, for that matter, talked about, and that prohibitions arise not out of an understanding of the 'nature' of what is prohibited but out of an understanding of the system of distinctions and classifications of which the prohibited item is a part. The reason that the ancient Hebrews refused to eat the flesh of the pig had nothing to do with the pig's intrinsic nature or incomparable filthiness, but everything to do with the fact that within the system for classifying animals set down in the *Book of Leviticus*, it was an anomalous creature, in this case incomplete – the pig parts the hoof but does not, unlike the cow, chew the cud; it is unclean, but only in the way that creatures which crawl or creep along the ground are unclean, being neither flyers nor swimmers. Had there been penguins in the ancient near East no doubt they would have been considered unclean too.

More importantly, while we may be tempted to argue that our ideas about pollution are scientific while those of non-literate cultures, for example, are symbolic, there remains plenty of pollution behaviour and boundary maintenance which is in its own way as symbolic and non-scientific as that of any non-western society. Hence:

> Dirt ... is never a unique, isolated event. Where there is dirt there is a system. Dirt is the by-product of a systematic ordering and classification of matter ... Shoes are not dirty in themselves, but it is dirty to place them on the dining table; food is not dirty in itself, but it is dirty to leave cooking utensils in the bedroom, or food bespattered on clothing; similarly bathroom equipment in the drawing room; clothing lying on chairs; out-door things indoors; upstairs things downstairs; under-clothing appearing where over-clothing should be ... In short, our pollution behaviour is the reaction which condemns any object or idea likely to confuse or contradict cherished classifications. (Douglas, 1966: 36–7)

There are two possible interpretations of this passage. The first is that before we classify reality or order it in any way, it is what the philosopher Kant called an 'infinite manifold', that any effort to bring everything under a single classification scheme is bound to fail, that no classification system is exhaustive, and that there will, therefore, always be items which fall 'outside', which belong to no category. The second is that it is the very process of classifying that creates those recalcitrant items, that they cannot become anomalies until this classification has begun. On this second interpretation, an item which is anomalous in one system may fit perfectly well within another. We could call these two interpretations the realist and the constructivist ones if you like. According to the first, classifying is akin to collecting, the material to be collected simply existing in the world, lying around waiting to be ordered in some way or another. According to the second, for all practical-symbolic purposes nothing has any significance until it is part of, or is an anomaly in relation to, a system. In this book I tend towards the second; the pig, anomalous in the ancient Hebrew classification of animals, is not the same as the pig, not anomalous in another system of classification. We do not have 'the same' animal classified in different ways, but rather different animals, different because of the fact of having a different significance attached to them. Our social lives are never lived outside a web of significances.

But the passage quoted here also contains a more straightforwardly empirical claim about the role of anomalies in cultures such as ours, a claim that we can be as intolerant of anomalies as cultures in which such anomalies are considered genuinely dangerous. So, for instance, while we may not put twins to death in the manner of some African societies that believe that only one baby can be born from a single womb, in so far as we 'do' pollution behaviour we have an awareness of anomaly which is at least as acute as theirs. This claim has evoked some lively reactions, notably this one from Rodney Needham:

> it cannot be alleged that an anomaly automatically gives rise to wariness or unease or a fear of danger. One proof of this is that everywhere people make up classificatory oddities: they are attracted by them, and it might even be said that they need them. As for people's response – they may pay them the respect due to gods ... or they may distrust them ... or they may find them entertaining. (Needham, 1979: 46)

Needham's statement is important because it appears to suggest that Douglas's work cannot account for variations and nuances of precisely this sort, and that she assumes that a fear of anomaly is an anthropological constant. This, along with a somewhat static account of social structure, may have been the impression given by *Purity and Danger* (1966), but in later works such as *Natural Symbols* (2003) and *Implicit Meanings* (1975) Douglas sought to develop an analytical framework in which it would be possible to make sense of the role and extent of classificatory practices in highly differentiated, highly individualised contemporary societies undergoing rapid social change.

> a classification system can be coherently organised for a small part of experience, and for the rest it can leave the discrete items jangling in disorder. Or it can be highly

coherent in the ordering it offers for the whole of experience, but the individuals for whom it is available may enjoy access to another competing and different system, equally coherent in itself, from which they feel free to select segments here and there eclectically, not worrying about the overall lack of coherence. (Douglas, 2003: 82)

Furthermore:

Some social structures can tolerate anomaly and deal with it constructively, while others are rigid in their classifications. The difference is probably the most important subject on which sociological research can focus. (Douglas, 1975: 227)

To provide for this focus Douglas developed the analytical device which most distinguishes her work. 'Grid and Group' is a simple and elegant way of representing both individual and collective cosmologies by locating them in an analytical space defined by the relationship between two variables: the extent to which a system of classification is 'shared'; and the extent to which the individual is dependent upon social pressures from the group of which he/she is a member.

No society is conceivable in which there are no shared systems of classification. Even our own is rendered coherent by the fact of classifications recognised in common. In Figure 3.2 on page 62, 'society as a whole' may be represented as a horizontal line drawn at some distance above the central horizontal line representing zero classification. The extent of it – how far across the diagram it goes – will depend upon the extent to which a society can tolerate individuals not being controlled by others. So, for instance, the societies studied by Durkheim and Mauss in *Primitive Classification* take the form of a short line high up on the right-hand side (A): there is a rigidly shared system of classification with little scope for individuals to exert pressure on the group. Modern western societies are characterised by a long line extending across to the left side of the page, less far above the line than in a pre-modern society (B). In other words, in so far as our society is stable, the scope for individual freedom of thought which is a central feature of it does not undermine the society's dominant classifications, which continue to have relevance to the way in which the members of those societies live their lives. A society subject to strong social revolutionary pressure is represented by (C) and may be under threat of what Durkheim called declassification, represented by 0 in the diagram (Starr, 1992).

If we can represent a society in this way we can also represent the biographies or current state of individual cosmologies too. Funes, for instance, might be said to have worked out a private system of classification, but it is close to being no system at all, and it is inconceivable that anybody else might learn it. Therefore he stands to the right of Figure 3.3, not so much controlled by others as unable to exert any influence on them. The case of Dr P. is different in that he has indeed something that might be described as a system of classification. He can handle abstractions, in particular abstract shapes, which are part of a publicly available repertoire of abstractions. He might even persuade others to describe parts of the world through the use of such abstractions rather than through individual names, and such redescriptions might be seen as poetic. But it is clear that Dr P. will influence nobody. This is important because we can identify positions to the left of the vertical, those which represent individuals who have influence over others. These may be like the Pope, who influences others while subscribing to a system of classification which is not his own; or artists or composers, situated in the bottom left-hand quadrant, who strive to develop and maintain, without compromise, their own system of classifications. Douglas's example in the 1970s was John Cage, but today we might refer to Madonna or Damien Hirst, all of whom are driven to reinvent themselves in the face of their possible incorporation into mainstream culture, and a potential drift towards the right of the diagram, where they would remain distinctive but without influence.

However, this is important too because 'Grid and Group' might provide us with a way of thinking about the problem of the 'anxiety of influence' which we referred to in connection with the classics. A classic author is one who may be said initially to occupy a point in the top right, absorbing an intellectual tradition, moving then to the bottom right, composing his as yet unrecognised work according to his increasingly individual system of classification, later moving to the left as his work becomes recognised. Moreover, as we will see, there is a curious, not to say eerie connection between Dr P's procedures and those of Talcott Parsons, Max Weber and any other sociologist who has sought to set down a battery of concepts and categories through which to generate descriptions which challenge or simply differ from the routine, everyday descriptions of ordinary actors. Parsons in particular appears to have derived his categories – in the early work, the pattern variables – from nowhere, at least not from any publicly available system of categories. Weber, by contrast, derived many of his from the publicly available and well-established system of concepts which constituted the German legal tradition (Figure 3.4).

The point of this discussion of Mary Douglas has been to show that much of what we call social order may be said to be rooted in the classificatory schemes that a society makes available to or perhaps imposes upon its members; they are of interest to students of social integration and to students of social

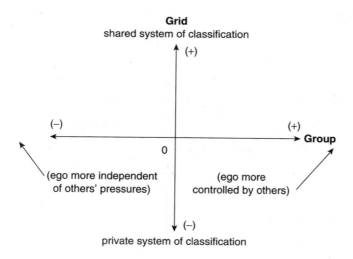

Figure 3.1

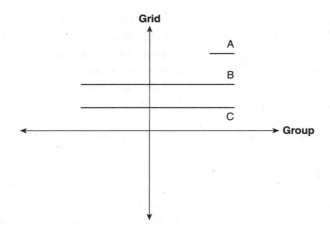

Figure 3.2

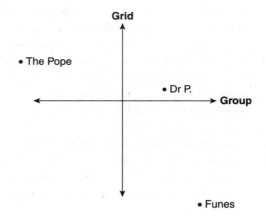

Figure 3.3

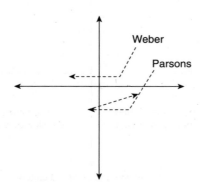

Figure 3.4

control. But it is important to realise that classification is not the only way to deploy categories in order to impose or make sense of social order. And nowhere is this better illustrated than in the special case of sociological theory itself. It is to this that we now turn.

Parsons: Classification as Sociology, Sociology as Classification

The work of Talcott Parsons has been called many things. One description of it is a 'giant filing system' (Craib, 1994: ch. 3). While there is truth to this, the classificatory logic emerges, so to speak, from a theory which, in its intention at least, is quite different. This is important because within some versions of sociology such a classificatory logic is there at the beginning as well as the end. Nowhere is this more evident than in statistically inspired accounts of inequality, where a population is simply divided into any number of groups derived from a sliding scale of income differentials. But it is also there in accounts of race, ethnicity and religion where, following an initial definition, little is said about the dynamic of the relationship between the groups.

Now, what happens in Parsons is different. We have already learned of his ambition to produce a 'complete description' of society. But a 'complete description' has nothing to do with 'covering' the whole of a population by means of a classificatory schema or a full-scale map of society. There is a classificatory logic at work in Parsons, but it emerges as a kind of secondary effect of the deployment of his primary categorical apparatus, the pattern variables. We saw in the last chapter how he described love by means of the pattern variable universalism–particularism, and it is time now to discuss this in more detail. The pattern variables were a schema Parsons invented in order to convey the idea that social action was structured in terms of a series of 'orientational' choices that individuals implicitly make and which are also institutionally embedded in social practices. These are set out in Figure 3.5.

PARSONS' PATTERN VARIABLES

PARTICULARISM/UNIVERSALISM – treat another actor EITHER as unique OR as a member of a class

ASCRIPTION/ACHIEVEMENT – treat another actor EITHER in terms of his/her inherited characteristics (e.g. as a member of the nobility whose criterion of membership is blood; or as a member of a race; as a woman) OR in terms of his/her qualifications (e.g. as a professional)

AFFECTIVITY/AFFECTIVE NEUTRALITY – EITHER respond to another actor emotionally OR exhibit distance/reserve

DIFFUSENESS/SPECIFICITY – treat another actor EITHER in terms of all of his/her characteristics and activities OR in terms of one activity

---

Figure 3.5

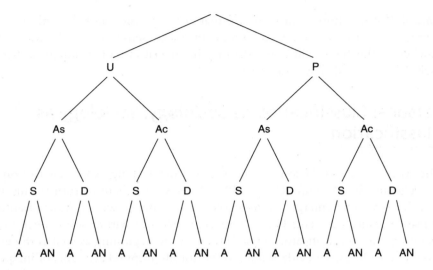

Figure 3.6

The story of the pattern variables as a device has been told countless times elsewhere; they are important here because it might be thought that Parsons has subjected the complexity and messiness of social life to a formula so simple and general that nothing much of any use can be said. Paradoxically, however, the logical import of the pattern variable schema is, as Wilhelm Baldamus pointed out thirty years ago, that it generates too many rather than too few possibilities.[2] For if in every situation there are four choices then we can represent them in the form of the branching diagram depicted on Figure 3.6, from which we can see that the upshot is a schema of 16 types of social situation, or rather, 16 pattern variable choice combinations.

Now if Parsons was simply a classifier we would expect him to have concluded that there were 16 types of social structure. In the early part of *The Social System* he implies as much, filling in the 16 boxes which are drawn by means of the pattern variable schema; we have what looks like a 16-fold classificatory schema. But this is hardly a classificatory schema in the biologist's or the natural historian's sense. For the latter's lifeblood is the collection of material and its ordering, or continuing arguments about where material already collected and named 'really' belongs. There is, for instance, an argument within evolutionary biology over which of the following two schemas is correct or appropriate.

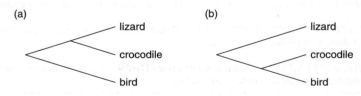

Figure 3.7

A lizard resembles a crocodile more than it does a bird, but from an evolutionary point of view (b) is more accurate. We might want to say that here 'nature' is 'socially constructed', but the point is that the lizard and the crocodile do exist, they are well understood, and their classification is no mere logical exercise. Even in the more overtly symbolic classificatory schemas studied by anthropologists from Durkheim to Douglas, there is no doubt about the existence of the creatures or plants which wait to have a meaning conferred upon them by ideas.

Parsons, by contrast, had not collected examples of interaction and subsequently attempted to make sense of them. Rather, *the 16 types of situation are generated solely by the pattern variables: they are mere logical possibilities.* Now, the point here is that if this 16-fold schema is not really a classificatory scheme or is unusable, it is not because it is too much of a shorthand, that 16 types of interaction are too few. On the contrary, they are too many. This is not as paradoxical as it sounds. The great political philosophers such as Aristotle, Montesquieu, or Marx managed to construct an entire political science or political sociology using a very limited number – three or four – of types of regime or historical period or type of legitimate authority; in the case of Aristotle or Montesquieu the only variation was the 'degenerate' form of each type. Weber constructed a theory of legitimate authority using three types, and Durkheim a theory of suicide using four types, only three of which he discussed at any length. Sixteen types of situation looks positively cumbersome by comparison, and the schema makes no sense at all if some of them are effectively empty boxes.

Parsons seems to have been aware of this; for example, in the chapter of *The Social System* entitled 'Types of Social Structure', in which he seeks to give concrete examples of what he is talking about, he makes use of only two of the pattern variable choices rather than the full four. Expressed in terms of Figure 3.6, the branching stops at the second stage. It is only the universalism/particularism and the achievement/ascription choices that interest him. This then gives him four types of social structure, as shown in Figure 3.8.

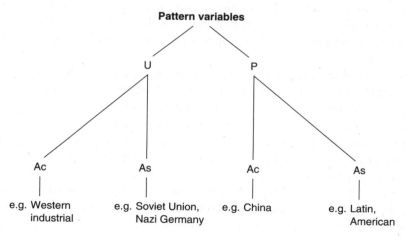

Figure 3.8

The distinction between the first and the second examples is interesting here because Parsons was writing at a time when theorisations of the relationship between the two core Cold War states themselves tended to fall into one of two camps: on the one hand, the theorists of industrial society argued that the West and the Soviet Union were converging on the same type of society centred on large industrial enterprises with enterprise managers, and driven by imperatives of growth and development; on the other, Cold War warriors insisted upon the existence of absolute distinctions between democracy and totalitarianism, or capitalism and communism. Synthesiser that he was, Parsons implicitly believed these to be stereotypical and partial descriptions, restricted to the economic or the political or the ideological aspects of the societies concerned. The combination of pattern variables was designed to show the relationship between the similarities and differences between the two societies at the level of social structure. Here he is on Soviet Russia:

> Because of the universalistic element there is the same emphasis on the sphere of occupation and organisation and its independence of kinship or narrowly defined community. However, there are certain important differences. First, the strong emphasis on classificatory qualities tends, in terms of social structure, to become an emphasis on status rather than on specific achievements. Hence the inevitable elaborate differentiation of roles where achievements are concretely of high importance and where universalistic criteria apply to them, tends to work out to a status-hierarchy where the accent is on what a given actor *is* rather than on *what he has done*. (Parsons, 1951: 192)

In view of our remarks in the last chapter about linguistic alienation, and about theoretical description's compensatory effects, there is much that could be said about this passage and the era in which it was written. For here, at a time when the truth about Stalin's crimes was not only becoming well-known but also being acknowledged publicly, Parsons' scientistic, bland formulation, however important it might be, could also serve as a distance-creating description of what others would have called tyranny or oppression or injustice. Parsons is usually described as a cultural conservative and as a representative of postwar American complacency; that may well be true, but the categories he deployed for the purposes of description made him a rather ineffective Cold War warrior.

The idea behind the pattern variables, however, was that these basic building blocks should be capable of generating accounts not only of large civilisational complexes or entire societies, but also of more concrete types of social situation. One example that demonstrates Parsons' ambition, and also his limitations, in this respect, is his description of the doctor-patient relationship (Parsons, 1949). Here one might have expected that a description of such a specific encounter between the incumbents of such well-defined roles would have, at least partly, followed the contours of the encounter itself. It might, for instance, have taken us inside the doctor's surgery and examined the interactional nuances of the encounter: use of language, gesture, differences of verbal repertoire between medical expert and person on the street. Instead, the most concrete level of description which Parsons achieves is one in which the doctor-patient encounter is held to be structured by means of the value-orientations characteristic of the 'professional pattern' peculiar to western industrial societies: what we discover by means of this description is that the doctor's orientation is typical for that of modern professionals more generally: it is, like that of the lawyer or the university professor, universalistic, achievement-oriented, specific and affectively neutral.

Dialectical Categories

The most sustained effort to develop a version of sociology that avoids classificatory reason is the work of the Frankfurt School of Social Research, in particular its most talented representative, Adorno. Adorno believed that classificatory reason was pervasive in society and rife within sociology, and that therefore any form of social thought that was to question society's dominant assumptions needed to be vigilant in its adherence to dialectical reasoning. This is not always appreciated by sociologists who often focus on his substantive diagnosis of the pathologies of modern society at the expense of an attention to the intellectual moves through which such diagnosis is made possible. *Dialectic of Enlightenment*, Adorno and Horkheimer's relentless dismantling of the shibboleths of western culture, is more often referred to than essays such as 'Sociology and Empirical Research' (Adorno, 1976a), the introduction to the German edition of Durkheim's essays (Adorno, 1976b) or the lectures now collected in *Introduction to Sociology* (Adorno, 2000). The whole thrust of Adorno's work is that it makes no sense to claim that the world is an arena of domination, injustice and alienation and to then express that claim in a language that is plain, direct and easy to understand. Plainness, directness and simplicity are not criteria of good style if the world is distorted, tortured and complex. Adorno himself undoubtedly took this point too far, but it is important to understand that he thought that a social science which tried to reflect the social world like a mirror was not only naïve but also complicit with it. For the same reason he had a disdain for 'realism' in culture, and a preference for the high modernism of writers like Beckett and composers like Schoenberg.

We will consider Adorno's critique of sociology in more detail below, but since elements of his critique of culture find their way into it we need to consider them here. The basic argument is that contemporary culture is pervaded by classificatory reason on a number of levels. On the most abstract level there is a series of categorical oppositions or dualisms that structure our perceptions of contemporary reality or at least lie behind it as its presuppositions: freedom/heteronomy, culture/barbarism, work/leisure, truth/falsehood, culture/industry, and hovering so to speak above all of them, enlightenment and myth. According to Adorno, we assume these oppositions to be absolute: hence 'culture' stands for what is elevated, sophisticated and nuanced, barbarism for its opposite; work is work, free time is free time, they are clearly different things. The dialectical approach to such phenomena is precisely not to argue that they stand at either end of a spectrum – in the manner in which Durkheim, for instance, arrived at his types of suicide – and that we should seek a third way between them, a pragmatic mean. Instead, he seeks to demonstrate the ways in which these categories operate historically, as part of the way in we structure experience. The argument is that there is always a point at which one pole of the opposition passes over into its opposite; that point occurs precisely when the separation between them is thought to be at its greatest. In the essay 'Free Time' he observes that in our society, in which individuals have available to them more formally designated free time than at any point in modern history, and in which therefore we tend to believe that 'work' and 'leisure' are opposites, the lack of imaginative resources with which to fill their free time leads people to seek forms of leisure which take on the characteristics of work: sport, which requires the kind of team discipline that is demanded in the world of work; or Do-It-Yourself, in which large parts of the weekend are devoted to the exercise of substandard craft skills.

Similarly in *Dialectic of Enlightenment*, the apparent opposition between freedom and necessity is called into question through the observation that the culture industry, through films and other forms of popular entertainment, markets not only its products but also the idea that our consumption of them is the product of individual choice. Choice is an illusion put about by those who market culture and who do so, moreover, by the ever more refined process of the differentiation of cultural products. Adorno and Horkheimer's formulation of this point recalls the Durkheim-Mauss-Douglas material we have just discussed:

> Kant said that there was a secret mechanism in the soul which prepared direct intuitions in such a way that they could be fitted into the system of pure reason. But today that secret has been deciphered ... There is nothing left for the consumer to classify. Producers have done it for him. (Adorno and Horkheimer, 1973: 124–5)

Put more bluntly, 'everyone is given a choice so that none may escape'. Confronted by a wealth of stimuli which threaten to overwhelm them, consumers are daily congratulated by the culture industry for having shown themselves able to operate with a public system of classification and to employ it in order to make their own decisions or lifestyle choices. But it is this very freedom of choice which is the manifestation of a kind of heteronomy, as when we express our free choice of the latest product by saying that we 'have to have' it. It is a tribute to Adorno's discernment that today we might make a similar observation about the role played by 'choice' in the reform of some public services: choice is not an illusion, but at the same time there is no choice but to make a choice.

Another example is provided by language. Many people believe that plain, direct speech is always preferable to abstraction and circumlocution. For Adorno, however, plain speaking is as often as not a device by which to make language impenetrable: '... the more purely and transparently words communicate what is intended, the more impenetrable they become' (Adorno and Horkheimer, 1973: 152). Or take the production of sexuality in popular entertainment, where more dialectical paradoxes arise. The 'graphic' depiction of sex in popular culture, which might be taken for openness or the throwing off of inhibition, undermines our capacity to imagine the possibility of sex for ourselves:

Works of art are ascetic and unashamed; the culture industry is pornographic and prudish. Love is downgraded to romance ... The mass production of the sexual automatically achieves its repression. Because of his ubiquity, the film star with whom one is meant to fall in love is from the outset a copy of himself. (Adorno and Horkheimer, 1973: 140)

Once you start to collect examples of this kind of reversal strategy – the most memorable are found in *Minima Moralia* – you can readily arrive at a litany of contemporary culture's shortcomings, so much so that Adorno's efforts to describe society dialectically begin to look suspiciously mechanical.

Be that as it may, the main thrust of his argument is that mainstream sociology is crippled by shared assumptions about the relationship between social reality and the categories through which we make sense of it. These assumptions are of neo-Kantian origin, the most important of which for us is that reality confronts the investigator as an infinite manifold of raw data, which are then ordered by means of subsuming them under categories. Such categories are properties of consciousness, and it is through these alone that the object of inquiry is *constituted*. The two most important consequences of this were the search for categories through which reality might be classified (empiricism), and the formulation of historical or social laws which they might be said to obey (positivism). An empiricist is not necessarily a positivist, and vice-versa, but in either case, two things happen. Firstly, concrete empirical reality is treated as an object of inquiry, so that concrete objects are treated as nothing more than examples or illustrations of general laws or of exclusive categories; secondly, in their reflection on their own procedures, both empiricism and positivism treat the order or lawfulness which is the product of their own consciousness as though it were a property of the object of inquiry itself. This confusion of the relationship between social reality and the categories of thought is an example of a much broader process that Adorno and Horkheimer dubbed the entanglement of myth and enlightenment.

At its simplest, enlightenment refers to the elimination of all forms of religious belief in favour of a secular understanding of human beings and their relation to the world. It is supposed to be the opposite of prejudice and superstition. But enlightenment has two meanings which stand in tension towards one another. Firstly, enlightenment implies a link between rationality and freedom, summed up in Kant's famous definition:

Enlightenment is man's emergence from his self-incurred immaturity. Immaturity is the inability to use one's own understanding without the guidance of another. This immaturity is self-incurred if its cause is not lack of understanding, but lack of resolution and courage to use it without the guidance of another. The motto of enlightenment is therefore: *Sapere aude!* Have courage to use your own understanding. (Kant, 1970: 54)

Because we all possess the faculty of reason, we all understand the idea of a liberal utopia of free, reasonable, mature individuals.

However, secondly, enlightenment refers to the rise of modern science and the theme of science as a tool with which human beings can achieve a domination over nature. It implies not maturity, but mastery, of both nature and society, what Weber called disenchantment; there is nothing in our world that cannot be explained by reference to calculable forces.

Now if you interpret enlightenment in the first sense, you will say that enlightenment is opposed to other, inferior ways of looking at the world, such as myth. Mythical thinking doesn't realise that the supernatural is just a mirror-image, or a projection, of human beings who have allowed themselves to be frightened by natural phenomena. Myth takes images of reality for reality itself. But Adorno and Horkheimer argued that by far the more important legacy of the enlightenment was its second sense, domination over nature, science, technology, and their harnessing for the purpose of capital accumulation. And if this is what enlightenment is, the distinction between myth and enlightenment is not as hard and fast as it seems. Enlightenment has more to do with human *self-preservation* than human maturity, and has no moral status at all. From the point of view of self-preservation, myth too is a form of enlightenment, and secondly, enlightenment can turn into myth, when scientific progress is worshipped as uncritically as any god, and when the search for the laws governing natural forces is driven by a fear of those very forces: 'enlightenment is mythic fear turned radical' (Adorno and Horkheimer, 1973: 16). This myth-as-enlightenment, enlightenment-as-myth theme is central to a dialectical understanding of enlightenment.

Adorno's point was that sociology is itself entangled in this dialectic, mastering social reality by means of arbitrary categories, but at the same time attributing reality status to the product of its limited imagination. He thought that this unstable combination of subjectivism and objectivism had lain at the heart of mainstream sociology since its emergence: the subjectivism comes from Weber, who sees social relations and institutions as ultimately reducible to the actions of individuals and who constructs a battery of arbitrary concepts – ideal types – with which to study those social relations and institutions; the objectivism comes from Durkheim, who hypostasises 'society' as a reality *sui generis*, wholly independent of individuals. On the one hand, there is bourgeois liberalism which lauds the autonomous individual while neglecting the movement of objective social forces; on the other, there is bourgeois reification which acknowledges those forces but conceptualises them idealistically, for instance as the conscience collective.

Fans of Adorno may see this as a caricature of his views, but if you read his introduction to the German edition of Durkheim's essays in sociology and philosophy (Adorno, 1976b), or his *Introduction to Sociology* (Adorno, 2000), you will see that it is not far wide of the mark. For instance, in his discussion of Weber's ideal types, of which more below, Adorno describes Weber's sociology (rightly as it happens) as being driven by a set of nominalistic procedures which he learnt as a lawyer and which coloured his own thinking:

> The difficulty of understanding legal thinking at all has always arisen at this point, from the fact that in this thinking systems of concepts which have been constructed, thought out in a very tangible sense of the term, have taken the place of the real circumstances and the real conditions affecting decisions. (Adorno, 2000: 120)

He then says that this jurisprudential approach is forced, by virtue of the fact that it is an approach to real, concrete social relations, to attribute to its categories a life they do not have. The best example in Weber is his three types of legitimate domination, which begin as heuristic devices intended to orient inquiry, but which are described at other times by Weber himself, and contrary to the most basic principles of neo-Kantian concept formation, as though they were real historical forces, capable even of being transformed into one another. For instance, Weber's famous theory of 'the routinisation of charisma', exemplified by the 'transformation of charisma in a democratic direction', suggests that these ideal types are no longer devices used by the historical sociologist but names for 'real forces'. Adorno thought that this move on Weber's part was understandable, but only because:

> even if one operates with concepts defined in a purely instrumental manner, the structured character of the subject matter asserts itself in such a way that something of the objective structure imposes itself on these operationally defined concepts. (Adorno, 2000: 123)

This weakness of classificatory reason, namely that only 'something of' the structure of the object studied is allowed to assert itself, cannot be corrected by seeking to know the object through

> the sum total of correct classifications of it. For this kind of thinking we would know an object once all possible correct classifications of it have been completed. But ... when truth is conceived according to the method of such judgements the concepts become purely classificatory, merely the common denominator of what is gathered under them. The objects become merely illustrative, of interest only as examples of the concept. (Jarvis, 1998: 165–6)

But if mainstream sociology: a) privileges method over material; b) is trapped in an undialectical opposition between subjectivism and objectivism; and c) is dominated in its empirical research procedures as well as in its theory by classificatory reason, what alternative does Adorno offer? Adorno was understandably reticent on this: his own efforts at mainstream empirical social inquiry did take him further than Simmel managed in his abandoned study of yodelling; he contributed to the radio research project organised by Paul Lazarsfeld, but he also participated in the ill-fated questionnaire-based study, *The Authoritarian Personality*, featuring the most leading questions in the history of survey research (Adorno et al., 1950; see also Adorno, 1998; for a brilliant anticipatory critique see Van Gennep, 1967: ch. 5).

Perhaps ironically for one who wrote so frequently of the complicities of 'bourgeois' thought, Adorno's most prescriptive statement about procedure is a plea on behalf of an old and venerable form of writing, one also favoured by Simmel: the essay. Indeed, he was most successful and persuasive when he adopted this form; the essays in *The Culture Industry* and *The Stars Down to Earth* are among his finest achievements (Adorno, 1991a, 2002). The virtues of the essay as the ideal vehicle for non-classificatory thinking are that it allows thinking to attend to what science might regard as transitory, inessential and marginal, and more importantly that it suspends the traditional concept of method. Thought's depth depends on how deeply it penetrates its object, not on the extent to which it reduces it to something else. The essay gives this a polemical turn by dealing with objects that would be considered derivative, without itself pursuing their ultimate derivation. (Adorno, 1991b: 11)

Moreover, the essay, rather than beginning with concepts which are defined in advance and then 'applied' in order to bring coherence to otherwise chaotic material, takes concepts which are already used unreflectively and subjects them to a process of reflection. Reflection here absolutely does not mean a search for the origins of their current meaning or an obscure etymological exercise or a search for their ultimate derivation, but rather a confrontation with other unreflectively employed concepts.

All its concepts are to be presented in such a way that they support one another, that each becomes articulated through its configuration with the others. In the essay discrete elements set off against one another come together to form a readable context; the essay erects no scaffolding and no structure. (Adorno, 1991b: 13)

In some ways this book follows the same procedure; there is no template against which all these theorists are being assessed, no synthesis of them is being offered, no hope that by combining each of their strengths and rejecting all of their weaknesses we might construct a better version of sociological theory.

And now Adorno makes a remark that reminds us of the whole problem with which we began this chapter, to Oliver Sacks's Dr P, and with him to the pattern variables of Professor P. For the question here is: how does the configuration of concepts in the essay do justice to the object of inquiry? The aim is to avoid a procedure in which we break something down into its elements and then order them in accordance with a science which strives for the 'elemental'. We must reject the version of the relationship between parts and wholes that defines mainstream social science:

The specific moments are not to be simply derived from the whole and vice-versa. The whole is a monad, and yet it is not; its moments, which as moments are conceptual in nature, point beyond the specific object in which they are assembled. But the essay does not pursue them to the point where they would legitimate themselves outside the specific object; if it did so, it would end up with an infinity of the wrong kind. (Adorno, 1991b: 14)

But, we might say, this is just what does happen when Dr P. tries to describe a rose and when Professor P. tries to describe the doctor–patient encounter; just as the rose becomes a convoluted figure with a linear green attachment, the doctor–patient relationship is a set of expectations which combine universalism, specificity, affective neutrality and achievement, while the Soviet Union is a combination of universalism and ascription. In each case, the moments of the phenomenon under investigation are conceptual; that is, they 'point beyond the specific object in which they are assembled'. The abstract shapes in Dr P's description could be deployed in the description of another quite different object; by the same token, Parsons' pattern variables are deployed throughout his sociology in order to describe many types of situation: doctors and patients, priests and congregations, the Soviet Union, love. Adorno's point is that in these cases the concepts deployed are legitimated entirely outside the specific object they are being used to describe. In Parsons' case what legitimates them is the pursuit of a science capable of generating a complete description of society. And because this is the logic of his deployment of these concepts as the 'moments' of this object, he hasn't really described the doctor–patient relationship at all, hasn't reflected on it, or put better, hasn't inhabited it in the way in which the essay can inhabit it. There is nothing in Parsons about the interactional nuances of the doctor–patient interaction, just as Dr P's description of the rose is not really a description of the rose. To be sure, his account is not beset by the problem of trivialisation that can occur when the ethnographer gets his or her hands on the minutiae of individual speech patterns and bodily-posture; it is driven by a concern with the orientation patterns characteristic of people living in mature industrial societies, and in this sense retains a sense of overall significance. But it is driven by the logic of what Adorno calls the 'general overview', which 'would be possible only if it were established in advance that the object to be dealt with was fully grasped by the concepts used to treat it, that nothing would be left over that could not be anticipated from the concepts' (Adorno, 1991b: 15). In this respect Parsons' *Essays in Sociological Theory* are not essays at all, more the turning over of a machine; the genuine essay, by contrast, 'has to be constructed as though it could break off at any point … An unequivocal logical order deceives us about the antagonistic nature of what that order is imposed upon. Discontinuity is essential to the essay' (Adorno, 1991b: 16).

Adorno is describing a kind of writing, but in the final chapter we will ask what sort of connection can be made, if any, between attitudes to sociological theory and attitudes to the art of living; part of the answer will involve a discussion of what Musil calls 'the utopian idea of essayism', the idea that an attitude to a kind of writing might also be an attitude to how to live.

For now, we need to take note of an important third approach to categorisation, one associated with a sociologist who both believed that what he was doing was science and who harboured a hostility to the essay as form, but who nevertheless developed an approach to categorisation which differs markedly from both the classificatory approach of Parsons and the dialectics of Adorno.

The Ideal Type

So many books have been written about Weber, so many textbooks have discussed his use of ideal types, so many introductions to sociological methods have made assumptions about their importance, that it would be hard to know what more there is to say on the topic. Here I will not so much offer anything new as place ideal types within the theoretical liberal universe of discourse of which we spoke earlier. Recall Baldamus's remark that there is only one theoretical method in sociology, the ideal type. By now it should be clear that this can be true only if we treat the ideal type as one of Wittgenstein's super concepts, a general term for the incomparable essence of sociological inquiry. But it is not; Weber's approach to the study of society is as distinct as anyone else's.

In the cases of both classificatory and dialectical categories, we have seen that there was a continuity of topic at least between the sense-making efforts of sociologists and those of ordinary actors: classification is something we do as competent social actors, even if the sociologist's (especially Parsons') and the actor's classifications might not be the same; and while 'thinking dialectically' is perhaps not the most routine everyday operation, Adorno tried to show, in a much more direct way than he himself admitted, the ways in which categories which are perfectly familiar to the layperson may be subjected to processes of transformation and mutation at the level of everyday experience ('work' and 'leisure', 'culture' and 'industry'). Adorno's essays may defamiliarise the social world, make it strange, they may shock the reader, but they do so in a way which does make a curious appeal to the reader's vision. Adorno believed that dialectics was not a scientific method to be applied mechanically in order to make sense of an otherwise senseless reality, but a way of bringing out the way the world worked.

Now much of what Weber wrote about the ideal type was written in order to secure the distinctive, scientific character of the social sciences, particularly the historical sciences. He never tired of stressing the artificial, unreal character of ideal types. He wrote most extensively about the ideal type in essays which are a model of how to ensnare the reader in complex circumlocution and burdensome detail. And finally he believed that in any case, science, with the ideal type at its heart, cannot tell us what to do and how to live! Nevertheless, when he comes to define what distinguishes the ideal type from what he calls 'merely classificatory concepts', he invokes a criterion which, far from being an abstruse technical one internal to social science, is grounded in something outside science. In other words, it is precisely when Weber, often after a tortuous exercise in self-clarification, comes to say what the ideal type is all about, that he justifies it in the non-scientific terms of which Adorno might have approved.

We cannot discuss the ideal type without saying something about Weber's epistemology. Weber repeatedly states that the reality which confronts the investigator is 'an infinite manifold', a plethora or chaos of phenomena, and that in order to know the world we are bound to be selective, to see it from certain points of view, and we are bound to order it in some way. As we saw, the construction of classificatory systems does this; the ideal type does it too, but in a different way. The first difference is that the construction of classificatory or taxonomic systems is based upon a simple realist epistemology, in which things are taken as they are and then placed here or there. Things are named, collected, ordered, but ordering is not seen as an act of cognition. The thing which is named remains the same after it is named. My classification system may be crude – snow, rain, sleet, clouds – or refined – seven types of snow, eight types of rain, cumulo-nimbus, stratus – but either way the more sophisticated version merely supplies me with more detail, and more importantly, once an individual phenomenon belongs in one class it cannot belong in another. A bumble bee cannot be a wasp unless we are interested solely in the fact that they are both insects, in which case they cannot be birds, and so on. By the same token, and to use more familiar examples, a member of social class 1A cannot be a member of social class 2C, a member of housing class 1 cannot be a member of housing class 5 (Rex and Moore, 1967). This comparison between insects/birds and social classes is no accident. Both Adorno and Weber were resolute in their opposition to the use of a classificatory logic for the social or historical sciences, since it reduced social inquiry to natural history.

Now this is important because Weber's work – specifically *Economy and Society* – is replete not just with ideal types but also with what look like classificatory typologies, that is, systems of categories the rationale for which seems to be to subsume everything under one category or another. The most obvious example would be his three types of legitimate domination. Legal-rational, charismatic and traditional domination appear to exhaust the field of domination in the same way in which the more elaborate classification systems of the natural sciences might exhaust their fields of inquiry. Similarly, every instance of action appears to be covered by the four-fold typology of value-rational, purpose-rational, traditional and affective action. 'Class, status and party' is another such typology. Yet 'the idea that the whole of concrete historical reality can be exhausted in the conceptual scheme about to be developed here is as far from the author's intentions as anything could be' (Weber, 1978: 216).

Weber does not always make it clear that these are not 'merely' classificatory categories but when he does – mainly in the essay 'Objectivity in Social Science and Social Policy' – he makes two closely related points. The first is that the ideal type is an artificial abstraction, a pure type which does not exist in reality but rather in the mind of the investigator. It is, as Weber himself says, a 'utopia' – we will come back to the irony contained in this expression – which literally means that it exists nowhere in reality. Instead, we can say that legal-rational domination, for instance, has a list of characteristic features. We can list them, and Weber does, exhaustively. We can do the same for the other types of domination. But the important point here is that no concrete case of domination will correspond fully to the image of domination contained in the ideal type. It will, rather, more or less approximate to it. And because of this, it will more or less approximate to one of the other ideal types at the same time. And this is the point: the ideal types are, unlike classificatory categories, not mutually exclusive when deployed in investigation. The same phenomenon can 'fall under' more than one category, something which is impossible according to a classificatory logic. So the ideal type is – and here Weber is completely in agreement with Adorno – 'a conceptual construct which is neither historical reality nor even the true reality. It is even less fitted to serve as a schema under which a real situation of action is to be subsumed as one instance' (Weber, 1949: 93). The ideal types are radically different from one another when set down as definitions, but the point of them is that they themselves are not the representation of reality but rather heuristic devices designed to orient and stimulate that representation, a means towards historical-sociological inquiry. At the same time, this does not mean that the categories which Weber constructs 'artificially' and to the clarification of which he devoted so much time in *Economy and Society* are plucked from nowhere. They are not like Parsons' pattern variables or the constructs of economic theory, however much Weber respected the latter. Weber is neither an idealist nor a formalist, terms which repeatedly crop up in the critical literature. So where do the ideal types come from?

The answer, ironically enough, is in many cases – from social reality – The ideal type is not an arbitrary abstraction imposed upon an unformed reality, but rather the 'one-sided' accentuation or exaggeration of reality, a reality which is itself already formed, shaped by human action into institutions and by human understandings into ideas about such institutions. Historians and empirical social scientists have such material available to them all the time. Weber, through a combination of monstrous historical erudition, sociological sensitivity and philosophical acumen, transformed this material into the battery of categories set down in *Economy and Society* and used them in the studies in the sociology of religion. His work is, if you like, the product of a 'dialectical' relationship between historico-sociological phenomena and their distillation/exaggeration into categories – ideal types – which might then be made use of by other scholars working in related but not identical fields.

But this still leaves us with the question of why Weber constructed the particular ideal types he did. This is the second of the points mentioned earlier. Ideal types may be derived from historical social reality but they are artificial enough not to be dictated by it. The answer that he gives in the objectivity essay is not the whole story but it is a considerable part of it: ideal typical concepts are not *generic*, i.e. classificatory, but *genetic*, i.e. having to do with causality. Causality here refers not to the mundane causality involved in constructing, say, five reasons why a particular war broke out, for it is possible that we might take an isolated historical episode like this and list the individual factors which caused it, and we might indeed produce an account which in one sense was a model of empirical causal inquiry. Weber is not interested in causality in this sense but in something much grander. The overriding criterion which drives the construction of ideal types is what he calls cultural significance: we construct ideal types not for the sake of a universal science of society, but because the light of cultural problems shines at this particular time in history on certain problems, on certain phenomena which are of significance to all those who find themselves living in our kind of society now. There are ideal types of social institutions – those of domination for instance – and of action and of political ideas – liberalism, conservatism, Marxism and so on. There are ideal types of historical processes as well. But in all cases the construction is driven by questions of cultural significance.

For example, the distinction between types of legitimate domination is not an innocent three-fold distinction, but is rooted in the historical experience of the modern West. The section of *Economy and Society* in which Weber defines these types begins with legal–rational domination, the type that has arisen most prominently in our type of society. Similarly, the distinction between asceticism and mysticism in the sociology of religion is no mere taxonomy, but is made by Weber in accordance with his sense of the cultural significance of ascetic practices for the emergence of the modern West. Similarly, terms like 'church' and 'sect' can be used classificatorily, distinguishing between phenomena which fall under one heading or another.

If however I wish to formulate the concept of 'sect' genetically, e.g. with reference to certain important cultural significances which the 'sectarian spirit' has had for modern culture, certain characteristics of both [church and sect] become essential because they stand in an adequate causal relationship to those influences. However, the concepts become ideal typical in the sense that they appear in full conceptual integrity either not at all or only in individual instances. Here as elsewhere every concept which is not purely classificatory diverges from reality. (Weber, 1949: 93–4)

Now Weber's work contains many ideal types of varying levels of generality. Some are general ideal types which might be deployed again and again across a range of individual inquiries. This is especially true of those found in Chapter 1 of *Economy and Society*, with its 'austere beauty'; some are less general, such as asceticism and mysticism; some are individual ideal types, including ideal types of processes as well as states of affairs, such as the process depicted in the Protestant ethic thesis or in the sociology of religion. These studies make full use of the more general ideal types found in *Economy and Society*. But the individual cases are never there simply to be classified, as Parsons classified Russia or China. Nor is Weber doing area studies.

Now it must be admitted that his early studies of medieval trading associations or ancient agriculture or the causes of the decline of ancient civilisations, and his daunting erudition with respect to a vast range of historical periods and cultures, sometimes strain the average reader's sense of what 'cultural significance' means. Still, the bulk of what is read today is of importance because of its overriding concern with the types of human being who inhabit our kind of societies and with the causes of their emergence. *Economy and Society* is in this respect not simply an encyclopaedia for a universal science, but a portrait, or rather the conditions of possibility for a portrait, of the emergence of European humanity – in its legal, religious, economic and political aspects. It deploys categories that may well have a distinct resonance only for Europeans who share its understanding of cultural significance, but that may also be treated as having a universal analytical scope, and be deployed by non-Europeans.[3]

So we have here a double movement. Historical and sociological inquiry is driven not by the goal of scientific purity but by extra-scientific questions – the large questions of our time. But it is just this extra-scientific agenda which demands that the historical and social sciences strive for clarity of categorical definition. As we will see in Chapter 7 when we discuss Weber's account of science and progress, this has him facing two ways at once, stressing the 'eternal youth' of historical science – new questions arise and 'the light of the great cultural problems moves on' (Weber, 1949: 112) – and at the same time setting down a battery of ideal types which continue to set the agenda for much conceptualisation within the historico-cultural sciences. This double movement, or better, this tension, is precisely Weber's strength; as a result of thinking of categories, and with them, inquiry, in this way, Weber manages to construct historical narratives which are more dramatic than the bland evolutionary schemas to which the Durkheimian tradition – Parsons, Luhmann, Habermas, even Gellner – has always resorted when trying to write about history, yet less dramatic and more sober than Adornian dialectics, which when it is applied to the analysis of social processes often consists of little more than hysterical outbursts. In other words, the ideal type was a central means by which Weber managed to be both less boring than Parsons and not as exciting as Adorno. Sometimes, though, his sentences were so long that there was also time for him to be both as boring as Parsons and as exciting as Adorno (Stern, 1992).

Conclusion

The aim of this chapter has been to get a handle on the differences between theorists' intellectual sensibilities by understanding the way they construct and manipulate categories. A commitment to classificatory or dialectical or ideal-typical categories is, seemingly, a commitment to one rather than another of the most basic building blocks of social science, a commitment that, because it is a fundamental choice, is bound to have consequences. While this may be true, categories do not exhaust the theorist's arsenal, and other types of commitment to other types of device may be just as consequential. One of those devices is metaphor.

It is tempting to say that whereas no theorist can live without categories, many can live perfectly well without metaphor, that categories are a necessity and metaphor a decorative or rhetorical luxury, frequently called upon but ultimately dispensable. The next chapter will suggest that nothing could be further from the truth.

4

Metaphors

The perfection of diction is for it to be at once clear and not mean. The clearest indeed is that made up of the ordinary words for things, but it is mean ... On the other hand the diction becomes distinguished and non-prolix by the use of unfamiliar terms, i.e. strange words, metaphors, lengthened forms, and everything that deviates from the ordinary modes of speech. But a whole statement in such terms will be either a riddle or a barbarism, a riddle, if made up of metaphors, a barbarism, if made up of strange words ... A certain admixture, accordingly, of unfamiliar terms is necessary. These, the strange word, the metaphor, the ornamental equivalent, will save language from seeming mean and prosaic, while ordinary words in it will secure the requisite clearness. (Aristotle, 1941: 1478)

Introduction

The three approaches to categories discussed in the previous chapter – classificatory, dialectical and ideal typical – may be treated as the product of purely intellectual commitments. But we also saw that the differences between them may amount to something more, namely a certain sort of political commitment: one might even speak of conservative classification (Parsons, Mary Douglas), radical dialectics (Adorno) and liberal ideal types (Weber). In fact, the attempt to link a sociological theory with the political beliefs of the theorist is a rather well-worn path, and so instead of following it here we will explore another one, asking about the sense in which the concepts or categories employed by a theorist can be said to rest upon another type of non-conceptual support: metaphor.

In a famous passage in *Leviathan*, Thomas Hobbes writes:

... the light of human minds is perspicuous words, but by exact definitions first snuffed, and purged from ambiguity; reason is the pace; increase of science, the way; and the benefit of mankind, the end. And, on the contrary, metaphors, and senseless and ambiguous words, are like *ignes fatui*; and reasoning upon them is wandering amongst innumerable absurdities; and their end, contention and sedition, or contempt. (Hobbes, 1991: ch. V)

This looks like a glorious contradiction, Hobbes seemingly unable to express his belief in scientific rigour and linguistic precision, and his disdain for metaphor, without himself resorting to metaphor; reasoning is described as a journey with a clear goal, not mere 'wandering'. It was Hobbes, too, who coined some of the most enduring metaphors in the history of political thought: the state is described as a mortal god and as an artificial man, and as the sea monster Leviathan; he writes of 'the body politic' where potentially seditious sects and other intermediate powers are 'like worms in the entrailes of a natural man'.

In fact, one can imagine writing the history of political theory as the history of its metaphors, which have been drawn from, among other areas, the family (the fatherland, the mother country), exchanges (contract theory), war, crafts (tending sheep, piloting a ship), engineering (Weber's 'politics is the slow, strong drilling through hard boards' [1994: 369], imagery that Weber adopted from Montesquieu's 'dull rasp which by slowly grinding away gains its end': Montesquieu, 1989: 243), and animals (the wolf in Hobbes, the fox and the lion in Machiavelli).

The sociological tradition too, though 'younger', is replete with metaphors: Weber gave us the 'iron cage', or rather he gave us 'a shell as hard as steel' (Baehr, 2001; Weber, 2002: 121); Marx says that the new society is contained in the 'womb' of the old, and that 'all that is solid melts into air', imagery that appears now in the work of Bauman (2000, 2003); Robert Merton made much of the phrase 'On the shoulders of giants' to convey our relationship with the history of ideas, a phrase that he himself borrowed from Bernard of Chartres (Merton, 1993); Ernest Gellner varies Weber's imagery, giving us 'the rubber cage' and uses the image of 'the big ditch' to convey the difference between the pre-modern and the modern world (Gellner, 1979: 145–7); Erving Goffman writes that 'in truth, in talk it seems routine that, while firmly standing on two feet, we jump up and down on another' (Goffman, 1981: 155). And then there are sociology's master metaphors, in which society 'itself' is imagined 'as' something: organism, cybernetic or autopoetic system, drama, game, text. The latest master metaphor to have attracted widespread interest is that of the network (Latour, 2005). And on top of all this the idea of a truth about society is haunted by Nietzsche's remark that truth itself is a 'moving army of metaphors' (Nietzsche, 1976: 47).

The pervasiveness of metaphor in the human sciences tempts us to explain it by saying that 'all language is metaphorical' and leaving the matter there, or, with George Eliot, that 'all of us get our thoughts entangled in metaphors, and act fatally on the strength of them' (Eliot, 1994: 111) and then heeding Hobbes's recommendation of vigilance in the face of the threat to clear thinking that the permanent presence of metaphor poses.

Neither attitude is especially productive; it seems more interesting to accept that metaphor in sociology is unavoidable and to make a distinction between metaphors that advance and those that hamper inquiry, or between metaphors that play an essential role in a theorist's thinking and those that are marginal to it. We will do this here, and will discover some surprising relationships between the use of metaphor, the tension between sociology as a literature and sociology as science, and the boundary between everyday and sociological reasoning.

You might think, for instance, that to draw attention to the role of metaphor in sociology is to emphasise the extent to which sociology is a literary rather than a scientific activity. Yet as we will see, it can be precisely through a reliance on an overarching metaphor that a sociologist seeks to establish his/her scientific credentials.

For our purposes, the most useful definition of metaphor for social scientific purposes has been provided by Geertz:

> a metaphor is a way of talking that works well in one field of inquiry and that is employed in an attempt to make sense of something in another field of inquiry; we resort to metaphor when we seek to make sense of something which is not comprehended by means of something which is comprehended better, but comprehended somewhere else. (Geertz, 1983: 22)

Obvious examples of the sociological use of metaphor in this sense are 'organism' and 'system': to see society as an organism is to draw upon language taken from outside sociology, namely human biology; to see society as a system is to draw upon the non-sociological language of cybernetics and information science. Other major examples are those of 'drama' or 'game', although here we should speak of synecdoche, since language pertinent to the description of one part of social life is used to comprehend the whole of it. As Erving Goffman once put it: 'the world is, in truth, a wedding' (Goffman, 1959: 45). For purposes of convenience we will include synecdoche under the broader heading of metaphor, because in both cases the issue will be the same, namely whether the metaphor or synecdoche is capable of generating a serviceable vocabulary for theorising.

Now Geertz's definition of metaphor is especially pertinent to sociology and helps us to understand why metaphor might be so pervasive here. The reason is not so much that 'all language is metaphorical', as that in sociology we are faced with a primary object of inquiry, society, that is particularly elusive. As Baldamus once put it:

> Although the word 'society' is nowadays constantly used by laymen in all sorts of political, economic and ethical debates, it is easy to see that it has no recognizable substance. Nobody knows what it means. (Baldamus, 1976: 5)

If Baldamus is right, it means that as soon as one begins to theorise about society, for instance by saying 'Gemeinschaft and Gesellschaft', or 'agency and structure', or 'macro- and micro-', or 'church and sect', one confronts the problem of 'dividing unknown entities'; the fact is that 'society' is not like an apple that you can cut in half and study. If 'society' is so elusive it is hardly surprising that sociological theorists with a grand ambition have searched other disciplines or domains of life, and felt free to do so, for images and ways of speaking that already 'work' elsewhere.

That is a little vague, and so before examining the use of metaphor within sociological theory I will have to try the reader's patience considering some technical questions that bear on metaphor in general but also on our inquiry here.

Five Aspects of Metaphor

i. Metaphor and Simile. The distinction between metaphor and simile may sound trivial, since both clearly involve appealing to the characteristic features of one thing in order to describe another. On the other hand, rhetorically there is an important difference between them: while simile takes the form 'A *is like* B', metaphor takes the form 'A *is* B'. There is a difference, for instance, between saying 'modernity *is like* an iron cage' and saying that 'modernity *is* an iron cage'. In the former case, two things which are different from one another are compared. In the latter, two things which are different from one another are identified with one another. Some say that metaphor is simply condensed simile, the difference between the two being that metaphor is simply 'more powerful: the direct attribution causes surprise, whereas simile dissipates this surprise' (Ricoeur, 1977: 53). Here, simile and metaphor are not fundamentally opposed because in both there is a tension between A and B, and this tension is never fully resolved. If A is 'my love' and B is 'a red, red rose', making the metaphorical statement 'my love is a red red rose' rather than using the simile 'my love is like a red, red rose' doesn't resolve it, even though the second sounds more romantic than the first (Craib, 1994: 39), and both of them more romantic that 'my love is like a red convoluted red form with a linear green attachment'. The love and the red rose remain different things. The metaphorical statement 'A is B' is an exercise in *predication* rather than identification, by which we mean that B is predicated of A, B is a quality which is held to be one quality of A, not something that A 'really is'. The statement 'modernity is an iron cage' or 'society is an organism' has the same status as 'Jack is a dull boy' or 'the sky is blue', the point being that just as Jack could equally be many other things as well as dull, so 'the iron cage' is just one of the many characteristics of modernity, and 'society' could be thought of as a text as well as an organism. This led Nelson Goodman to his famous statement that: 'Metaphor is an affair between a predicate with a past and an object that yields while protesting' (Goodman, 1968: 69).

ii. Substitutive v. Interactive Metaphor. In a classic essay Max Black distinguished between what he calls the *substitution theory* and the *interaction theory* of metaphor. According to the substitution theory, 'the focus of a metaphor, the word or expression having a distinctively metaphorical use within a literal frame, is used to communicate a meaning that might have been expressed literally' (Black, 1962: 32). Metaphor here has a more or less decorative purpose, allowing us perhaps to find a concrete referent for an abstract concept, but no more; so that if we say 'Richard is a lion' when we mean 'Richard is brave', we are not adding anything new to an account of Richard's bravery. The metaphor has a literal equivalent. Against this view, Black defended I.A. Richards' interaction theory, according to which in metaphor we have two thoughts of different things placed together, with the reader being invited to connect them.

Clearly, the invitation is not open, because the point of the metaphor will be to make us think about A by reference to the characteristics of B, and to do so in such a way that our attention is drawn towards the respects in which A has the characteristics of B and away from the respects in which it does not. So 'man is a wolf' invites us to consider what Black calls a set of 'associated commonplaces' about wolves and construct corresponding implications about man which inevitably push into the background any human features which cannot be spoken of in the language we would apply to wolves. More interesting for our purposes is the idea that the effectiveness of a metaphor can depend upon the writer's capacity to vary the implications of the literal expression. A zoologist for instance might give an account of wolves in which 'man is a wolf' implied something more attractive than that man was a rapacious, aggressive killer. Making sense of man here depends upon a set of deliberately constructed implications. As Black puts it, metaphors 'can be made to measure and need not be hand-me-downs' (Black, 1962: 43).

This is interesting for us because within sociology we can make just such a distinction. The organised and sustained use of metaphor involved when we say that 'society is X' requires the theorist to specify what is meant by an organism or a cybernetic system, what the structural features of a text are, before he or she tells us that society 'is' an organism or a cybernetic system or a text. By contrast, when someone says 'modernity is an iron cage' we can all visualise, without much prompting, what an iron cage is along with its associated 'commonplaces' (a prison or place of confinement). Between these two extremes lies Goffman's drama metaphor. Goffman does not need to elaborate the implications of the theatre or theatricality, and in resorting to them he appeals to the reader's already existing sense of what drama is. Nonetheless, having gained the reader's acceptance of this basic image he needs to push its implications further by means of a series of conceptual elaborations erected, so to speak, on this foundation.

In the end, Black drew the pragmatic conclusion that it makes less sense to say that the substitution or the interaction theory of metaphor is correct than to say that some metaphors are of one type and others are of the other type. The point is, however, that the first can be replaced by literal translations, and that if this happens we may lose some of the charm or drama that the metaphor created for us, but none of the cognitive content. As with categories that do not seem to be doing very much work (Parsons' pattern variables from the last chapter), we feel that we could have said it all more simply and directly. On the other hand, interactional metaphors are not expendable, the subsidiary subject giving insight into the principal subject. A literal translation would cause a loss of cognitive content, would reduce our knowledge of the phenomenon under investigation. 'The relevant weakness of the literal paraphrase is not that it may be tiresomely prolix or boringly explicit (or deficient in qualities of style); it fails to be a translation because it fails to give the insight that the metaphor did' (Black, 1962: 46).

iii. Level of Discourse and Level of Words. A third distinction, in many ways for us the most important, is that between two levels at which metaphor is operative:

the level of words/sentences and the level of 'discourse'. We can say that metaphor at the level of words or sentences serves the purpose of dramatisation, while, metaphor at the level of discourse serves the purpose of systematisation. The most famous dramatic metaphor in the history of sociology is doubtless Weber's image of the 'iron cage'. Yet despite its influence and the discussion it has generated, one cannot say that it has any systematic relationship with Weber's vision of sociology as a whole. It is simply a powerful image at the end of a sustained historical inquiry and works at the level of words, not at the level of discourse. By contrast, we can see the writings of Talcott Parsons or Niklas Luhmann or Jon Elster as the working out of a single metaphor for an overarching systematic purpose: society here is a cybernetic system (Parsons, Luhmann) or a game/series of games played between utility-maximising actors (Elster). And for much of his career Erving Goffman deployed the image of society as a drama, a kind of master image in relationship to which the details of his work – his words and sentences – make sense.

A sociological theorist's work may be peppered with metaphorical statements (level of words/sentences) while his or her work as a whole (level of discourse) is not defined by any particular vision; conversely, it may be that a theorist's entire project is describable as the working out or elaboration of a single metaphor (level of discourse) while his or her writing itself largely avoids the use of metaphor at the level of words/sentences. Sometimes the metaphorical statement may be both a dramatic aside and an indication of the nature of the writer's thought as a whole. When Marx, for instance, says that the beginnings of a new society are contained within the 'womb' of the old, he is not only deploying a fine image but giving a shorthand but not entirely misleading statement of his overall philosophy of history; 'revolutions' are not wholly unpredictable ruptures – rather, some of the necessary conditions for, say, communism, are already developed within capitalism at the point at which capitalism is predicted to collapse.

Incidentally, this distinction between systematisation and dramatisation – whether or not these procedures are helped along by metaphor – gives us another sense of the meaning of the 'classics'. The work of all of the founding figures of the discipline displays a capacity for both. Marx gives us long passages of systematisation in *Capital*, but dramatisation in his often vituperative and critical writings. Weber wrote the encyclopaedic *Economy and Society* but also withering articles on the future of Germany. Durkheim was committed to sociology as a science, but also wrote haunting passages in *Suicide* about the anomic individual's relationship to time. If talk of the decline of the classics makes sense it may be because these two activities, as well as the concerns with Generalities II and III we met with in Chapter 2, have tended to drift apart. Today there is much systematisation without dramatisation (systems theory, rational choice, critical realism) and vice-versa (much of cultural studies, Bauman, Beck, Giddens).

iv. Words and Images. A fourth distinction is that between words and images. We are perhaps tempted to say that the use of metaphor in sociology involves the substitution of *images* for *concepts*; we speak readily of Durkheim's or Marx's 'image of society' (Poggi, 1972), as though we were being invited to visualise society in some way or another, to picture it. If we describe as metaphorical statements such as 'society is a system' or 'society is a game' or 'society is a drama' and so on, we seem to want to visualise something. I myself invoked Plessner's idea of 'different eyes' in the introduction. Yet this is not always the right way of putting it; metaphor, insofar as it involves trying to make sense of something not comprehended by a resort to something which is comprehended, but comprehended somewhere else (Geertz's definition with which we began), more often than not replaces one way of talking with another way of talking rather than replacing words with images; for many prominent sociological theorists, the point of a metaphor is to persuade us to think of A in terms of the commonplaces or constructed implications associated with B, not merely in terms of an image.

v. Images and Models. A fifth distinction may help us to appreciate the distinction between images and words: that between metaphors and models. Let us say, then, that even if a penchant for metaphors is a penchant for images, in sociological theory, a metaphor may be worked up into something more organised and systematic: models, or well-defined and often elaborate batteries of categories. Such models may arise from an initial hunch or gesture which is then developed into something more by the theorist, often in the course of empirical inquiry. Goffman's work is an example, the 'drama' metaphor providing, initially, some terminology, some imagery indeed, but Goffman himself then elaborates it into the books we know as *The Presentation of Self in Everyday Life* or *Relations in Public*; he does so, moreover, in such a way that the eclectic range of empirical material itself contributes to the development of the model of society as a drama. Hence his discussion of 'front and back regions' owes as much to the ethnographic material on crofting communities as it does to the image of front stage and back stage in the theatre. The empirical material is not there simply in order to be 'fitted in' to the model as an example fits into a system of classification.

By contrast, models which have no obvious connection with social life may be already available elsewhere, and imported wholesale into sociology. Luhmann and Parsons' systems theory is characteristic, as is the use by rational choice theorists of models taken from the study of economic behaviour.

But what is a model? When we think of a model we think perhaps initially of a scale model such as a ship in a bottle or an enlarged version of something very small, such as an insect. The purpose of a scale model is to show how something works, how it looks, and the change in size is designed to bring certain features of the original into perspective. But at bottom a scale model merely imitates its original. A second type of model is the analogue model, in which the original is represented in a new medium, and where the aim is to represent its structures rather than its sensible features. An example here would be a hydraulic model of an economic system. Thirdly, we have a purely theoretical model: whereas the first two can be physically constructed, the theoretical model cannot. It exists solely in language. The example given by Max Black is Maxwell's 'representation of an electrical field in terms of the properties of an imaginary incompressible fluid'. The point here is that no such fluid is actually there to look at, but rather, the idea of a fluid makes it possible to express and explore a certain set of mathematical relationships which could not have been explored otherwise. As Paul Ricoeur puts it:

> The important thing is not that one has something to view mentally, but that one can operate on an object that on the one hand is better known and in this sense more familiar, and on the other hand is full of implications and in this sense rich at the level of hypotheses. (Ricoeur, 1977: 285)

Within the natural sciences the use of such models is controversial; Karl Popper argued that the logic of scientific discovery is a process of deduction which does not require the use of models. For others, models provide scientists with an imaginative detour by means of which an original object of inquiry can be redescribed as something else. Regardless of just what the relationship is between reason and imagination, in the natural sciences it is clear that the construction of models is restricted by the existence of rules according to which statements for one domain can be translated into those for another.

Now if we say that the natural sciences are governed by two logics, of argumentation (deduction, proof and so on), and discovery (which may or may not involve the use of models), in the social sciences it is perhaps better to speak of three logics: argumentation, discovery, and invention. And given what we have said about the difference between model and metaphor, we can ascribe models to the logic of discovery and metaphors to the logic of invention. This means that the use of models in the social sciences pulls in two directions, on the one hand in the direction of truth (logic of argumentation and discovery) and on the other in the direction of the original impulse to construct the model in the first place (logic of invention). In Ricoeur's terms, it is rich not only in hypotheses (direction of truth) but also in sheer suggestiveness. The social scientist has to remain true, in other words, both to the truth and to his original basic intuitions about the nature of the social world and the place of human beings in it. This means that the sociologist is freer than the physicist to exercise his or her imagination, but also that this very freedom is a constraint: there may be more scope for the use of apparently arbitrary metaphors and the models to which they give rise, but at the same time their very 'free' use confronts the sociologist with the fact that, however obscure 'society' is as an object of inquiry, it is constituted in some way by actors who themselves deploy metaphors to make sense of the world. The sociologist is restricted not only by the standards or prevailing attitudes of a scholarly community but also by the fact that the very objects of his inquiry are themselves amateur social theorists. This last point – what Anthony Giddens calls the 'double hermeneutic' – has generated whole libraries of commentary, much of it now gathering non-metaphorical dust, but the point here is that while it is easier to say that society is a game or a drama or a system than it is to say that the universe is shaped like a disc, it is also easier to say that it is not.

This means that there is frequently something absurd about the spectacle of major theorists sticking resolutely to their master images and painstakingly constructing models of society in the face of the ready availability of other metaphors and models. The uncomfortable fact is that, as Clifford Geertz has observed in his classic essay 'Blurred Genres', a particular model, which its author believes helps us to make sense of all we need to make sense of, is almost certainly better at making sense of some facets of social experience than of others. It may be that war is politics by other means, but is love? There may be some aspects of social life which are, as structuralists used to say, structured like a language, or susceptible to analysis which uses similar resources to those which are used to analyse texts, and it may be liberating to say that a society is 'readable':

> To see social institutions, social customs, social changes as in some sense readable is to alter our whole sense of what such interpretation is and shift it toward modes of thought rather more familiar to the translator, the exegete, or the iconographer than to the test giver, the factor analyst, or the pollster. (Geertz, 1983: 31)

The attraction of such models is their promise to provide us with something more than a shift in perception, namely a logic of discovery in which the whole of social life can be seen as a system, a game, a drama, a text. But at best, so Geertz implies, they provide less of a totalising, overarching theory of society than a way of grasping certain kinds of social relationship but not others.

Now, not all of the theorists who have had an impact on sociological theory would accept this characterisation of their achievements. On the contrary, many have strived for 'the only way' to do sociology, and if you were to tell them that there are extensive areas of social life on which their theories cast the weakest of lights they might be surprised. Max Weber once said that to succeed in modern life one needed to put on blinkers, and he was right. Yet there is a difference between blinkers donned by those who see a need for them and blinkers which, so to speak, grow on the sides of the head as a result of a certain attitude to looking. I think that the latter happens with Parsons and Luhmann and to a lesser extent with Elias. Not many theorists would be prepared to follow Goffman's more modest line:

> This book is about the organisation of experience ... and not the organisation of society. I make no claim whatsoever to be talking about the core matters of sociology – social organisation and social structure ... I personally hold society to be first in every way and any individual's current involvements to be second; this report deals only with matters that are second. (Goffman, 1974: 13)

Goffman's tongue may have been in his cheek when he wrote this, but in much of his work he is more aware than most of his own limits; he says 'I must be allowed to pick my level', but believes that others are free to pick theirs. In so doing he anticipates an important warning from Richard Harvey Brown: 'it is unclear how the root metaphors of the organism or machine could be conjoined with consistency to those of drama or game. Efforts to integrate paradigms have remained a congeries of fragile patchworks' (Brown, 1992: 225–6).

This reminds us of the theme of theoretical liberalism, and if it is true, it places a considerable burden of responsibility on the theorist who does make use of such metaphors. Metaphor can be worn lightly and make an arresting appeal to the reader's vision (as Wittgenstein says, 'a good comparison refreshes the understanding'); but it can also become a burden or a prison or a fetish – or an iron cage for that matter – in which the theorist's account of society becomes dogmatic and inflexible (when, as Wittgenstein says, 'the engine is idling'). Or to use a more familiar vocabulary: in sociology as in life, there are living and dead metaphors, metaphors that seem to do some work for us by enabling us to see something or talk about it in new ways, and those that obstruct our view or involve us in needless circumlocution. What Michael Oakeshott once said of philosophers applies equally to sociological theorists:

> ... if it requires great energy of mind to create a system, it requires even greater not to become the slave of the creation. To become the slave of a system in life is not to know when to 'hang up philosophy', not to recognise the final triumph of inconsequence; in philosophy, it is not to know when the claims of comprehension outweigh those of coherence. (Oakeshott, 1996: xv)

Oakeshott's distinction between coherence and comprehension is perhaps too sharp. But the point is well taken: an obsession with coherence can produce a blinkered vision, while a measure of incoherence, while it may lead to chaos, may well be an adjunct to curiosity, the stop that keeps the door to significance open.

Figure 4.1 expresses an evaluation of the use of metaphor by prominent sociological theorists, and does so in terms of some of the ideas we have just reviewed; it divides theorists into what appear to be successes and failures – those whose metaphors are alive and those whose metaphors are dead – though the distinction is not quite the same as that between 'readable' and 'unreadable'.

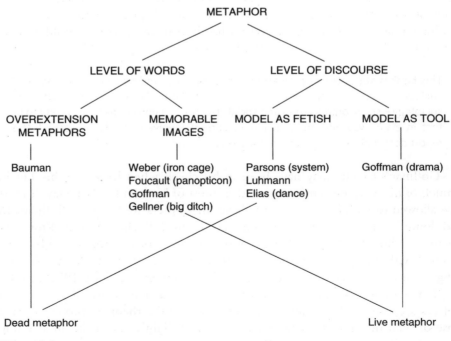

Figure 4.1

Investigating Sociological Theory

Living and Dead Metaphors in Sociology

In the next section, dead metaphor at the level of discourse is illustrated by Parsons' systems theory and Elias's figurational sociology; dead metaphor at the level of words is illustrated by the work of Zygmunt Bauman. Living metaphor at both levels is found in the work of Erving Goffman. To this distinction a rider should be added: we will discuss dead metaphor through the idea of a 'hypertrophy of metaphor'. This seems like an odd way of going about things because hypertrophy means not death but uncontrolled growth. But the point is one about usefulness and uselessness: a metaphor that has been allowed to get out of control or to go beyond the limits of its own usefulness is, theoretically, in terms of its capacity to generate new descriptions, to allow us to see with different eyes, dead to the world of inquiry.

Hypertrophy of Metaphor at the Level of Discourse

Parsons

At the start of this chapter we saw Aristotle cautioning us against the overuse of metaphors and 'strange words' because they may lead either to a riddle (metaphors) or to barbarism (strange words). His recommendation that their use be leavened with plainer speech was never taken up by Talcott Parsons, whose work is generally seen as a riddle and a barbarism combined. Nevertheless, it would be foolish to dismiss the entirety of Parsons' work on these grounds; the system metaphor clearly proved capable of generating descriptions of the social world that had a measure of plausibility and persuasiveness, even if in the end the effort to make it work triumphed over a sense of what the effort was for: once he has hit upon the system as a metaphor for society, the moves he makes are governed more by the need for coherence – of the system – than by a quest for comprehension – of the social world. In this section it is important to bear in mind that, although we will refer to concepts and conceptual hierarchies, because they are brought to the understanding of society from outside sociology, from another domain of inquiry in which the concept of system works and makes sense, they are metaphorical in Geertz's sense of the term. Moreover, as we will see, there are strange metaphorical moves at work within the overall system framework.

Parsons' blind commitment to his own way of seeing is expressed very well in the following passage:

> A society is a type of social system, in any universe of social systems which attains the highest level of self-sufficiency as a system in relation to its environments ... This definition refers to an abstracted system, of which the other, similarly abstracted subsystems of action are the primary environments. This view contrasts sharply with our common sense notion of society as being composed of concrete human individuals ... We cannot argue the merits of these two views of societies here. But the reader must be clear about the usage in this book. (Parsons, 1969: 10)

Curiously enough, 'the usage in this book' did yield, if not empirical insight as common sense might define it, then at least a distinctive way of thinking about and describing the dilemmas and problems facing contemporary western societies, and in particular the conditions under which liberal democracies are able to reproduce themselves. In the last chapter we encountered the pattern variables as part of the answer to the problem of order; the later model of society as a 'system' is intended to do the same sort of job. Parsons gave a typically clumsy definition of 'system' in an encyclopaedia article of 1968. System

> ... refers to a complex of interdependencies between parts, components; and processes that involves [sic] discernible regularities of relationship, and to a similar type of interdependency between such a concept and its surrounding environment. (Parsons, 1968: 458)

Parsons sometimes refers to 'living systems', so that the 19th-century image of an organism suggests itself, but what he is really after is the idea of survival, perpetuation and reproduction of any coherent set of interdependencies. He says that in order to reproduce itself a system must fulfil four functions, which he calls 'adaptation', 'goal–attainment', 'integration', and 'latency'. Where Parsons got them from is as big a mystery as the origin of the pattern variables. He wrote some frankly deluded articles about the 'development' of his thought but left us none the wiser about why any system should have to fulfil four rather than three or five functions. We will return to this question of 'how many functions?' in the next chapter. To anticipate: you can draw more elegant and flexible diagrams if there are four functions than you can if there are three or five. Do they help us to think better about society?

Let us say that adaptation refers to ways of getting and allocating resources from the external world or environment; that goal–attainment refers to ways of ensuring that important general tasks are accomplished (such as the distribution of roles); integration to ways of ensuring that actors fill their roles (e.g. through formal–legal or informal norms); and latency to ways of keeping the system as a whole in a state of equilibrium (e.g. through ultimate values, beliefs). The interesting thing about the model is that you can break the system down into subsystems, and say that each function is said to be carried out by a particular subsystem of the system as a whole, so that in the case of the system we call 'society', or rather of society when it is called a 'system', adaptation is the job of the economy, goal–attainment of the polity, integration of what Parsons calls 'the societal community' (the non–state sector, legal system and so on) and latency of the 'pattern–maintenance' subsystem (religion, education and so on).

The key to any system is the relationship between what Parsons calls its inputs and its outputs, the point being that a system will receive inputs from its external environment and, as a result of the action peculiar to it, generate some 'output'. The full story of how this works has been told many times before (Alexander, 1987). Our question is whether this model, which was inspired by an initial metaphor, can enable us to say something interesting or whether it blinds or restricts us. The point is that Parsons was being wholly disingenuous when he referred to 'discernible regularities of relationship', as though it were a simple matter of 'looking' or a more complex matter of engaging in experimentation or statistical investigation, neither of which he in fact attempted. The four subsystems of the social system are institutional sectors, and it is they, according to Parsons, which are the parts whose interrelationship we should be examining (Lockwood, 1988). These parts were famously represented by means of the diagram shown in Figure 4.2, consisting of four boxes (we will have more to say about diagrams in the next chapter).

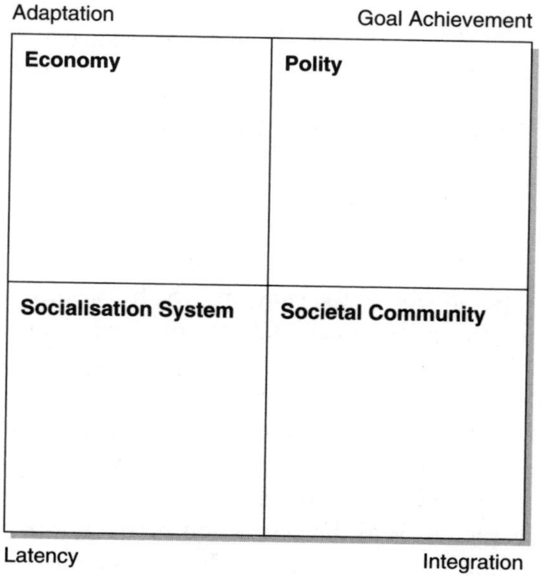

Figure 4.2

Left on their own, the boxes are just boxes. What gives the diagram some life and meaning is the arrows which Parsons sometimes puts in, sometimes leaves out and sometimes draws, so to speak, in invisible ink. Parsons thought, or he wrote as if he thought, that each subsystem produced something, an output, after having received an input from each of the other subsystems, these inputs being in turn their outputs. Including all the arrows at once, as Parsons often did, is confusing, so Figure 4.3 shows the basic idea for the political system.

The political system's task is to set goals for the society as a whole, and in order to do that it must continue to create an output, which Parsons calls 'power'. It can only do this if it receives inputs from the other three subsystems: money from the economy, 'influence' from the societal community (as a result of the activities of pressure groups, trade unions, public opinion and the like) and 'value commitments' from the pattern maintenance system. When this happens, power becomes an input for those other subsystems. And if all is well, so it seems, and so the conventional story goes, society is a system of harmonious and mutually reinforcing functional relationships between subsystems.

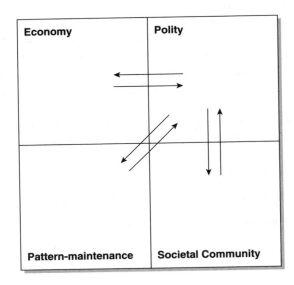

Figure 4.3

There are two points about the way in which Parsons manipulates both conceptual and metaphorical hierarchies. In the previous chapter we saw that the four pattern variable choices were of equal weight when discussed abstractly as a list, but resolved themselves into a hierarchy in the analysis of types of social structure, so that the universalism-particularism and ascription-achievement variables were the ones we needed in order to distinguish between – to classify – different societies; affectivity-affective neutrality and specificity-diffuseness suddenly dropped out of the picture. With his distinction between four functions Parsons again thinks of the functions hierarchically, only this time the diagram masks it; his original discussion of the four functions presents them as a list, with latency at the bottom and adaptation at the top, but with an arrow running up the side of the list to indicate that the priority runs from bottom to top. In order to make sense of society, then, you have to realise that basic values are key to maintaining the overall character of society and the direction of change. Because he thought of societies as self-equilibriating systems, Parsons took the organisation of information to be a more important factor in ensuring their perpetuation than was the mobilisation of energy. Values are high on information if low on energy, while adaptation to circumstance requires a lot of energy but is low on information. The model here is that of a washing machine: the washing machine's motor uses a lot of energy, but the key to the machine's operation is the information contained in the programme cycle. Switching to the right programme is a low energy activity, but without it the machine would not operate (Craib, 1994). The point, however, is that because he wanted to find a way of representing the interdependencies between the different parts of a society, Parsons resorted to the diagram for which he became famous. Once he did so, the hierarchy became less clear, for it appears that on this flat plane each subsystem has equal weight and significance. The arrow that previously conveyed hierarchy by means of a straight vertical would now have to loop round the right-hand side of the diagram before it reached the adaptation function, and so the sense of hierarchy would be lost. The fact that it is lost, and with it the emphasis on norms and values at the expense of power and money, helps to explain why a number of neo-Marxists with a more materialist bent were able to take Parsons more seriously than they might have done had the four functions been displayed as a simple vertical list.

This is not an abstruse point. We need to be sensitive to issues such as conceptual hierarchy because it points us towards just where the centre of gravity of a theorist's work lies, something that theorists have a habit of not always making explicit. A sense of the logic of theories and of how they work sometimes only emerges in the course of exposing oneself to them and to the manner in which they make their claims on us as readers. For example, Parsons did not say explicitly that 'the social world is a flat surface divided into four squares', but he did draw a diagram that made it look that way; this had consequences for the way in which he was able to think about society, for as Philip Manning has pointed out, the flat square allows you to think that you are looking at society as a whole, whereas a cube, for instance, would not, since you cannot look at a cube without having part of its surface hidden from view (Manning, 2005).

The conceptual hierarchy that gives priority to values over energy has been alluded to quite often in the secondary literature on Parsons; but less attention has been given to the fact that there is another type of hierarchy at work, one that appears at first to be the reverse of the one we have just discussed. This hierarchy emerges when we consider the fact that Parsons makes use of metaphor at, so to speak, a lower level of abstraction than the one on which he sees society as a system. Parsons says that power is an output which serves as an input to the other subsystems. But it is also something internal to the political system, just as money is internal to the economy. And Parsons describes money and power not quite in the way that you or I might describe them. He calls them 'symbolic media of exchange'. By this he means that, for the economy to function, money must not be understood as a merely physical thing in your pocket, but as a means of exchange which transcends actual exchanges. Money can also be accumulated, it can be invested and gain interest, or exist as credit. Money today exists in vast quantities as electronic impulses and signals rather than as paper. Without a banking and finance system (which is in fact a subsystem of the economic subsystem), none of this would be possible.

Now the point here is that Parsons will describe power in the same terms that he has employed for the description of money. It has been said countless times that power is 'an essentially contested concept', in other words that sociological and political theorists have never come to an agreement about what it is because no such agreement is possible (Poggi, 2001; Lukes, 2004). Indeed, you can get a good sense of how a theorist thinks about society by examining his or her theory of power. What does Parsons say about it? He says that power can be accumulated, can be banked, can circulate as a resource independent of those who possess it; it is a property of the system, not of individuals or groups; it is exercised but not possessed. This view of power was at the heart of his dispute with Wright Mills, for whom struggles for power are a zero–sum game.

According to this view, power is a thing, to be thought of as property, something that one can have or not have, or possess more or less of. The amount of power in any society at any time is finite, so that if I have 70% of it you have 30%.

Now we could treat Parsons' way of seeing power as the product of his insightful empirical observations of modern society, for instance, of the fact that the collapse of a democratically elected government does not mean the collapse of the state and its institutions, that institutional power seems to exist independent of the incumbents of office. However, it is not; it is entirely the product of the way in which he theorises it, and central to this is the fact that in order to help him understand something that would otherwise be not well understood – the elusive phenomenon of power – he mobilises a metaphor, the metaphor of money; we don't understand very well what power is, but we do understand what money is, or understand it better. So why not talk about power as if it were money?

> I assert with some confidence that ... the power equivalent of the creation of credit by banks can and does occur, and that there are in political systems phenomena strictly parallel to ... inflation and deflation in the economic sense. The scientific consequences ... are surely not trivial. (Parsons, 1969: 41)

> The politically significant parallel to what Keynes called 'saving' is the withholding by constituents of support that can be potentially given to political leadership, possibly 'hoarding' it, possibly 'investing' it in directions other than the support of current and possibly routine leadership. (Parsons, 1969: 47)

This does not make Parsons an economic determinist, because he is simply making use of money as a metaphor. But he does effectively argue that power is something less comprehensible than money and that it is by resorting to what we do know about money that we can make more sense of power.

But that is not the end of the story, because if this wasn't enough, Parsons is not sure that he knows quite so much about money either; in fact he calls it a symbolic medium of exchange, and this involves him in a further metaphorical move. For money is being seen here as a means of communication, and the means of communication we understand better than money, in fact best of all ... is language. Parsons makes it as plain as Parsons can:

> Money not only resembles a language, but it is a very specialised language through which intentions and conditional consequences of action are communicated. (Parsons, 1969: 40)

So language is a metaphor – not a simile – for money, which in turn is a metaphor for power.

Amazingly enough, this enabled Parsons to develop a model of politics and power in which he was able to say some important things about liberal democratic societies, such as that, in a properly functioning polity the incumbent of legitimate political office is a custodian and executor of a power which exists independent of actors, a power which will not disappear with the actor's defeat because it is not 'his' to exercise or to take away with him. It may have required a laborious journey, but in the end Parsons arrived at an account of power which seems to hold at least as much if not more plausibility than the power-as-property views of Wright Mills. If the reason that Parsons did not believe that power was a zero–sum game had as much to do with his theorising as with his attendance to what was going on around him, that should not be held against him even if the theorising itself might be; there is more than one theoretical route to the same or similar conclusions about the 'nature' of a phenomenon such as power. The idea, for instance, that power is something that is exercised rather than possessed or owned, has been treated by fans of Michel Foucault as one of his great insights; Hannah Arendt's concept of power also has affinities with this.

Although it will not be attempted here, comparing views of power is a worthwhile pedagogic exercise from which one can learn a lot about differences in theoretical sensibilities, more than one can learn, I think, from differences that occur between theorists in more well-defined subfields of sociology. 'Power', like 'society', is an essentially contested concept. For a variation on the non-possessive concept of power we turn now to a figure who found Parsons even more uncongenial than Wright Mills did, but who also felt the need to resort to metaphor in order to make sense of it: Norbert Elias.

Figurational Sociology

Norbert Elias repeatedly stated his opposition to Parsonsian sociology. Nicos Mouzelis has suggested that we take this idea of opposition seriously and see them as being a mirror image of one another, so that the one is as limited as the other but, just because of this, can help us see what the other makes us blind to (Mouzelis, 1995: 71). Mouzelis thinks that the limitations of both arise from the defective way in which they address one of the most venerable puzzles in sociological theory, the relationship between agency and structure, with the result that while both offer a distinct and, in their way, coherent account of what social structures are, they remain blind to, unable to handle, literally silent on, entire swathes of the social world. Mouzelis sees this as a problem of inadequate concept formation. But here we will see it in a different way: as an example of how theorists can become prisoners of their most productive and fertile metaphors and models. I call Elias a theorist here despite the fact that his reputation rests less on his contribution to sociological theory than on his historical sociology, most notably *The Civilising Process*, and the empirical generalisations concerning social processes which are derived from it. The basic historical claim is that the history of Europe can be written as one in which, with the development of the division of labour, and the emergence of states possessing a monopoly of the means of violence, there develop increasingly long and complex chains of interdependence between social classes. This in turn means that in order to gain political and economic power individuals and groups have need of increasingly complex and subtle means, such as forward planning and the deferral of gratification. The mechanisms of external constraint give rise, over the course of centuries of development, to personality structures in which a capacity for self-constraint is internalised. Elias's shorthand term for the first stage of this development – roughly from the Middle Ages to the middle of the 18th century in France – is 'the transformation of warriors into courtiers'. With the triumph of modern capitalism the primary source of external constraint is no longer what he calls the 'royal power mechanism' but the market: there is no other way to pursue power or wealth in the modern world than by engaging in the sort of rationalised, self-disciplined conduct upon which Max Weber had laid so much stress. This in turn then contributes to the development of peculiarly modern senses of shame and embarrassment.

In the original concluding reflections to The *Civilising Process*, the theoretical claims at work in this historical sociological project are expressed pretty directly, and there is no sustained use of metaphor in the extended sense in which it appears in Parsons' systems theory. Nevertheless, in the late 1960s, when sociology was dominated by functionalism and challenged by phenomenology and symbolic interactionism, Elias felt the need to make much more explicit the vision of sociology contained in his earlier works, and to show all of them why they were wrong. The result is the introduction to the 1968 edition of *The Civilising Process*, and *What Is Sociology?*, written in 1970. Both contain hostile references to Parsons, but more importantly, both make use of metaphors and models in order to create and sustain a more precise account of the meaning of terms like 'interdependence', 'power differentials', and 'social structure' – sociology's bread and butter, to put it in the language of English cuisine. The metaphorical imagery is more than a dramatic aside:

> ... the rationalisation of conduct is an expression of the foreign policy of the super-ego formation whose domestic policy is expressed in an advance of the shame threshold. (Elias, 1982: 294)

> Monopolies of physical violence and of the economic means of consumption and production, whether coordinated or not, are inseparably connected ... *Both together form the link in the chain by which men are mutually bound.* (Elias, 1982: 321)

For one who wished to emphasise the non-deterministic features of his work this is an unfortunate image, albeit one with a respectable pedigree. Indeed, Elias himself is aware of the constraining effect of the 'wrong' metaphors. He tries to steer clear of one in particular, that of what he calls 'the inner man', *homo clausus*, seen as divided from 'society' by an 'invisible wall'.

> One is satisfied with the spatial metaphor of 'inside' and 'outside', but one makes no serious attempt to locate the 'inner' in space' ... this preconceived image of *homo clausus* commands the stage not only in society at large but also in the human sciences. Its derivatives include not only the traditional *homo philosophicus*, the image of man of classical epistemology, but also *homo oeconomicus, homo psychologicus, homo historicus,* and not least *homo sociologicus* in his present-day version. The images of the individual of Descartes, of Max Weber, and of Parsons and many other sociologists are of the same provenance. (Elias, 1982: 249)

This image of a static individual positioned over against a 'society' external to it is described as a 'blind alley' or as a 'conceptual trap' which needs to be 'prized open … in such a way that the two concepts are made to refer to processes' (Elias, 1982: 250). Elias makes clear that this way of thinking about the individual and society is not a theorist's fantasy but is itself the late modern product of the very long-term historical developments which he analyses. *Homo clausus* is, if you will, a metaphor we modern individuals live by; but for that very reason, *it is not a useful metaphor for the description of the history of how we came to live by it.* We saw in Chapter 2 how the sociologist's capacity to describe involves an act of distancing. The point, however, is that the capacity for distancing is one which is built into the personality structures of modern individuals in such a way that they can abstract their selves clean out of their social conditions and contexts and think of themselves as autonomous, ahistorical beings, or 'unencumbered selves' as they are sometimes called. Elias proposes that the sociologist engage in a further act of distancing in order to see this ahistorical self as being itself a late product of historically specific developments. And the only way in which this can be done is through imagery which does justice to the processual and conflict-ridden nature of social life. For all the abstruseness of his theorising, Parsons operated with a conventional image that was too much a part of the society he was trying to study, the image of a 'closed' personality set over against society as a 'system'. The Parsonian image of the human being that Elias was criticising in Leicester in 1968 was the same as the one that Adorno was criticising in Frankfurt; it is an image of the human being that is both 'over-socialised' and 'over-psychologised'.

Elias's alternative is the concept of 'figuration', a 'structure of mutually oriented and dependent people'. Society does not exist 'both' in the individual and in a system somewhere else; it is nothing other than the 'network of interdependencies formed by individuals'. Now it is not immediately obvious that 'figuration' means anything more than 'system' does, and so sensing this, Elias thinks that another metaphor will help.

> What is meant by the concept of the figuration can be conveniently explained by reference to social dances … The image of the mobile figurations of interdependent people on a dance floor perhaps makes it easier to imagine states, cities, families, and also capitalist, communist and feudal systems as figurations … One can certainly speak of a dance in general, but no one will imagine a dance as a structure outside the individual or as a mere abstraction. The same dance figurations can certainly be danced by different people; but without a plurality of reciprocally oriented and dependent individuals, there is no dance … It would be absurd to say that dances are mental constructions abstracted from observations of individuals considered separately. The same applies to all other figurations. Just as the small dance figurations change – becoming now slower, now quicker – so, too, gradually or more suddenly, do large figurations we call societies. (Elias, 1982: 262)

It is tempting to dismiss this, and to ask whether, having already spoken of human beings being bound together by 'chains', it is entirely sure-footed to say that they are able to dance in them. Yet one can see that Elias badly needed an image on which to hang the term 'figuration' if it was to appear less abstract than Parsons' 'system'. Wanting to convey the idea that there is no version of 'society' which is not constituted, enacted and performed by its constituent members, he says effectively that all forms of organisational and group life are akin to a dance. At one level, there is nothing wrong with this image, because it does the job asked of it, namely to convey the sense in which and the (limited) extent to which we can legitimately speak of social structures being independent of the individuals who make them up: there are only dances in so far as people actually dance, there is only social interaction in so far as people interact, no 'interaction order', no 'society', separate from these activities. But it is not obvious that such an image can generate much of a research programme or lead to conceptual innovation. Could it, for instance, provide for a new set of categories for political analysis? Does Elias believe that we could replace 'monarchy', 'democracy' and 'aristocracy', or traditional, charismatic and legal-rational authority, with 'mazurka', 'tango' and 'the Gay Gordons'?

The second major objection Elias had to Parsons was that his sociology was static not only because of its commitment to *homo clausus* but also because it had no adequate account of the dynamics of social conflict. If conflict – over resources, power influence and so on – is to be theorised seriously, imagery drawn from a harmless leisure pursuit like dancing – a largely cooperative enter-prise – will hardly fit the bill. It is not surprising then that, in looking for a metaphorical image that could be worked up into a model, Elias abandoned the dance and fastened upon the competitive game. Elias believes that simplified models of competitive games can make more sense of the figurations, webs of relationships and so on of which individuals find themselves part. Elias refers to

> the image of people playing a game as a metaphor for people forming societies together ... One only needs to compare the imaginative possibilities of such static concepts as the individual and society or ego and system with the imaginative pos-sibilities opened up by the metaphoric use of various images of games and players; the comparison will help us to understand that these models have served to unleash our powers of imagination. (Elias, 1978: 131)

However, the point of a model or metaphor is that for it to be convincing and productive, let alone 'unleash the powers of our imagination', it needs to do the work which no other device can do, it needs to define the terms in which something can be predicated of the subject in question, or in the case of society, constituted in theory. There is an irreducibility about metaphor, because it is the 'better understood somewhere else' through which we try to make sense of the 'less well understood here'. So if we say that 'modernity is an iron cage', we do not first explain what an iron cage is and then apply it to moder-nity, rather we assume that the reader will have sufficient understanding of the imaginative implications of the iron cage image for a description of them to be superfluous. Similarly, when Marx and Engels say, in *The Communist Manifesto*, that 'a spectre is haunting Europe', they do not define 'spectre', for this would destroy the rhetorical force of describing communism in these terms. Although the term 'spectre' suggests that a peculiar conception of historical time is at work in which something that is not yet born can already be a ghost, the point of the whole exercise is communism, not ghosts, a point that seems to have been missed by Jacques Derrida (1994).

What happens when Elias starts to make a list of the types of games he has in mind? Beginning with a 'primal contest' without rules, we are then led through two-person games in which players have a measure of control over each other, however great the 'power-ratio' between them; 'multi-person games at one level' in which A is playing against B, C, D jointly but separately, or against all of them as a group; multi-person games on several levels which become too complicated for individual players to have a sense of all the appropriate moves (Elias, 1998b).

Two observations may be made about Elias's discussion of games: firstly, there comes a point where Elias constructs a table enumerating 'increases in number of possible relationships relative to the number of individuals in a web of relationships', an exercise that curiously resembles Parsons' list of all the possible pattern variable combinations we referred to in Chapter 3; secondly and more importantly, Elias introduces two further, more complex games: the first are what he calls 'two-tier games', in which all players remain interdependent but in which a small group of players coordinates the game while the rest, on the lower level, are 'peripheral figures, mere statistics' (Elias, 1998b: 90); the second are those in which those on the lower level influence the game to such an extent that those on the upper level have to take them into account as much as those on the upper level. Both of these games are too complicated for any individual to be able to make sense of them on their own.

Yet it is at just this point, where more complicated relationships are addressed, that Elias's model breaks down and becomes redundant. One can see this by reading the titles of the sections in which these more complex games are discussed: they are called 'Two-tier games model: oligarchic type'; and 'Game models on two levels: simplified increasingly democratic type'. What has happened here is that the model, which is supposed to cast new light on questions of political culture by introducing us to a set of implications which are formulated independent of political power, 'somewhere else', itself has to be re-described for us, the readers, in the language with which we are familiar from that very political culture. Elias wants us to understand what he is talking about, and helps us by using terms like 'oligarchic' and 'democratic', terms that are drawn straight from the realm of inquiry that the model was supposed to help us understand. Which means in effect that the types of games cannot be types in their own right. Like dances, games do not seem to be able to produce a new way of seeing.

Perhaps the model of the 'game' is best seen less as something that leads to a re-description of social and political relationships than as Elias's own theoretical response to the competitive pressure placed upon him by Parsonian functionalism in the 1950s and 1960s. Perhaps 'game models' are not really models at all, but Elias's attempt at a rational reconstruction of the implicit reasoning that had informed the historical sociology he had practised so successfully thirty years before. But as such, they point up very usefully the restricted view of the social world that Elias's sociology gives us. If Parsons' later work is committed to the master metaphor of the system and so allows us to 'see' and talk about only institutional logics of action, Elias's historical sociology allows us to see and talk about only conflictual relationships between groups – primarily social classes – and to write an entire history of Europe since the Middle Ages that refers only in passing to developments in, say, science, religion or philosophy: in Elias's world, the world he creates for us on the page, there is no Renaissance, no scientific revolution of the 17th century, no Reformation, no Enlightenment. This does not mean that Elias is unaware of them, but that, given his commitments, commitments that he sought to express by means of metaphors of chains, dances and games, they cannot be spoken of.

In this section, then, we have seen two theorists (we could have chosen many others) drawn to metaphor at the level of discourse, and we have raised some doubts about the scope of the legitimate claims that could be made on behalf of such metaphors as system, dance or game. The next section discusses theorists who deploy metaphor not at the level of discourse, in order to define an entire approach to theorising, but at the level of words.

Hypertrophy of Metaphor at the Level of Words: Bauman

If the systems theorist or the follower of game models has his blinkers on too tight, or concentrates his vision so tightly that, like the magnifying glass on a sunny day, it burns a hole in the paper, our next theorist has no such encumbrances. Lacking blinkers, and seemingly curious about everything, he looks about him in all directions. Nothing escapes his gaze. But can he see the wood for the trees?

In the work of Zygmunt Bauman you will look in vain for an overarching metaphor at the level of discourse that then defines a model of social analysis. This in some ways makes his enormous output – to use the language of systems theory – all the more bewildering. Systems theory or game theory has a remarkable but in some ways understandable generative capacity, in that once you have mastered the apparatus it can often be a matter of feeding in the material – relationships between institutions, relationships between people – turning the handle and hey presto. But in Bauman there is a positive disdain for the system or for systematic inquiry of any sort. In themselves, the impulses which drive such an approach are no bad thing. But the price is what might be called cultural diagnosticism combined with a hypertrophy of metaphor at the level of words, something particularly evident in his more recent books.

In this section we will see that Bauman's use of metaphor is not always successful, for two reasons: firstly, metaphor is never deployed at the level of discourse, so that the work contains no vision of sociology as a distinct intellectual exercise, no clearly defined apparatus for studying society. Instead we are invited to a rich and often persuasive display of the author's diagnostic and imaginative sympathy. There is, in other words, no systematisation but plenty of dramatisation in his work. Even this would not be crippling if metaphor was used for the witty aside, or to present a pithy and pregnant shorthand version of an argument already established. But Bauman at times has more grandiose aims; not exactly for a conceptual framework, but certainly for something which is required to do a good deal of work. The most widely quoted example is his account of the 'gardening state', which he uses in both *Modernity and the Holocaust* and *Modernity and Ambivalence*.

It is certainly true that in the interwar period a number of theoreticians, including those close to the leadership of Nazi Germany, themselves employed metaphors derived from gardening, explicitly describing the health of the state in terms derived from the activity of weeding out and re-planting. But Bauman wants to claim more for this idea, namely that the image of gardening accurately conveys the relationship between Enlightenment ideas and the administrative practices of modern states since the 18th century; moreover, once we understand the ways in which modern states routinely deploy a classificatory logic to distinguish between healthy plants and weeds, between the normal and the pathological, we can understand much of what made the Holocaust possible. Hence the title of his most well known book. But here, in the face of the mountain of existing scholarship on the modern state and its administrative apparatus, as well as the large variety of ways in which the polity has been envisioned by influential political philosophers (recall our list at the start of this chapter), the suggestion that the metaphor of 'gardening' is a helpful way of thinking about modern politics as such seems to be over-egging the pudding.

Much the same can be said of his more recent notion of 'liquid modernity'. While there is some truth in the idea that social institutions in modern western societies – particularly those connected with economic and cultural life – have lost some of their capacity to influence individual conduct in a manner that is stable over time, and while it may be true that those individuals are, taken in the round, increasingly faced with the need to be adaptable, flexible agents of their own fate, subject to the need for re-skilling, the extent to which this is true varies enormously from country to country and between institutional sectors in any one country; 'liquid modernity' is the sort of image that is unlikely to lead to anything one could call a serviceable model of social analysis, because the only 'implications' and 'hypotheses' it is capable of generating are unlikely to take us very far beyond the question of 'how liquid' Britain or Spain really are, a somewhat thin and watery return in an area – the historical sociology of modernity – already fairly rich in analytic and diagnostic possibility. Marxist historians, for instance, even if they pay lip service to the phrase 'all that is solid melts into air', mostly conduct sober and solid historical materialist analyses of the relationship between economic, political and cultural forces, rather than extending the metaphor of liquidness – which Marx offered as a dramatic aside – into any and every area of social life.

The point to remember here, however, is that there is nothing in principle wrong with the use of extended metaphor, only that it requires considerable skill. As we will see below, Erving Goffman, for all the criticism which has been directed at the procedure, was a master of it. The key is being able to show that the initial image has enough productive potential to help us make some sense of the variety of social phenomena to which it is to be applied, and to describe them in new and arresting ways. This requires something more than simply arriving at an initial image and then listing as many properties as you can think of which are associated with it. The metaphor has a chance of being extended successfully only when there is a sense of connection between those properties and the reality they are expected to illuminate.

Two images from *Liquid Modernity* – and we could have chosen many more – demonstrate that something is being demanded of them which they will struggle to provide. The first occurs near the beginning, where Bauman discusses the apparently limited sense in which modern societies are open, or 'hospitable to critique':

> The kind of 'hospitality to critique' characteristic of modern society in its present form may be likened to the pattern of a caravan site. The place is open to everyone with his or her own caravan and enough money to pay the rent. Guests come and go; none of them takes much interest in how the site is run, providing the customers have been allocated plots big enough to park the caravans, the electric sockets and water taps are in good order and the owners of the caravans parked nearby do not make too much noise and keep down the sound from their portable TVs and hi-fi speakers after dark. Drivers bring to the site their own homes attached to their cars. (Bauman, 2000: 23)

And so on for another half a page.

Here he is again, writing about types of 'explosive', short-lived and transitory community which, he believes, are characteristic of today's world.

> The name 'cloakroom community' grasps well some of their characteristic traits. Visitors to a spectacle dress for the occasion, abiding by a sartorial code distinct from those codes they follow daily – the act which simultaneously sets apart the visit as a 'special occasion' and makes the visitors look, for the duration of the event, much more uniform than they do in the life outside the theatre building. It is the evening performance which brought them all here – different as their interests and pastimes during the day could have been. Before entering the auditorium they all leave the coats or anoraks they wore in the streets in the playhouse cloakroom (by counting the number of hooks and hangers used, one can judge how full is the house and how assured is the immediate future of the production). During the performance all eyes are on the stage; so is everybody's attention ... After the last fall of the curtain, however, the spectators collect their belongings from the cloakroom and when putting their street clothes on once more return to their ordinary mundane and different roles. (Bauman, 2000: 200)

Not content with this, Bauman almost immediately adds that 'carnival communities' seem to be another fitting name for the communities under discussion, and that 'cloakroom or carnival, the explosive communities are as indispensable a feature of the liquid modernity landscape ... The spectacles, the pegs and hangers in the cloakroom and the crowd-pulling carnival fairs are many and varied, catering for any sort of taste' (Bauman, 2000: 201).

Bauman may well be on to something in his emphasis on the limited ways in which critique in the name of group interests can be sustained, or on the way in which long-term collectivities based upon interests are being challenged by more short-lived forms of community based upon criteria of membership which are fleeting. But in order for the metaphors with which he seeks to depict this state of affairs to be effective, there needs to be a sense that the details of his master image bear some resemblance to the details of his argument. In the case of the caravan site, 'money to pay the rent', 'allocated plots', 'electric sockets and water taps', neighbours' 'hi-fi speakers', and 'after dark'; and in the case of the cloakroom, 'evening performance', 'coats and anoraks (!)', and 'hooks and hangers' have to have a metaphorical function of their own, have to be such that they can do some work for us in our efforts to understand society better than we could without resorting to them. Yet it should not take you long to see that the apparent detail cannot hide a certain barrenness in this image, that, rather than provide us with a set of tools with which we can make sense of society, Bauman has sought to give us a set of immediate, striking images of certain aspects of society. There is an urgency about all of his recent books which many readers find attractive. But if you read those books through it will be hard to mistake the literal-mindedness that pervades them. The metaphors in Bauman, far from being part of an allusive or 'poetic' style in which the sense of things emerges only gradually and indirectly, are all consistent with an attempt to tell it to you straight. There is no extension of metaphor or deepening of significance or enrichment of implication here, merely a description of what a caravan site or a cloakroom looks like.

In defence of Bauman it might be said that these passages are so weak that they do not so much undermine his argument as clutter it; this talk of caravan sites and cloakrooms is so redundant, so rhetorically moribund, that we would do best to ignore it. The problem with this view is that Bauman himself seems oddly attached to these images. Nowhere is this more true than in his use of the metaphor of gardening to describe the practices of modern states. Yet while certain policy-makers may themselves have made use of such imagery, the idea that these self-descriptions can illuminate the workings of modern states sits uneasily with the far more interesting and nuanced account of the state functionary given by Bauman himself in *Modernity and the Holocaust* (Bauman, 1988: ch. 2).

Another way of putting this would be to say that there are metaphors in Bauman, but that they do not generate new descriptions. There is description aplenty, of course, but it is not theoretical description, or put better, it is description which owes nothing to a distinctive approach to theorising, but everything to the author's intuitive sense of things, and his capacity to appeal rather directly to the reader's own instincts. For all the passion and often genuine seductiveness of his style, there is in his work no real conceptual or methodological innovation, be it strictly sociological or interdisciplinary, and no sense of the heroic striving and failure which, as we have seen, is the mark of the discipline's greatest exponents. As Bauman himself might have put it: it seems that, in Bauman's work, sometimes the baby of analytical rigour is thrown out with the bathwater of science, and discharged into the sewerage system of discarded paradigms which, if our pipes are not properly laid, may well seep into the soil beneath the garden of sociology and reduce the value of the property as a whole.

Living Metaphor at the level of words and discourse: Goffman

For an example of work which makes use of metaphor more effectively, and which does so both at the level of discourse and at the level of words, we turn now to Erving Goffman. Few who have written about Goffman have failed to say at least something about the use of metaphor in his sociology. The point here will be to show you how, handled properly, metaphor can be the sociologist's light cloak rather than its iron cage. 'Handled properly' here refers not only to the skilful deployment of metaphor in description and argument, but also to the sociologist's sense of distance towards the metaphors to which he is committed. Nobody was more aware than Goffman of the limits of the categories and metaphors he used, limits a sense of which he often conveys through metaphor itself: in the 'Author's Note' to *Relations in Public* he writes: 'I snipe at a target from six different positions; there is no pretence at laying down a barrage. The result is chapters, but wayward ones' (Goffman, 1971: 9); in *Forms of Talk* he will 'lumber in where the self-respecting decline to tread. A question of pinning with our ten thumbs what ought to be secured with a needle' (Goffman, 1981: 2); at the end of *The Presentation of Self in Everyday Life*, his attempt to see social life as drama, he cautions the reader against any overestimation of the status of what was 'a rhetoric and a manoeuvre' on his part, going so far as to say that 'here the language and mask of the stage will be dropped. Scaffolds, after all, are to build things with, and should be erected with an eye to taking them down' (Goffman, 1959: 246).[4]

These pithy shorthand accounts of the status of his work are one example of Goffman's use of metaphor at the level of words; another is his use of asides deploying a range of imagery from that of battle – in which individuals construct an 'encircling barricade' around themselves (Goffman, 1961: 24), or are left to 'bleed to death from the conversational strategies performed on them' (Goffman, 1971: 95) – to that of love-making, as when individuals are described as embracing a role and being embraced by it (Goffman, 1961: 94–5). A more elaborate use of metaphor at the level of words is contained in the following passage in which Goffman uses an arresting image in order to summarise an argument or observation and bring a passage to a conclusion.

> In middle-class society, care in the use of eyes can be readily found in connection with nakedness. In nudist camps, for example, apparently considerable effort is taken to avoid appearing to be looking at the private parts of others. Topless waitresses sometimes obtain the same courtesy from their patrons, especially when engaging them in close serving. A rule in our society: when bodies are naked, glances are clothed. (Goffman, 1971: 70–1)

At other times, he goes further, ending a paragraph with a metaphor but in such a way that, although the passage may have come to a conclusion, discussion of its import is expected to continue. For instance, in the 1961 essay 'Role Distance', Goffman argues that the concept of 'role' – at the time one of sociological theory's magic words – entails both that an individual 'give' only part of himself to whatever activity is demanded of him as an incumbent of a role, and that any one role will involve not one but a collection of required performances that the individual is not free to take or leave as he wishes. Here is how he puts it:

> The role perspective has definite implications of a social-psychological kind. In entering the position, the incumbent finds that he must take on the whole array of action encompassed by the corresponding role, so role implies a social determinism and a doctrine about socialisation. We do not take on items of conduct one at a time but rather a whole harness load of them and may anticipatorily learn to be a horse even while being pulled like a wagon. (Goffman, 1971: 77)

Here, the 'harness load' metaphor enables Goffman to summarise an argument about the possibly burdensome nature of role obligations, much in the way that 'glances are clothed' completes the previous example; but here he goes further, extending the metaphor in order to convey a sense of the practical variation in the relationship between freedom and constraint, individual uniqueness and social obligation, personal initiative and unavoidable restriction. He does so in a way that leaves this relationship open; we may learn to be a horse, but we might not, remaining a wagon; even if we do 'learn to be a horse' we may learn 'anticipatorily', which introduces an element of temporal inexactitude and even scepticism towards our ability to act autonomously. But does this have to imply that to be a horse here means to be in control of one's destiny? Isn't a horse a beast of burden, full of strength and power but also subject to the will of its master? Then again, what if the one being pulled by the horse is also holding the reins? Or John Wayne in *Stagecoach*, leaping from the carriage onto the horse in front of it? The point here is that Goffman completes his account with an image which is simple, yet pregnant, suggestive of a definite kind of relationship, but flexible enough to generate further discussion about the precise way in which the version of the relationship we are interested in works itself out. In short, it opens up a horizon of implication and invites us to walk towards it. In this sense it has a different rhetorical function from Weber's iron cage of modernity or Marx's spectre of communism, because these images are there largely to bring an account to an end (*The Protestant Ethic*) or set it in motion (*The Communist Manifesto*). It is also an image of a type of action, pulling and being pulled. Bauman's images of caravan sites and cloakrooms, by contrast, are images of physical spaces; even if such static imagery is serviceable, imagine trying to generate a discussion about, say, community and identity in modern society on the basis of questions like: 'what if the electricity isn't working?' or 'what if we are handed the wrong anorak?'.

Now these examples of Goffman's use of metaphor at the level of words might be taken as evidence of a certain literary talent, on the basis of which we could conclude that, in addition to being blessed with sharp powers of observation and a keen analytical mind, he wrote well. But this would be to treat metaphor as mere decoration, whereas Goffman had a grander intent, deploying metaphor not only for the purpose of the witty aside or pregnant summary, but also at the level of discourse, as a means of organising an entire body of inquiry. Goffman takes it as self-evident that the drama metaphor can do this job: 'Scripts even in the hands of unpractised players can come to life because life itself is a dramatically enacted thing. All the world is not, of course, a stage, but the crucial ways in which it isn't are not easy to specify' (Goffman, 1959: 78). Yet this negative statement of a positive claim also hints that 'grander intent' does not mean that Goffman's use of 'drama' is comparable to Parsons' use of 'system'. Parsons had no distance at all towards the 'system' metaphor, and neither he, nor Elias for that matter, would have written: 'the introduction is necessarily abstract and can be skipped' (Goffman, 1959: 10). Goffman displays the same distance towards the drama metaphor at the start of *Frame Analysis*. 'All the world is not a stage – certainly the theatre isn't entirely. (Whether you organize a theatre or an aircraft factory, you need to find places for cars to park and coats to be checked, and these had better carry real insurance against theft.)' (Goffman, 1974: 1). Much of social life is not subject to the uncertainties and vulnerabilities that pervade our efforts to maintain a sense of reality, so that these efforts take place against a background of things such as car parks and cloakrooms – Bauman take note! – that are real and solid and not of much interest to the sociologist of face-to-face interaction, or for that matter to anybody else. Moreover, Goffman is not afraid to mix his master metaphors with others brought in for supplementary purposes. In *The Presentation of Self in Everyday Life*, for instance, the metaphor of drama is combined with that of a game; in *Frame Analysis* the metaphor of a frame is combined with that of 'keys and keying' taken from music. Sometimes the supplementary metaphor is a one-off:

> Our activity, then, is largely concerned with moral matters, but as performers we do not have a moral concern with them. As performers we are merchants of morality. Our day is given over to intimate contact with the goods we display and our minds are filled with intimate understandings of them; but it may well be that the more attention we give to these goods, then, the more distant we feel from them and from those who are believing enough to buy them. (Goffman, 1959: 244)

This looks like a recipe for the 'fragile patchwork' that Richard Harvey Brown feared. But it also reflects Goffman's reluctance to commit himself too heavily to his metaphors, and an attendant willingness to allow the inquiry to be driven – pulled? – forward as much by the vast and eclectic body of empirical material he collected as by the unfolding of any one model; indeed, the sheer volume of material to which the dramaturgical metaphor or that of 'frame' appears applicable forced Goffman to develop an initial orientation into a bewildering array of lower level conceptual constructs even within the confines of the master metaphor itself: thus, in the case of drama, we also have performance, audience, front, setting, impression management, props, enactment; in the case of a frame, keying, designs, fabrications, laminations (Williams, 1983).

Finally, some remarks about Goffman's overall intellectual style, because in the end that is what our discussions of all our heroes are about; a kind of sensibility, a relationship to social reality. The first point arises from a critique of Goffman contained in Clifford Geertz's essay 'Blurred Genres'. Geertz writes:

The writings of Erving Goffman ... rest ... almost entirely on the game analogy. (Goffman also employs the language of the stage quite extensively, but as his view of the theater is that it is an oddly mannered kind of interaction game – ping-pong in masks – his work is not, at base, really dramaturgical.) ... Social conflict, deviance, entrepreneurship, sex roles, religious rites, status ranking, and the simple need for human acceptance get the same treatment. Life is just a bowl of strategies. (Geertz, 1983: 25)

This is premature – on this account, Goffman could never have written an essay like 'Face Work' or developed a concept like 'civil inattention' or referred to the 'little pieties' by means of which each of us helps others to maintain or save face, refuses to notice their slips and interactional misdemeanours, 'honours' the other's self (Manning, 1989). To be sure, Goffman's world contains conmen and crooks aplenty, but it is not constituted or defined by their game-like behaviour.

Later in the same essay Geertz makes a more telling point about Goffman, albeit inadvertently, in the course of a criticism of the anthropologist Victor Turner: 'This hospitableness in the face of cases is at once the major strength of the ritual theory version of the drama analogy and its most prominent weakness. It can expose some of the profoundest features of social process, but at the expense of making vividly disparate matters look drably homogeneous' (Geertz, 1983: 28). There are two problems here: the number of cases embraced by a particular perspective; and disparateness versus homogeneity. On the first, for any attempt to study something as general as 'face-to-face interaction', the infinity of possible examples is clearly both a temptation and a challenge. Here Goffman's work may be contrasted with that of comparative historical sociologists who generally work with a handful of cases. Barrington Moore based a theory of modern dictatorship and democracy on eight cases, his student Theda Skocpol formulated a theory of modern revolution on the basis of just three (Moore, 1977; Skocpol, 1979). But the second point is that the contrast between Skocpol and Goffman is not strictly one between few cases and many cases, and this, I think, is the source of Geertz's misgivings about Goffman. Geertz's version of how to do anthropology is not dissimilar to Skocpol's of how to do comparative historical sociology. He once said, 'the anthropologist doesn't study villages, he studies *in* villages', by which he meant that the anthropologist's task is to perform what he called a 'thick description' on a quite specific ethnographic case, and in so doing illuminate the manner in which an entire society or a culture holds itself together. The classic example of this approach is his essay on the Balinese cockfight, which is 'about' cockfighting in Bali but only in so far as it is an account of the way in which Balinese society tells a story to itself about the things that matter most to it. Cockfighting is only interesting from this contextual point of view (Geertz, 1973).

By contrast with this concentrated ethnographic performance, Goffman's work is peppered with examples of strips of interaction taken from all over the world, from different historical periods, and from different genres – newspapers, memoirs, philosophical treatises, social psychology journal articles, field notes; instead of doing ethnography, Goffman takes ethnographic fragments and places them where they will fit within the overall architecture of his books. Thus the section of the chapter called 'Performances' in *The Presentation of Self* contains material on, among other things, London clubs, Chinese public ceremonies, estate agents' stationery, hospitals, army barracks, undertakers, sales offices, Adam Smith, the caste system, and Scottish crofting communities. Material taken from these same sources will then crop up in another chapter dedicated to another aspect of interaction (the similarity with Simmel is palpable). The same is true of *Frame Analysis*. The upshot of Geertz's objection is that this, combined with Goffman's wilful construction of formalised vocabularies, produces description aplenty, but description that is thin compared with the detailed, layered, thickly descriptive ethnographic study of one or two cases in which a complex way of life might be laid bare. The little worlds – of salesmen, clerks, diplomats, con artists and gamblers – from which Goffman takes his materials are constantly being broken down and their parts redistributed across the landscape of Goffman's books, fitted, according to Geertz's critique, into the procrustean bed of Goffman's master metaphors. Or most of them at any rate. Goffman did write an entire Master's thesis on the world of the petrol pump attendant, and his PhD was about the crofting communities that keep appearing in most of his books; among his published works, *Asylums* is clearly a concentrated effort to stay with a discreet object of inquiry, the social situation of the mental patient.

However, even in his most theoretically ambitious books, in which a master metaphor is mobilised in the most sustained way, Goffman does not reduce the disparate to the homogeneous in the way that Geertz implies. We can get a sense of this – and of Goffman's relationship as a professional sociologist to the social world – if we examine two passages in which Goffman describes matters that have been addressed by Parsons and by Adorno and, for that matter, many others. We will see the difference between the way Goffman constructs generalisations about social life and the way Parsons and Adorno do it, the difference consisting in Goffman's respect for disparateness as opposed to Parsons' and Adorno's tendency to reduce the social world to drab homogeneity. This may sound peculiar in view of what we said in Chapter 3 about the difference between classificatory and dialectical sensibilities, but there are numerous passages where even negative dialectics becomes something of a dogmatically applied formula rather than a nuanced engagement with social reality. Note here too that the difference between a sensitivity to disparateness and a reduction to homogeneity cuts across the difference between metaphorical and non-metaphorical theorising; forcing the social world into a straitjacket can be done by the overzealous development of categories or by a fixation with metaphor at the level of discourse; openness to nuance may be achieved by the skilful use of categories or by the apposite deployment of metaphor.

For instance, Parsons achieves – if that is the right word – the first position both by means of the system metaphor – witness his theory of power – and by the application of the pattern variables to anything and everything – recall his description of love in Chapter 2. Perhaps the most significant arena in which he deployed them was in his study of the professions. The tendency towards achievement-based, universalistic, affectively neutral, and specific roles and modes of world orientation was a general feature of modern industrial society. This means that when he describes the doctor–patient encounter Parsons does so just as he might describe that between lawyer and client, professor and student. Indeed, whatever the doctor's manifest function may be – to make the patient better – his latent function is to 'bring the patient back into line', to recall the patient to a world in which objective scientific knowledge has become a cultural touchstone, and reinforce the professional pattern. Exactly the same thing is done by the professor who marks the student's essay or the lawyer who handles a client's case. But how does Parsons know all of this? Has he conducted empirical inquiries or done ethnographic work on these matters, inhabited the settings in which these outcomes are achieved? Of course not! Everything follows, as everything must, according to a categorical logic as it follows according to a metaphorical logic when he uses the language of systems.

Compare this with a passage in *The Presentation of Self* in which Goffman is discussing the notion of 'front'. Front is 'that part of the individual's performance which regularly functions in a general and fixed fashion to define the situation for those who observe the performance'. He then notes a tendency for routines, particularly work routines, to develop social fronts that cut across the peculiarities, the contents if you like, of the particular job at hand. Thus, 'many service occupations offer their clients a performance that is illuminated with dramatic expressions of cleanliness, modernity, competence and integrity. While in fact these abstract standards have a different significance in different occupational performances, the observer is encouraged to stress the abstract similarities' (Goffman, 1959: 36). Put like that, it seems that Goffman is describing the same generalised ethos of service that Parsons writes about. But the point here is that the generalisation refers not to society-wide norms and values that operate outside the contexts in which they are performed, but to a tendency that emerges pragmatically and whose course Goffman seeks to follow:

> ... the current tendency for chimney sweeps and perfume clerks to wear white lab coats tends to provide the client with an understanding that the delicate tasks performed by these persons will be performed in what has become a standardized, clinical, confidential manner ... in factories, barracks and other large establishments those who organize [them] find it impossible to provide a special cafeteria, special modes of payment, special vacation rights, and special sanitary facilities for every line and staff status category in the organization. (Goffman, 1959: 36–7)

Put another way, non-contingency is one of the contingencies of social life; it is not, as it is in Parsons, something that is provided for by society-wide norms and values to be expressed by means of fundamental categories. Rather than the complete description of society – for which Parsons strove by means of a rigid and all-embracing terminology, both conceptual (pattern variables) and metaphorical (language of systems theory) – Goffman gives us a wide-ranging description of society by means of flexible and adaptable metaphors combined with localised supplementary concepts.

A similar contrast can be made between Goffman and Adorno. We saw in the last chapter that one of Adorno's criticisms of classificatory reason was that it treated individual phenomena as mere 'examples' or 'instances' of a class of phenomena; in Adorno's language, the object was made to go into the concept 'without remainder'. Adorno himself proposed the essay as a literary genre that might escape this kind of trap. But at the same time, this apparent sensitivity to nuance is vitiated by his attachment to what can only be called 'magic words or phrases'. One of these is 'instrumental reason', meaning the tendency of the means of action to turn into its end. Because Adorno tended to see this happening everywhere in capitalist societies, even his finest essays on culture, such as 'Free Time', tend to force disparate matters into the same mould. Here he is, for instance, on gender relations:

> Taken in its strict sense, in contradistinction to work, as it at least used to apply in what would today be considered an out-dated ideology, there is something vacuous (Hegel would have said abstract) about the notion of free time. An archetypal instance is the behaviour of those who grill themselves brown in the sun merely for the sake of a sun-tan, although dozing in the blazing sun is not at all enjoyable, might very possibly be physically unpleasant, and certainly impoverishes the mind. In the sun-tan, which can be quite fetching, the fetish character of the commodity lays claim to actual people; they themselves become fetishes. The idea that a girl is more erotically attractive because of her brown skin is probably only another rationalization. The sun-tan is an end in itself, of more importance than the boy-friend it was perhaps supposed to entice. (Adorno, 1991a: 191)

Compare this vituperative and entirely speculative piece of culture criticism with the following passage from Goffman:

> American college girls did, and no doubt do, play down their intelligence, skills and determinativeness when in the presence of datable boys, thereby manifesting a profound psychic discipline in spite of their international reputation for flightiness. These performers are reported to allow their boy friends to explain things to them tediously that they already know; they conceal proficiency in mathematics from their less able consorts; they lose ping-pong games just before the ending: 'One of the nicest techniques is to spell out long words incorrectly once in a while. My boy friend seems to get a great kick out of it and writes back: "Honey, you certainly don't know how to spell"'. (Goffman, 1959: 48)

Now it may be that Goffman has no interest in criticising this state of affairs. The point here, however, is that this is a statement about gender relations seen in the context of the way status differences are performed; in this passage he is addressing one of several examples of behaviour – all of which are empirically established cases – in which individuals downplay their social status, wealth, intelligence or other attributes that might otherwise be seen as positive. Their reasons for so doing may vary both across and within societies – certainly they have to do with more than the mere calculation of advantage – so that although Goffman will string them all together as part of the same analysis, the analysis itself is more localised; he is hesitant to link them by seeing each one as yet another exemplar of the workings of 'capitalism', 'modernity', 'patriarchy' and so on. Having picked his level, in other words, he largely sticks to it. Compared to this, Adorno's way of connecting the activity of girls sunning themselves on the beach with 'the fetishism of the commodity' appears trite and forced.

Conclusion

If we have concentrated here on a few examples of the use of metaphor in sociology, it was in order to be able to point up the theoretical problems that can arise in their deployment rather than to provide a detailed inventory. The reader is invited to draw his or her conclusions about my interpretations of these particular thinkers but to look for similar problems and questions in the work of others. One general remark, though, is perhaps in order. If reason needs imagination, if conceptualisation needs metaphor, then it needs it for the task of describing the social world more persuasively, in such a way that we are able to see or talk differently. Goffman, for instance, says that his dramaturgical metaphor is scaffolding that can be taken down when its job is done. This makes it more substantial than a light cloak that can be cast off at will, but a temporary or interim device none the less. Yet often in the history of socio-logical thought, either because of the megalomaniac ambitions of the theoret-ical genius or because of the need of less able scholars for an intellectual security or for something larger to which to attach their individual projects, fate decrees that metaphor becomes an iron cage.

There is a further point that we merely hinted at here: the use of metaphor has nothing necessarily to do with the quest to make sociology a more literary or artistic activity; when it is resorted to at the level of discourse this is perfectly consistent with a striving towards science and away from literature. Indeed, the history of science can be written as a history of the metaphors that even the hard sciences have resorted to. In the next chapter we will see that the rela-tionship between sociology as science and sociology as literature is also com-plicated when we observe the use that sociological theorists make of diagrams; only here, the surprising thing is that a device that might be thought to lend inquiry a more scientific air may push it even further away from it than metaphor can.

5

Diagrams

Diagrammatic reasoning is the only fertile reasoning. If logicians would only embrace this method, we should no longer see attempts to base their science on the fragile foundations of metaphysics, or a psychology not based on logical theory; and there would soon be such an advance in logic that every science would feel the benefit of it. (Peirce, 1958: 459)

The previous two chapters explored tools that can be argued to be crucial to the theoretical enterprise. Without categories and metaphors the theorist would not be able to generate much talk about the social world. Although some may say that ontology is more important than epistemology, that the first move is to say what the social world 'is' and what is in it, and only then to worry about how we can know it, you cannot make sense without tools to make sense with. Categories and metaphors are indispensable.

In this chapter we will ask whether the same can be said for diagrams. At first it might seem that diagrams are a peripheral matter, or at best what the literary theorist Gerard Genette called a paratextual one, belonging to the class of phenomena that includes acknowledgements, indices, prefaces and appendices. On closer inspection, however, there turns out to be more to diagrams than that; theorists do make use of them, and do so often enough for them to be worthy of discussion here. In the last chapter we downplayed the role played by images in the use of metaphor, saying that metaphor is not a matter of substituting images for words but of substituting one way of talking for another way of talking. Nevertheless, we are still entitled to ask about the ways in which sociologists make use of visual representations, if only for the reason that if they are there on the page it must be because the theorist believes that they make a difference to the argument. Even Wright Mills, who can hardly be characterised as an esoteric thinker, wrote that 'charts, tables and diagrams of a qualitative sort are not only ways to display work already done; they are very often genuine tools of production' (Mills, 1960: 213).

Let us, then, take Wright Mills at his word and ask whether the diagram aids the production of knowledge or hampers it. Is the diagram an adjunct to the words on the page, a mere pedagogic device, or does it have an independent cognitive potential? Furthermore, in what direction is sociology pushed by theoretical diagrams? Do they take sociology towards natural science or towards literature or art? Although the use of diagrams might seem like a clumsy attempt to push sociology towards mathematics and physics, as we will see, they can also suggest a relationship between sociology and primitive or abstract art; some of the diagrams in sociological theory books – both works of theory and books about theory – even resemble the symbolism found in the world religions. The use of diagrams does not, notably, push sociological theory towards literature, although there is scope for considering even that relationship (Mitchell, 1981; Adler, 2003).

The point here is that, just as the use of metaphor does not necessarily push sociology in the direction of literature but may be consistent with a need to give sociology a scientific status, so the use of diagrams does not necessarily push sociology towards science but may be consistent with the need to give a theory a more accessible aesthetic form. This is not always appreciated in the sparse literature on diagrams in theory. For instance, in one of the few sustained treatments of the topic, Mike Lynch sees in diagrams 'a rhetorical mathematics that conveys an impression of rationality', a sceptical view that leads him to propose a choice between diagrams which seek this rationality and (inevitably in his view) fail, and diagrams which are used 'parodically' or 'deconstructively' by those who know that such rationality can never be achieved in the social sciences (Lynch, 1991). The problem with this is that it leaves out the possibility that some diagrams are not seeking an impression of rationality at all, either drawing on unacknowledged pre-modern or non-rational resources or being used for aesthetic purposes from the beginning. So while some of the diagrams employed by sociologists are undoubtedly driven by a quasi-scientific ambition, some of them look more like diagrams with much older lineages, both pre-modern and non-European. In order to make sense of them, we may have to look beyond sociology to other fields of knowledge, such as art history, mathematics and the physical sciences, and the history of religion.

The last may come as a surprise, but there is a range of legitimate perspectives from which to think about the significance of these marks on paper, these lines, arrows, circles and squares and boxes. At one end of the spectrum, so to speak, we can discuss them in terms of a logic of visual perception, in which we speak of a diagram purely in terms of what Rudolf Arnheim called 'configurations of visual forces'. Here we can ask whether the theorist's diagram works as a diagram, whether the theorist has the capacity or the talent to make the diagram do the work he requires of it, about the tendencies at work in the lines and shapes themselves. At the other end we can draw upon ideas from the history of religion and ask whether it is wholly accidental that sociologists, for instance, repeatedly operate with a threefold typology of types of power (economic, political, ideological) – which can be represented in certain ways and not others, e.g. by a three-sided pyramid or by a triangle – or a fourfold typology of systemic functions – which can be represented by a square divided into four – or with dualisms or pairs of opposites which can also be combined in a two-by-two table with four cells. And once we have done this we can ask a more basic question: are a theorist's diagrams any good? Do they bear the burden which has been placed upon them? And if they do not, what are they doing on the page?

The art historian Ernst Gombrich once wrote, in praise of the diagram:

A relationship that would take so long to explain in words that we might lose the thread ('she is the wife of a second cousin of my stepmother') could be seen on a family tree at a glance. Whatever the type of conception, whether it is a chain of command, the organisation of a corporation, a classification system for a library or a network of logical dependencies, the diagram will always spread out before our eyes what a verbal description could only present in a string of statements. (Gombrich, 1996: 56)

This is an admirably succinct statement of the virtues of the diagram, but it describes, so to speak, the ideal diagram; it assumes that every diagram is in some way successful and leaves open the question of whether the diagram presents merely a visual version of something otherwise expressed in words – in which case the diagram is simply a miniaturised, shorthand translation of something that remains what it is after the translation – or a transformation such that the ideas rendered in diagrammatic form are different from those conveyed in words. And it leaves out entirely a third possibility, one identified by Baldamus, who, in a neglected essay on Habermas writes that:

the following section aims at an analysis of the logical foundations of the *Theory of Communicative Action*. More specifically, I shall examine the method by which the graphical diagrams, vaguely called 'conceptual schemes', have been constructed. In the 'secondary literature' it is widely assumed that the diagrams are used for didactic purposes, i.e. to make the sophisticated verbal text accessible to undergraduates. But this is a mistake. The truth is that without the diagrams the whole theory would break down. (Baldamus, 1992: 102)

This is a strong claim and possibly an exaggerated one, but it is made about a book containing 40 diagrams, all of them in tabular form and deploying a variety of (sometimes contradictory) dyadic and triadic categorical distinctions. Baldamus implies that what might appear to be a short–cut device to aid comprehension is rather the container within which the basic substance of the theory is condensed. This means that the undergraduate seeking a short-cut through the diagrams is unlikely to get any further than the experienced scholar who takes the long route through the text. They are there and demand our attention as much as the text does. We do not have to agree with Baldamus that 'the whole theory' stands or falls with the diagrams to see their importance.

In order to make some progress here we need to make a number of distinctions: between levels of importance which can be attached to diagrams, between the levels of abstraction at which they operate, between types of diagram, and between the purposes for which they are constructed.

An inventory of purposes might look like this:

i)   diagrams whose point is to make clearer the structure of a theorist's own theory or thinking, such as Parsons' box diagrams in *Social System*, or Elias's representation of power relationships in *What Is Sociology?*, what Eric Dunning called 'the false teeth' (Mennell, 2006).

ii) diagrams designed to represent the way in which other theorists represent a social process, such as Lévi-Strauss's diagram of different historical chronologies in *The Savage Mind* (1972), Ernest Gellner's account of the anthropological imagination in his essay 'Concepts and Society' (Gellner, 1973), Baldamus's account of the branching logic of Parsons' pattern variables (see Chapter 3), or Wolfgang Schluchter's diagrammatic representation of Weber's sociology of domination.

iii) diagrams designed to represent the structure of social relationships for the purposes of inquiry in a manner such that it might be usable by other theorists; examples here include Parsons' and Smelser's AGIL schema in *Economy and Society* (1958), and Mary Douglas's 'Grid and Group' (Douglas, 2003).

iv) diagrams designed to represent the world view of an entire society, such as Pierre Bourdieu's account of the Kabyele in *Outline of a Theory of Practice* (Bourdieu, 1977), or Bruno Latour's anthropological diagrams of the modern world view in *We Have Never Been Modern* (1993).

v) diagrams designed to depict the whole of a society's social structure once and for all, such as Ernest Gellner's and Lenski's diagrams of agricultural society, or W.G. Runciman's efforts in *The Social Animal* (1998).

An inventory of types of diagram would have to include:

i) tables and box diagrams containing words (Parsons, Habermas)
ii) quasi-mathematical diagrams:

  a. graph-like ones involving Cartesian co-ordinates depicting change over time or location in social space (e.g. Douglas's 'Grid and Group')
  b. Venn diagram-like diagrams.

iii) diagrams making use of arrows in order to depict strength of forces or directions of influence (Parsons, Münch, Levine, Collins).
iv) figurative/topological diagrams aimed at depicting stable social hierarchies (Gellner, Runciman) or cycles of reproduction of social structure (Giddens).
v) emblematic diagrams, in which abstract shapes (boxes, circles, triangles) containing labels, words or categories are arranged in a bounded or unbounded space.

Finally, we can construct a sliding scale of diagrammatical weight. At one end would be diagrams that are central to a theory, at the other, diagrams that are there for purposes of illustration alone or, while sincerely meant, so misleading/ineffective as to be redundant. As we will see, there is something unsatisfactory about diagrams at each end of the scale, since they are either so heavy that they burden the inquiry as a whole, or so light that they add nothing to it. Somewhere in between are diagrams that have a chance of acting as a genuine cognitive tool, going beyond mere illustration by doing something that the text cannot do, taking the reader to places he or she would not otherwise have explored, having a life of their own yet without leading the reader to believe that by knowing the diagram he or she thereby knows the social world. Lynch has called the diagram which has this quality 'a pictorial work space' (Lynch, 1991: 7). This is important because it means that, contrary to what one might think, the diagram which has a measure of autonomy from the text which gave rise to it is by no means a fetishised object representing a failure of the author's conceptual facility. In fact, if the theorist is to contribute to the collective enterprise of sociology, then the diagram which can be made use of by others may be part of that contribution, part of an intellectual community's shared inventory of visual method. As with all successful methods, one would not have to refer constantly to the theoretical moves which gave rise to it; and it may be flexible enough to be adapted for different purposes from the one for which it was originally devised.

Here there is an important difference between mathematics/physics and sociology. While mathematicians and physicists may argue with one another about the relative dignity of algebra and geometry, they all use diagrams and do so frequently. Moreover, while they may not always have access to a fixed set of standard diagrams, there is always a sense that whatever diagram emerges at a particular stage in a line of reasoning, it is not the product of caprice. The mathematician's drawing of a circle or a triangle or square or the path of a projectile is closely bound up with the algebraic expression or formula to which the diagram is tied. While there has been lively debate in the history of mathematics about whether diagrams can function autonomously as means of proof (Shin, 1994), the diagram is never arbitrary, nor is it an illustration of the meaning of a formula or an alternative way of getting at what the formula cannot get at. πr^2 is the formula for the area of a circle; $y = \sin(x)$ gives you the characteristic sine curve: the diagram and the algebraic expression form a closed, mutually implicative universe. They are not two different attempts to represent an external reality. At most, we might ask whether there is an abstract concept – a Platonic idea – which is separate from both of them and lies behind them, though even here it may be that we only think that there might be when we are able to make the connection between the algebra and the geometry (Mitchell, 1981). The representation of the path of an orbiting planet, drawn to aid a mathematical calculation, is not an exercise of creative imagination, but part of the evidential proof which the physicist is undertaking. Admittedly, in some branches of the natural sciences (astronomy is a good example) there is a debate over the relative importance of what Peter Galison has called image data in the form of visual representations and logic data in the form of numbers as sources of knowledge of the physical universe (Galison, 1997).

Be that as it may, visual representation in the natural sciences may be a teaching aid, a clue to the truth, a thing of great beauty, or even a controversial source of knowledge; what it cannot be is pregnant with meaning, or a symbol with religious overtones. It has no implicative horizon, it either aids in the pursuit of truth – mathematical, physical – or it does not. This is why the natural sciences and mathematics have developed standard diagrammatic repertoires, systems of notation which can be learned and used by all members of a scientific community.

In sociological theory, by contrast, diagrammatic representations are neither image nor logic, and standardisation has never been achieved or really attempted, although as we will see, Parsons – and more particularly his followers – did believe that he had constructed a diagrammatic representation of his ideas that achieved more than merely an iconic or emblematic status, becoming a portable version of the theory itself. Aside from cases in which the discussion is clearly about statistics or quantifiable relationships between variables – in which case a standard diagram from the appropriate field of knowledge can be used – theorists will often enough have a blank sheet of paper in front of them and, in the absence of anything obvious to put on it, come face-to-face with their own creativity. Or the lack of it. This can result in diagrams so simple as to appear hardly worth the effort, such as this from John Scott's (1995: 244) account of the difference between Marx and Habermas (see Figure 5.1).

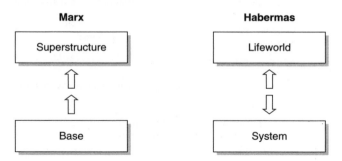

Figure 5.1

On the other hand, the theorist's lack of creativity may be combined with his or her need to communicate the complex character of his or her own thinking in diagrammatic form, something exemplified in Figure 5.2 by the German theorist Richard Münch (1988: 140). For what it is worth, the diagram is called 'Dispositions of the personality system'.

Although they are drawn for different purposes, the weakness of both diagrams is that little thought seems to have gone into what the connection is between the diagrammatic and the verbalised versions of a theory; in particular, neither diagram is much of a visible work space, such work as is done here being performed by the arrows, about the function of which neither writer is very forthcoming. The effect of both is a kind of redundancy, the reader returning straight to the text for a further clarification of terms rather than 'thinking with' the diagram.

The burden of proof for the theorist who wants to use diagrams as Wright Mills suggests they should be used, as a means of intellectual production, is to seek a more sophisticated relationship between text and diagram, in which the diagram really can do work which the text cannot, or in which there is a dialectical–hermeneutical interplay, a continual movement from text to diagram to text. Some theorists have sought to create this impression through a series of diagrams, building from a simple figure, taking the reader along with them, adding complication to the next diagram, and so on. But as Lynch has suggested, when the theorist makes use of a single diagram drawn for didactic purposes, as often happens in introductory theory textbooks, this movement can get reduced 'almost to a motion between largely redundant expressions written on separate surfaces' (Lynch, 1991: 7).

On the Non-Originality of Sociological Diagrams

I suggested that, in the absence of a standard repertoire of theoretical diagrams, this redundancy – exemplified in the diagrams from Scott and Münch – might be attributed to the fact that the theorist has to work alone in order to

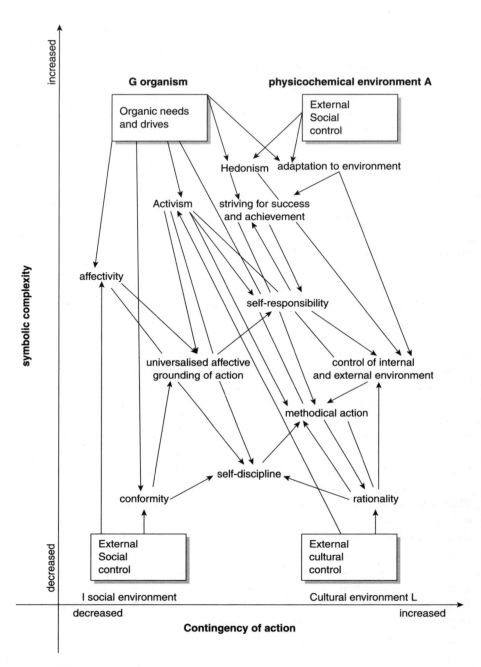

Figure 5.2

construct them, and that all of them are condemned to arbitrariness. In fact, the situation is both more and less troubling than this. It turns out that, despite the claim – or excuse – that used to be made about sociology being a young science, the manner in which sociologists use diagrams often owes much to pictorial devices that have been with us for a long time. Sociology

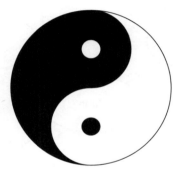

Figure 5.3

deploys an inherited symbolism. Consider, for instance, the fact that one of the most frequent uses of a diagram are to depict an interaction of some sort: between social groups, between individuals and social groups, between social groups and society, interaction involving social hierarchies, and so on. In an essay first published in 1960 (Arnheim, 1966), Rudolf Arnheim discusses the use of depiction in Taoistic cosmology (see Figure 5.3), with its famous diagram called the *T'ai-chi tu*, 'the great map of poles', showing the Yin and Yang principles, which manages with a few lines on the page to depict the idea of periodic repetition, the eternal return of the same, the existence of two opposed principles which are yet not separate from one another; one can speak of the 'centres of gravity' of the two tear-drop shaped halves, and of the different rotational tendencies which depend upon the initial orientation of the halves, and so on.

It will come as a surprise to nobody to learn that sociology has nothing to match the symbolic power and potential of such an apparently simple device. But Arnheim works up to his account of the *T'ai-chi tu* by discussing – and dismissing! – some simpler ways of depicting the interaction between the basic features of Taoistic cosmology: he calls them 'mutual bombardment', 'circularity', 'network', and 'hierarchic differentiation'.

Now in the last twenty years in more theoretically-oriented sociology, particularly in the sociology of science, a fashion has emerged for what has come to be called 'network theory', or 'Actor Network Theory' (Latour, 2005). As its biggest fans appear to regard it as something of a conceptual breakthrough, let us see what Arnheim had to say about 'networks' in 1960.

> Interaction can also be approximated conceptually by a network of one-to-one relations between units or groups of units. Such a network can be illustrated by another section of the ... 'Diagram of the Supreme Ultimate', depicting the system of the five elements. The identical principle is applied, for example, in our modern European 'sociograms', which purport to describe and measure the social structure of a group by determining the relations between any two members separately. Needless to say, the sum of individual influences does not represent the dynamics of the group any more than do the relations between the five elements add up to the physical interaction constituting the universe. (When I speak of 'the interaction of everything with everything' I am using network language, *faute de mieux*). (Arnheim, 1966: 229–30)

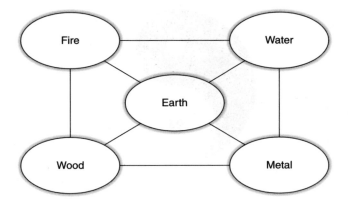

Figure 5.4

The 'Diagram of the Supreme Ultimate', which is in fact a series of diagrams, was first set down in the 11th century AD. Here is part of it (see Figure 5.4). Anyone who has studied sociology at school will have seen something like it before.

Fill in the circles with different words – like economy, polity, culture, science, law and so on – and, while you would be reluctant to call it 'the diagram of the supreme sociological ultimate', you might recognise the sort of thing that you find in sociology textbooks. Diagrammatically, then, there is nothing especially new about the way in which sociological theorists, for whatever purposes, have depicted the interaction between elements or between the 'parts' of a society. Even if one were to disagree with my assessment of the Münch diagram referred to earlier, the one that made us scream, the pictograms of the Eastern religions have already furnished its basic moves.

This need not be seen as sociology's failure to arrive at a system of genuinely modern signs. As Arnheim himself writes:

> Geometrically simple shapes emerge everywhere at an advanced stage of mental development because they are accessible to the limited organisational powers of a simple mind. They are retained in advanced civilisation for the purpose of schematic, symbolic or so-called ornamental representation because they provide the most clear-cut images of the most basic configuration of forces that continue to underlie man's life, and ... man's thinking, even in refinement and complexity. (Arnheim, 1966: 243)

In other words, if the lack of an agreed–upon symbolism is a theoretical short–coming or a sign that sociology can never be a unified science, the simplicity of the geometric shapes it deploys for diagrammatic purposes is not. Nor, if those diagrams have such a long pedigree, do we have to say that sociology, with its enlightenment pretensions, has become fatally entangled in myth. But when we see the connection between a sociological diagram and its origins we may understand why sociologists might be reluctant to see their diagrams as fully symbolic devices rather than as heuristic ones. Were sociological theory to embrace all of its diagrams wholeheartedly, it might be forced to acknowledge the non–scientific character of its representational procedures. The pragmatic response to this is to say that many diagrams in sociology – those which bear no resemblance to the 'modern' diagrams and graphs in mathematics or physics – may well be the product of 'the limited organisational powers of a simple mind', but for that very reason their simplicity may be considered a virtue – if, that is, they, like well used metaphors, can generate an implicative horizon or condense a complex argument into something more manageable.

Does sociology have available to it a set of such resources that are, so to speak, its own? Perhaps the most famous example of a successful, universally known diagram in sociological theory is Parsons' square divided into four smaller squares, representing his AGIL schema of the four functions of a system. In the last chapter we said that it was not clear where Parsons got the idea of the four functions from, nor for that matter where he got the idea of the fourfold set of pattern variable choices, or why these were always a choice between two rather than three alternatives. Indeed, there does appear to be something arbitrary about the choice of four functions rather than five or three, although as we said in Chapter 4, four functions did allow Parsons to represent society as a flat plane, and thereby to 'see' society all at once, so to speak. By the same token, we may ask why it is that political theorists from Aristotle to Weber and beyond have had resort to threefold typologies: think of Aristotle's monarchy, democracy and aristocracy, Montesquieu's republican, monarchical and despotic government, Comte's three stages of historical development – theological, metaphysical and positive – Weber's three types of legitimacy, or the threefold distinction between types of power – economic, political and ideological – to be found in Gellner, Runciman, Althusser, Mann, Poggi and many other historical sociologists. And why should structuralists want to construct a science of society on the basis of binary oppositions? Why should critics of structuralism have spent so much time and effort denouncing or deconstructing 'problematic' dualisms? What is so important about the number two? Without wanting to enter too far into the world of numerology, it is remarkable, in the vast secondary literature on sociological theory, how few commentators have sought to explore these questions. Consider, for instance, this passage from Carl Jung:

> As compared with the Trinitarian thinking of Plato, ancient Greek philosophy favoured thinking of a quaternary type ... The quaternary is an archetype of almost universal occurrence. It forms the logical basis for any whole judgement. If one wishes to pass such a judgement, it must have this fourfold aspect. For instance, if you want to describe the horizon as a whole, you name the four quarters of heaven. Three is not a natural co-efficient of order, but an artificial one. There are always four elements, four prime qualities, four colours, four castes, four ways of spiritual development, etc. So too there are four aspects of psychological orientation, beyond which nothing fundamental needs to be said. In order to orient ourselves, we must have a function which ascertains that something is there (sensation); a second function which establishes what it is (thinking); a third function which states whether it suits us or not, whether we wish to accept it or not (feeling); and a fourth function which indicates where it came from and where it is going (intuition). When this has been done, there is nothing more to say ... The ideal of completeness is the circle or sphere, but its natural minimal division is a quaternary. (Jung, 1970: 167)

There is no evidence that Parsons had the slightest interest in numerology or in Jungian archetypes – forms or shapes of non-rational thought which are held to persist in the 'collective unconscious' even of people living in the modern West. But his entire 'mature' theory is couched in terms of a fourfold division of functions, functions which he is supposed to have arrived at through a heroic act of individual theoretical will.

The point is this: although Parsons thought that he could generate every possible set of social relationships by combining a few basic elements, his generative logic, far from being modern, bears a striking resemblance to some features of medieval alchemy. If that sounds far-fetched, compare Parsons' AGIL diagram with those found in the writings of Ramon Lull, the 13th-century Catalonian philosopher and eccentric who, following a vision on Mount Randa in Majorca, devoted his life to the development of a system which would unite all branches of knowledge and with it all of the Abrahamic religions. His *Ars Magna* devised a logical system in the form of concentric discs divided into sections, each section having the name of a quality or element. Rotate one disc while keeping the others still, and keep doing it for each disc, and you can generate all possible combinations of qualities. In his *Ars Demonstrativa* he developed a system of logic which could be used for astrological and alchemical purposes. The whole system rested upon the four elements – air, fire, earth, water – each of which was given a letter, ABCD. The 12 signs of the zodiac were each assigned one of the elements, so that three of them shared the same element. And each of the seven known planets was given its own element, apart from mercury – the physical substance crucial to alchemical processes – which had all four. Mostly Lull's system was represented by a circle with the 12 signs of the zodiac around the edge, and lines would be drawn connecting the three signs which shared the same letter. But in the *Ars Demonstrativa* we find the diagram shown in Figure 5.5, a square. Now there are two interesting features of this system. One, as Frances Yates put it, is that 'it is always an *ars combinatoria*. It is not static, but constantly moves the concepts with which it is concerned into varying combinations' (Yates, 1982). Secondly, the importance of the four elements was they could be assigned to a series of phenomena at varying levels of abstraction.

Clearly, there is no precise fit between Lull's square of elements and Parsons' diagrams in *The Social System* or the AGIL diagrams. But the combinatory logic at work in Lull, in which a few basic elements are used to generate a series of phenomena at lower levels of abstraction, bears enough resemblance to Parsons' generation of concrete types of society from a few basic pattern variables, or for his resort to the AGIL schema in his later writing, for the connection to be worth making. Moreover, in Lull there is in fact a hierarchy between elements that appear to be equal in weight. The same is true of Parsons. In Chapter 3, I suggested that in the pattern variable schema, universalism/particularism is more important than specificity/diffuseness. In the AGIL diagram of the 'mature' period, Latency (bottom left box) is more important than Adaptation (top left box). To say that there is a connection between Lull and Parsons is obviously disturbing to Parsons' admirers and perhaps even to his detractors; yet it is hard to avoid the thought that, regardless of his desire to provide sociology with

The Square of Elements

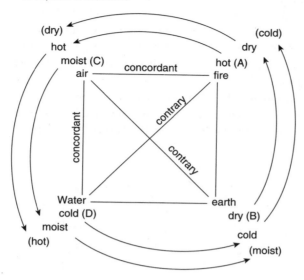

The Elemental Spheres (the sublunary world) with the lighter elements outside and the heavier inside.

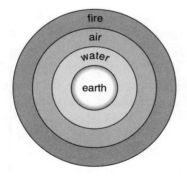

Figure 5.5   The elements and the figures of the *ars demonstrativa*

firm, rational foundations, to make it into the nearest thing to science of which sociology is capable, and to provide it with a standard repertoire of diagram-matic representations of society, his resort to diagrams pushed him at least as far in the direction of astrology and alchemy as in the direction of physics. Parsons is not alone in this respect. There is a very alchemical-looking diagram in Wilbert E. Moore's book, *Social Change* (Moore, 1963: 76).

If we refer to the affinities between Lull's and Parsons' diagrams it is partly because Parsons' followers made so much of the AGIL diagram. You might even say that it was part of the means by which his work became a classic, a portable device for the transmission and dissemination of great thoughts, something that may have begun as a visible work space – and in skilled hands might still be used as one – but

Diagrams

123

ended up as something which could be analysed through iconography and symbolism, as well as in terms of its own internal logic. In Parsons' case the analysis reveals a *reductio ad absurdum*: for once you say that society consists of four subsystems and represent them in the form of a four-cell diagram, there is no reason why any one cell – which is itself a system – should not be divided further into its own subsystems, and so on, until society has been broken down into its most basic units.

For the satirically minded, Parsons' diagrams (see Figure 5.6) provide rich pickings, the process of subdivision being one in which the object of inquiry seems to disappear down the plughole (Baldamus, 1976: 115).

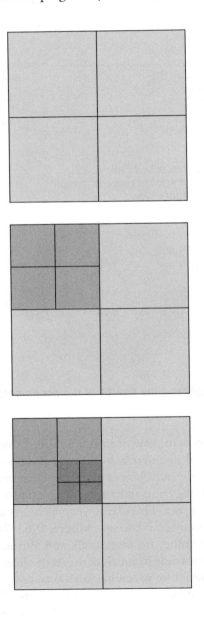

Figure 5.6

Curiously enough, for Parsons himself it seems to have provided the potential for progressively greater levels of concreteness, the level of abstraction being lowered each time the box is divided into four. At least that is the only conclusion that can be drawn from the book that he co-wrote with Neil Smelser, *Economy and Society* (1958). The focus here is on the economy, or expressed in terms of the AGIL schema, the top left hand square. This, like any other, can be subdivided into four squares, each of which can be subdivided in turn, and so on. The process only comes to a halt when the theorist cannot think of anything to write in the new boxes that are constantly being generated. It did come to a halt, but not before Parsons and Smelser had managed to come up with more ways of filling the boxes than many others would have managed. Starting with the basic functional differentiation of society, we have Figure 5.7.

The first move is to say that the Economy (the top left hand box) is itself functionally differentiated (see Figure 5.8).

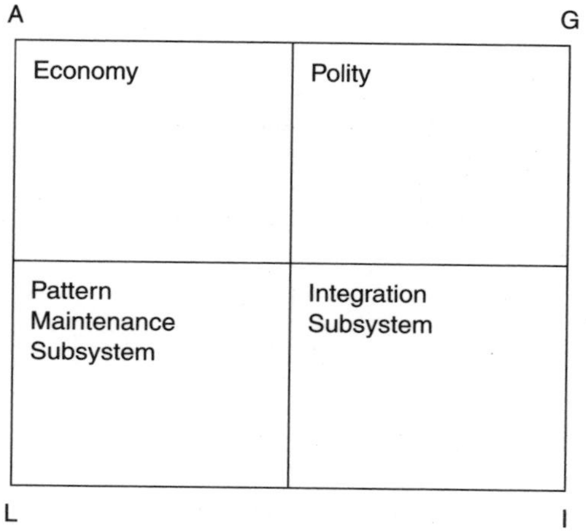

Figure 5.7

So far so good. But then Parsons and Smelser were forced by their own logic to claim that each of these subsystems was also functionally differentiated, which resulted in 16 more boxes with 16 more pieces of text to be written. I will spare the reader the whole story, but over the page is their diagram of the internal differentiation of the economic commitments sub-system (Figure 5.9). The signs of desperation are clear.

Parsons and Smelser's book is now of little or no interest, but once again it shows what can happen when theorists allow their reasoning to be dictated by their tools; here diagrams, albeit simple ones, undermine rather than aid the theorist's efforts to make sense of the social world. While not quite conforming to Lynch's view of them as 'pictures of nothing', they do not look like much of a pictorial work space either, and seem to support the view that the diagram in sociological theory can never be such a space in the same way that the diagram in physics can be.

Nevertheless, in the right hands, the diagram might still be a tool of knowledge production, going beyond the text but without turning into a theorist's fetish or quasi-religious symbol. The fact that there will never be a standard

Diagrams

125

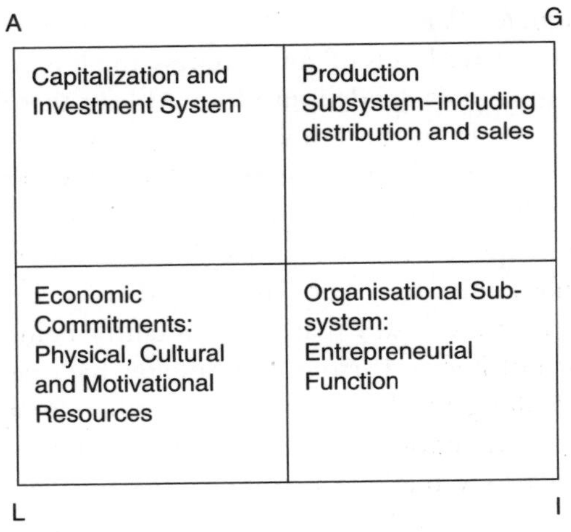

A   G

Capitalization and Investment System	Production Subsystem–including distribution and sales
Economic Commitments: Physical, Cultural and Motivational Resources	Organisational Sub-system: Entrepreneurial Function

L   I

Figure 5.8

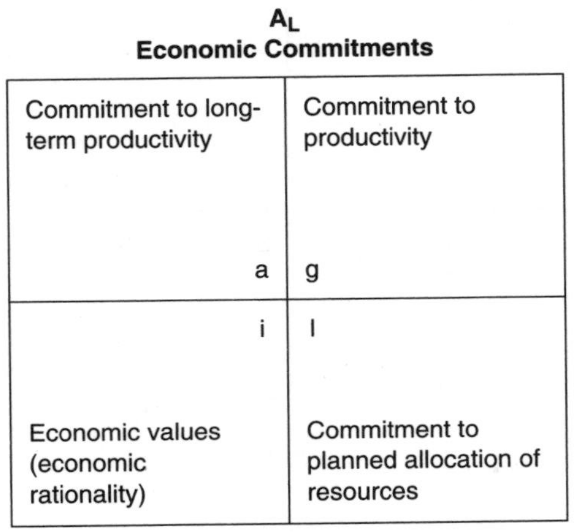

A_L
Economic Commitments

Commitment to long-term productivity	Commitment to productivity
Economic values (economic rationality)	Commitment to planned allocation of resources

With the central markers: a | g and i | l between the cells.

Figure 5.9

diagrammatic repertoire either for sociological theory or for sociological sub-fields should not discourage us from distinguishing stronger diagrams from weaker ones. According to what criteria should we do so? If we cannot aspire to the sociological equivalent of geometry or to a system of notation like Peirce's existential graphs or Venn diagrams, or to the diagrams made famous by Richard Feynman in physics (Feynman, 1990), our criteria are bound to be pragmatic: do they aid description in the way that Gombrich suggests they can, or serve the purpose for which they were intended? Let us pursue this question by looking at three types of diagram from the list we made earlier: those which seem to offer a figurative image of society as a whole; those which describe a relationship between social forces or tendencies; and those that try to depict the logic of theorising itself.

Investigating Sociological Theory

126

Diagrams of Society

In *The Social Animal* Runciman writes:

> ... the simplest and probably most familiar, representation of a society, is as a triangle – a few people at the top, rather less powerful people in the middle, and the mass of the powerless at the bottom. By way of contrast, Aristotle's putatively stable society can then be represented as a broad, flattish diamond – a small elite, a big middle class, and a small category of powerless unfortunates at the bottom. (Runciman, 1998: 69).

He then gives an example of a more complicated version – 'more sophisticated' in his words – of the diamond, Lenski's representation of a 'typical agrarian society' in *Power and Privilege* (Lenski, 1966: 284).

Why a triangle? Why a distorted diamond? Why these sweeping elongated divisions of the diamond? Because society looks like that? Because this is the

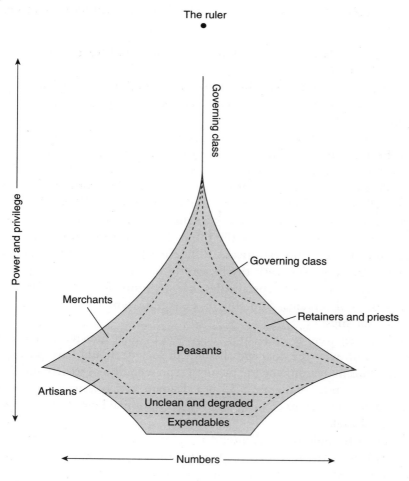

Figure 5.10

shape which intuitively springs to mind when we are asked to visualise society? Hardly. The reason is that the point of such a diagram is to represent society from a particular point of view, in this case, that of the distribution of power. Because of this, Runciman can see Lenski's diagram as important – along the right lines – but inadequate. The figure in the diagram is two dimensional, the two dimensions being power and 'numbers', which invites us to see power as something that is undifferentiated. By contrast, Runciman, along with many other theorists who subscribe to the Indo-European classification of human societies into warriors, priests and workers, believes that there are three types of power – economic, political and ideological – and that we need a diagram to match.

> This means that the logical way to visualise the social space within which more and less powerful roles are located is as the space enclosed between three coordinates joined at right angles, and since degrees of power are generally conceptualised in a metaphor which equates more power with a higher location and less power with a lower one, any society can be represented as an inverted pyramid and its constituent roles as vectors within it. (Runciman, 1998: 71)

Leaving aside Runciman's curious use of the word 'vector', the resulting figure looks like Figure 5.11.

It is a three-dimensional object for the depiction of social hierarchies. Two very different possibilities can be registered using the same basic shape (see Figure 5.12).

Three points can be made about these diagrams and the claims made on their behalf. Firstly, Runciman himself admits that this 'is no more than a device to make vivid the three-dimensionality of social structure ... diagrams like this can't reflect the fact that one person can occupy and perform more than one role, as well as move from one role to another' (Runciman, 1998: 72). In other words, it is not a visible work space but a means of initial orientation.

Secondly, the commitment to the three-dimensionality of social structure implies that there is no significant difference between military and non-military political power, with the bizarre result in this case that the second diagram, with its cast of typical roles, has no room for political leaders or activists or civil servants. And this in a diagram which purports to depict power hierarchies!

Thirdly, even were it an accurate depiction of such hierarchies, there is no obvious reason why the conceptualisation of society should have power at its heart and thus no reason why the pictorial representation of society should take this form. For instance, Figure 5.13 is a diagram which Ernest Gellner often employed. It is a diagram of an agrarian society, just like Lenski's. Or rather, not like Lenski's at all.

Neither a triangle nor a diamond nor, for that matter, an inverted pyramid, this diagram is intended to depict a society in which there is a clear separation between the ruling strata and the rest of society, such that while those ruling strata may be internally hierarchic and share more or less the

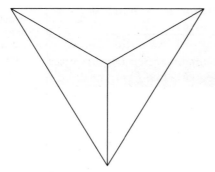

Figure 5.11

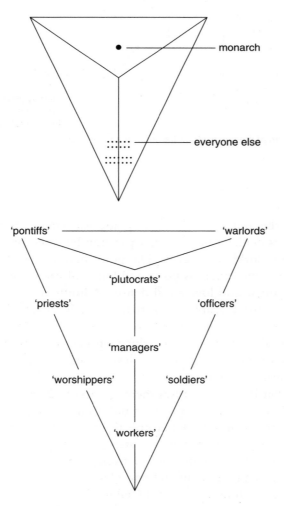

Figure 5.12
From W.G. Runciman (1998) *The Social Animal.* London: HarperCollins.

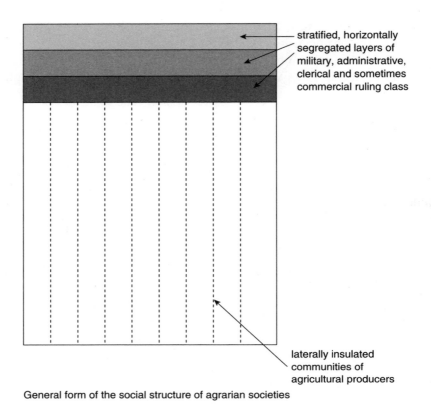

stratified, horizontally segregated layers of military, administrative, clerical and sometimes commercial ruling class

laterally insulated communities of agricultural producers

General form of the social structure of agrarian societies

Figure 5.13

same culture, the rest of society does not participate in it. In addition, the vertical lines depict a horizontal separation between non–ruling groups, or 'segments' in Durkheim's terms. The point here is that this is a relatively static society in which there is no shared high culture or means to communicate or transmit it, and low social density. Admittedly, on its own the diagram is no more of a visible work space than Runciman's, but given the purpose at hand – in Gellner's case, to discuss the lack of mobility in societies on the far side of the 'big ditch' which separates modern from pre-modern societies – this rectangular figure is no less a plausible image of society than Runciman's inverted pyramid.

Note here that in all these cases there appears to be no obvious need for a diagram; a kind of diagrammatic impulse takes over, but the result can often seem arbitrary, not least because the theorist is using a diagram to depict one particular thing – here the structure of agrarian society – rather than making use of a recognisable pictographic repertoire that might be used elsewhere. In the light of the completely different representations of agrarian society given by Lenski and Gellner, Runciman's inverted pyramid does have the virtue of looking like a more general device for studying the distribution of power in any sort of society at any time. But here again, in the absence of any thoroughgoing account of the logic of diagrammatic abstraction, the prospects for its becoming a general pictorial currency look slim. Certainly, it does not look as though it will do for the sociology of power what kinship and other diagrams have done for social anthropology (Gell, 2006).

Diagrams of Social Dynamics

We turn now to diagrams which seek to depict not only the relative positions of social actors – hierarchical or otherwise – but also the dynamics of their interaction, not only the existence of the different parts of a society but also the ways in which they are related both to one another and to the individual. Such diagrams may or may not incorporate an explicit attempt to depict changes over time. In mathematics the usual way of doing this is to depict time as moving from the left to the right of the page. Figure 5.14 is a very simple sociological version, incorporating a clear attempt to visualise changes in the relationship between agency and structure (Archer, 1982).

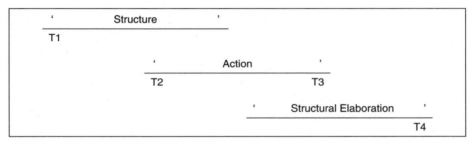

Figure 5.14

It is fairly obvious that for a diagram like this to mean anything a good deal of textual support is required, otherwise the existence of four rather than 16 or 24 points in time is an arbitrary choice, as is the decision to start with structure. The placing of wide quotation marks around the concepts would also require a good deal of explication.

Curiously enough, this diagram makes no use of one very common device, the arrow. Sociological theorists, as we saw in the cases of John Scott and Richard Münch, have a penchant for arrows, but what is remarkable is how seldom they are used for the obvious purpose of depicting temporal change, and how often they are deployed as physicists might deploy them, to depict lines of force or directions of influence, without any clear account of why an arrow is thick, thin, full, or dotted. Paul Klee once wrote that 'the father of the arrow is the thought, how do I expand my reach? Over this river, this lake, this mountain? ... It is the contrast between power and prostration that implies the duality of human existence. Half winged, half imprisoned – this is man!' (Klee, 1978: 54). Without wanting to become involved in the metaphysics of arrows, one might expect that if a theorist believes that an arrow is worth drawing then he or she would define its meaning and function, and give some thought to the way in which it is intended to structure our perception of the social world. For instance, the fat arrows in John Scott's diagram of the relationship between system and lifeworld in the thought of Habermas bear an uncanny resemblance to those in Klee's painting 'Separation in the Evening', and although one doubts whether he would welcome the association, is there any more reason to see them as a piece of physics than as a piece of art? Klee had some thoughts on triangles and pyramids, too: is Runciman's inverted pyramid any more scientific than it is metaphysical (Rosenthal, 1982)?

We will end this chapter with an instructive example of what can happen when such strictures are ignored. For now, consider a diagrammatic schema which makes use of arrows and which we encountered earlier, in the chapter on categories. Mary Douglas's 'Grid and Group' (Figure 5.15) diagram comes closer to being a visible work space than anything we have considered so far, not least because it resembles the most successful mathematical visualisation of all, Cartesian coordinates. Firstly, it presents two sliding scales – of degrees of social control over individuals, and of publicity/privacy of a system of classification. One of the functions of the diagram is to plot the course of an individual biography in relation to these issues. And Douglas readily describes individuals and social groups as being located in 'quadrants', or 'having spiralled down to the left' or 'moved gradually to the left' as they got older. The diagram is also a device for locating cosmologies, both individual and collective, and for tracing historical variations in such cosmologies. Since all societies require a commonly acknowledged set of classifications, 'society as a whole' may be represented in such diagrams as a horizontal line drawn at some distance above the central horizontal line representing zero classification. The extent of it – how far across the diagram it goes – will depend upon the extent to which a society can tolerate individuals not being controlled by others. So, for instance, the societies studied by Durkheim and Mauss in *Primitive Classification* take the form of a short line high up on the right-hand side (A). Our societies are characterised by a long line extending across to the left side of the page, less far above the line than in a pre-modern society. In other words, in our society there is relative freedom from group control along with scope for the development of private schemas of classification alongside, though not necessarily competing with, a dominant classification scheme shared by all (B). A modern society which is subject to strong social/revolutionary pressure – towards what Durkheim called declassification – is represented by (C).

'Grid and Group' works because the space which it defines is one of possibility; every point can potentially be occupied but tendencies towards certain combinations of degrees of group control, rigidity of classifications, and social stability or instability can be depicted. If it is a map it is a map of pressures, social change and social tensions. It is not the classification of society but a representation of the dynamic relationship between classification (grid) and social control (group). To be sure, its burden is to represent social control along a single dimension (degree of control by others) in order to depict the character of a society in its entirety, and thus it might be thought to offer little sense of the

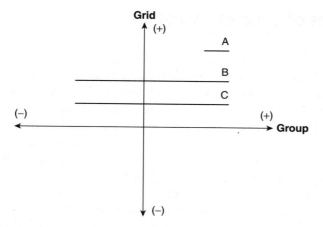

Figure 5.15

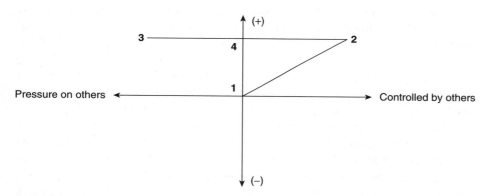

Figure 5.16

institutionally differentiated nature of social control. Yet there is no reason why one should not be able to plot the range within which different institutions operate by means of a line drawn on the diagram for each institution. Nor are we prevented from using it to depict the course of an individual biography, as Douglas demonstrates in her account of the life of St Augustine.

Figure 5.16 depicts the course of Augustine's religious development. It begins at the centre of the diagram with his conversion to Christianity. At this point there is no determinate classification system either collective or individual and it is not possible to speak of his being influenced by or influencing others. Augustine then accepts the creed and a circle of like-minded friends and moves up into the top right quadrant; he becomes Bishop of Hippo and a judge and legislator, and so moves all the way across into the upper left quadrant; after the Vandals attack Northern Africa and his people desert, 'we shift him back to the mid-point where the classifications are as strong as ever for him, but he has no influence on anyone or they on him' (Douglas, 1975: 225).

Diagrams

133

Diagrams of Theoretical Logic

Finally, we turn to diagrams the object of which is to depict the architecture of a piece of theorising itself. For instance, Gellner's essay 'Concepts and Society' contains a diagram (see Figure 5.17)which represents the way in which consideration of the context surrounding a sentence uttered in another language has an effect on the anthropologist's judgement of that sentence (good/bad, plausible/implausible). The diagram works because each element has a purpose: the arrows represent translations from initial sentence to language of the investigator and between that and judgement of worth. The idea that the final destination of the arrow (judgement of the sentence) is dependent on context is marked by a circle, which if you think about it makes sense because we intuitively perhaps think of context in terms of what is 'around' something. This then allows the idea that the greater the degree to which context is invoked, the greater the refraction of the original sense of the sentence. Of course the whole exercise only works if it is presented in a series of diagrams rather than in one which is already finished. But that is how Gellner presents it, as a brief visual narrative in which G = Good, B = Bad, S = Sentence, C = context (Gellner, 1973).

Now, we could dissent from the argument; context may as well refract an attractive sentence in such a way that it becomes an unattractive one: a statement which sounds attractive may then resonate within a certain political environment. The statements of thinkers like Carl Schmitt and Martin Heidegger have been contextualised in this way by those who disagree with their present-day admirers. And it is not clear that the 'refraction' of which Gellner speaks does not take place after the initial translation into English. Nevertheless, the diagram itself is a usable shorthand, it is a tool with which one can think about the processes through which the anthropologist makes sense of an unfamiliar culture. And it is such a tool because once its workings have been explained it can, so to speak, operate alone, independent of the words which initially supported it. In Chapter 2 we spoke of the necessary linguistic alienation to which theorising gives rise. Here we have a case of necessary alienation through diagrams, in which the diagram can be addressed in its own terms, not because it is a world unto itself, but because it makes possible a more focused argument by virtue of the fact that it condenses the terms of that argument into a dynamic visual form.

By the same token, there are diagrams of intellectual processes that seem to be devoid of imaginative implication; there is nothing one can 'do' with them. The most extreme example is one drawn by Claude Lévi-Strauss in *The Savage Mind*. Lévi-Strauss is arguing against the idea that 'history' can be a category of understanding, on the grounds that 'history' in the singular cannot be given any meaning, or for that matter any political valency; historians operate with different chronologies, chronologies which cannot be coordinated with one another: the order of millennia and those of centuries of weeks or days are irreconcilable. Each class of dates has its own dignity: it may 'refer back to another class' but it

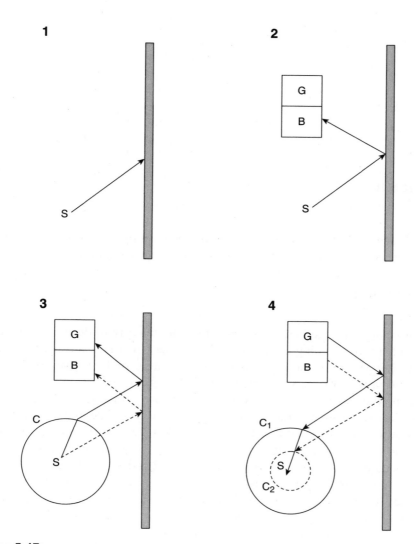

Figure 5.17

cannot aspire to that class's 'principle of intelligibility', from which point 'the discontinuous and classificatory nature of historical knowledge emerges clearly'.
One implication of this is political: if 'history' in the singular is an incoherent
category, then appeals to 'history' as a justification for political action are also
incoherent. This is an interesting and important argument that had considerable
resonance in France at the time that it was written, especially as it was directed
against one of France's leading intellectuals, Jean-Paul Sartre. However, the interesting point for us is that Lévi-Strauss chose to represent the idea of incommen-
surable chronologies in the form of a diagram (Figure 5.18).

It is hard to see how such a diagram has any explanatory or interpretative
potential of its own, how we could take if from the context of its emergence
and do something with it. While it has the virtue of being uncluttered with

Figure 5.18

words, without Lévi-Strauss's words in the body of the text it is helpless, mute. It is the diagrammatic equivalent of a private language (Andreski, 1972).

Conclusion

We cannot do justice here to the quantity and diversity of diagrammatic styles available to the sociological theorist. Nor is it easy to arrive at other than pragmatic criteria for what a diagram should contain or look like. But we can demand of it that it make a difference to the argument, that it serves the purpose the theorist has in mind for it, that it is more than a private language, and that, like categories and metaphors, it contains at least a degree of imaginative implication. In short, that it is not wholly useless. Lévi-Strauss's diagram is useless not so much because it is devoid of words — in this respect it is more of a true diagram than any others we have considered — but because we don't know how to make identical rows of dots and spaces look different from one another. Other diagrams are useless because they consist almost entirely of words or groups of words connected by lines or arrows. Such diagrams may be simple/primitive, such as those drawn by John Scott; or, like those of Münch, so complex that the graphic devices are in need of replacement by comprehensible prose.

We finish with an example of a more obviously achieved uselessness. *The Constitution of Society* (1984) is Anthony Giddens' most ambitious book, the one which comes closest to being a definitive account of his theory of structuration. It also contains a number of diagrams: sometimes they consist of a list of concepts or buzzwords already found in the text; sometimes these letters have a box placed around them, sometimes they don't. Sometimes the boxes are connected by a line; sometimes they are connected by arrows. Sometimes the arrows are solid; sometimes they are broken. Sometimes the arrows go up and down alongside the words; sometimes they are long, sometimes they are short. Take, for instance, Figure 5.19.

In this diagram Giddens wishes to convey his own ideas about multiple temporalities; here the idea is that the individual actor always has a relationship to three orders of temporality: day-to-day experience which is recurrent/

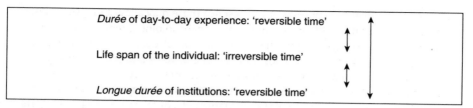

Durée of day-to-day experience: 'reversible time'

Life span of the individual: 'irreversible time'

Longue durée of institutions: 'reversible time'

Figure 5.19

repetitious, his/her own life span which has directionality, and the long-term existence of social institutions whose rate of change is too slow for the individual to perceive it. The two small arrows convey the relevance of the two orders of reversible time to the individual human life; the long one the fact that day-to-day life and the *longue durée* of institutional existence also have a relationship to each other which is independent of the life of any one individual. As a teaching aid one can see that such a diagram is useful. But it is so self-contained, so much designed to represent an idea that Giddens happens to have about temporality, that once its function within Giddens' own mode of reasoning has been established, it is hard to see what use anyone else might make of it.

Then there are diagrams which, in order to be comprehensible, require textual support but do not really receive it. Figure 5.20, for instance, is a diagram from *The Constitution of Society* (1984: 121).

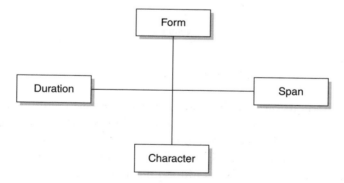

Figure 5.20

As it stands, it is not clear why the words (are they categories?) are in boxes, why there are two pairs of them, whether the pairs are conceptual opposites or merely different 'aspects' of something, or what kind of connection, in the absence of arrows, is being conveyed by the connecting lines. Perhaps, then, Giddens' own account of what the diagram means will help:

A useful classification of modes of regionalization might be offered by figure 7 [Figure 5.20]. By the 'form' of regionalization I mean the form of the boundaries that define the region. In most locales the boundaries separating regions have physical

Diagrams

137

or symbolic markers. In contexts of co-presence these may allow a greater or lesser number of the features of 'presencing' to permeate adjoining regions. As has been mentioned, in social gatherings the regionalization of encounters is usually indicated only by body posture and positioning, tone of voice and so on. In many such gatherings, as regionally bounded episodes, encounters may be nearly all of very short duration. Walls between rooms, on the other hand, may demarcate regionalisation in such a way that none of the ordinary media of co-presence can penetrate. Of course, where walls are thin various kinds of interruptions or embarrassments to the closure of encounters can occur. Aries, Elias and others have pointed to the ways in which the internal differentiation of the houses of the mass of the population since the eighteenth century has been interrelated with changing aspects ... (Giddens, 1984: 121–2)

As a cognitive device the diagram is made redundant by the fact that the text which is supposed to ground it or contextualise it – and, given the simplicity of the diagram, might have done – leaves it hanging in the air. The shape of the diagram, the use of the cross, suggests an account in which the items at each end are opposites. But 'form' is hardly the opposite of 'character', nor is it obvious that 'duration' is the opposite of 'span'. Compare Giddens' diagram with Carl Jung's depiction of Plato's theory of the creation the world (Figure 5.21).

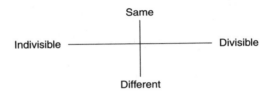

Figure 5.21

Admittedly, on its own the diagram conveys little information, but it is in its own terms simple and coherent, and ready for Jung's explication of it.

It is doubtful whether any amount of text could have made clear the implications of the next diagram (Figure 5.22), again from *The Constitution of Society* (Giddens, 1984: 289). It would require a measure of bravery and inventiveness, for instance, to interpret the arrows, so much so that one is tempted to say that a reader confronted with this diagram is likely to respond to the arrows in much the same way as Wittgenstein's recalcitrant pupil who 'reacted to the gesture of pointing with the hand by looking in the direction of the line from finger-tip to wrist, not from wrist to finger-tip' (Wittgenstein, 1997: §185).

Diagrams like this are an example of what can happen when a talented theorist tries to overcome some of the shortcomings he detects within his own theoretical tradition, jettisoning the older solutions to problems of concept formation on the grounds that, however aesthetically elegant they may be, they are overly simplistic. Unfortunately for Giddens, elegance and simplicity have been at the heart of diagrammatic symbolisation since well

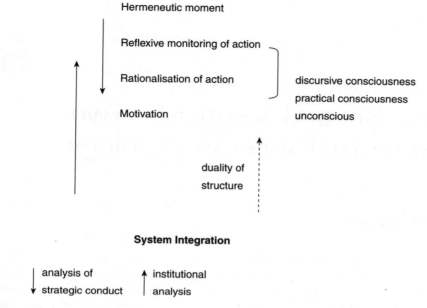

Hermeneutic moment

Reflexive monitoring of action

Rationalisation of action   discursive consciousness
                                   practical consciousness
Motivation   unconscious

duality of
structure

System Integration

analysis of   ↑ institutional
strategic conduct   analysis

Figure 5.22

before sociological theory. As another Viennese philosopher, Otto Neurath, pioneer of the international picture language, put it:

> A good teacher is conscious that only a certain amount of knowledge will be kept in mind. So he puts into his picture only what is necessary. He is of the opinion that a simple picture kept in the memory is better than any number of complex ones which have gone out of it. (Neurath, 1980: 28)

6

Cynicism and Scepticism: Two Intellectual Styles in Sociology

Introduction

There is something human and moving in the pursuit of the 'truth' about society, and in the record of striving and failure that is the history of that pursuit. So far we have read some classics of sociological theory from the point of view of the categories they deploy, the metaphors they use, the descriptions their work generates, and even the diagrams they use, and we have seen some of the limits of theorising that a discussion of them can reveal. This chapter raises some broader questions about intellectual style in sociology; the next asks whether sociological theory has anything to tell us about that old problem, the art of living.

For the sake of convenience, and to bring together themes from earlier chapters, two broad intellectual styles will be identified: I will call them cynicism and scepticism. Although the use of any single distinction like this might strike the reader as simplistic, as we saw in the chapter on categories, the history of entire civilisations may be studied on the basis of twofold or threefold categorical distinctions, so the use of such devices is not in principle too crude for the more local history of sociological theory (Dawe, 1978; Lockwood, 1988). Whether 'cynicism and scepticism' fit the bill remains to be seen. In a badly neglected paper Phil Strong lumped them together in an argument about sociology's 'imperialistic' attitude to the objects of its inquiry (Strong, 1979). His point is well taken, but as we will see I think that it applies more to the work I will call cynical than to that I call sceptical. When Robert Merton used the term 'organized scepticism' to describe part of the 'normative order' of science he meant something other than cynicism (Merton, 1996).

The distinction between cynicism and scepticism as approaches to sociology may be thought to have affinities with the one made by Michael Oakeshott between two styles of politics, the politics of faith and the politics of scepticism (Oakeshott, 1996). But the politics of faith for Oakeshott was defined by the collective pursuit of human perfection, that is, with utopianism, while the politics of scepticism was defined by the rejection of utopianism. In contrast, Chapter 7 will suggest that the idea of individual utopian striving can be made consistent with rather than antagonistic to a sceptical approach to inquiry, and that this individual utopianism is a different thing from the politics of faith that does sometimes hover over the writings of those I will call cynical sociologists.

There is another distinction between cynicism and scepticism; scepticism involves a greater readiness to take the very idea of intellectual styles seriously. This means that the difference between cynicism and scepticism itself is likely to be of greater interest to the sceptic than to the cynic. One might even say that only a sceptic could have written this book, were it not for the fact that that is a cynical observation (Horkheimer, 1995).

In this chapter the difference between them will be illustrated by their approaches to culture. Sociological theory at its best can make us sensitive to questions of world-orientation, and it is perhaps through our involvement in or relationship to culture that such questions can become urgent for us. Weber says that 'we *are* cultural beings', which means for him that we are equipped with the capacity to distance ourselves from reality, to then attach significance to things in reality by relating them to values, and thereby to orient ourselves in the world. In studying culture we are studying sources of world-orientation for cultural beings, sources of orientation which include ideals about how to live, about the relationship between human beings and nature, about the relationship between the sacred and the secular, about history, time, meaning, and so on. And if we understand politics as it has been understood by the tradition of classical political philosophy – that is, as more than a mere 'sphere' of activity – then politics too refers to the most basic questions regarding the human condition.

But the reason that politics and culture are useful arenas in which to characterise the distinction between cynical and sceptical modes of theorising is that in many versions of sociological theory, these senses of politics and of culture as sources of world-orientation are obscured, or ignored altogether. When that happens, politics, for instance, then belongs to a logic of social interests, and culture becomes the expression of the pursuit of social status or class/gender/race position. Sometimes, politics and culture are brought together and then neglected together, so to speak, as when some neo-Marxist authors make use of terms such as 'hegemony', 'ideology' or 'symbolic violence'.

Cynicism and Scepticism as Approaches to the Study of Culture

Cynicism as a philosophy, as both a mode of inquiry and an approach to living, can be traced back to the ancient world, in which it sat alongside the philosophies of Plato or Aristotle or the Stoics. Our interest is in cynicism as a modern intellectual procedure and as a modern social attitude. The difference between the two is neatly summed up by Simmel.

> The cynicism of antiquity had a very definite ideal in life, namely positive strength of mind and moral freedom of the individual. This was such an absolute value for cynicism that all the differences between otherwise accepted values paled into insignificance. Whether a person is a master or a slave, whether he satisfies his needs in an

aesthetic or unaesthetic manner, whether he has a native country or not, whether he fulfils his family obligations or not – all this is completely irrelevant for the wise person, not only in comparison with any absolute value but also in that this indifference is revealed in their existence. In the attitude which we nowadays characterise as cynical, it seems to me decisive that here too no higher differences in values exist and that, in general, the only significance of what is highly valued consists in its being degraded to the lowest level, but that the positive and ideal moral purpose of this levelling has disappeared ... The nature of the cynic – in the contemporary sense – is most clearly demonstrated in contrast with that of the enthusiast. Whereas the curve of evaluation of the enthusiast moves upwards and lower values strive to be raised to the importance of higher values, the evaluation curve of the cynic moves in the opposite direction. His awareness of life is adequately expressed only when he has theoretically and practically exemplified the baseness of the highest values and the illusion of any differences in values. (Simmel, 1980: 255)

For the modern cynic, then, the highest ideals are the product of less elevated motives, apparently universal claims are rooted in particular interests, ideas are the expression of material forces, permanent human problems are historically specific ones, the validity of a way of thinking or mode of human sensibility is inseparable from and/or reducible to its social origin. Whatever else works of art or poetry or philosophy are, they cannot be direct sources of inspiration or wisdom, cannot appeal to the reader or listener's vision, which is always mediated or situated or a child of its context. In this chapter we will treat this cynicism as an intellectual attitude alone, although it is worth remembering that for Simmel it was linked to the role of money in a capitalist economy. In an economy in which everything has its price, non-economic values such as honour or virtue or beauty can easily be drawn into the orbit of business (Sloterdijk, 1987: 315–17). It is tempting to speculate whether one can take this further and ask whether, when they say that universal or enlightenment values are 'really' the expression of gender or race prejudices, today's radical academics are displaying a sensibility first made possible by the money economy.

Scepticism, by contrast, is a style of thinking which, while it may be moved to establish a relationship between ideas or values and 'something else', is more hesitant to say precisely what that relationship is and is willing to allow, without having to subscribe to a belief in canons or in works of enduring human worth, that such works may have the power to detach themselves from the context – political, argumentative, economic or otherwise – in which they first arose. The values or principles which those works contain may make a claim on those who know little or nothing of those ideas and values' origins (Rose, 1981; Bergner, 1982). The sceptical attitude is defined by a pervasive doubt, yet it is a doubt directed towards a different place from that which catches the cynic's eye; the sceptic will claim not that the highest values are really something else or a vehicle for baser motives, but that, owing to the fact of our human finitude, the recalcitrance of a complex social reality or the weight of tradition, these values, even when they have emancipated themselves from their social origins, and lofty as they may be as ideals, can never be fully realised, that the gap between intention and fulfilment can never be closed.

Certainly, cynicism is not distinguished by virtue of the attempt to make a link between an intellectual or artistic phenomenon and its context or conditions, because some such move is common enough in many versions of sociology, especially in the sociology of culture. But there are several ways in which the link can be made between works of art or literature and the larger context to which they are to be related. It is worth noting how frequently the more long-running discussions in both sociology and cultural studies are a variation on the debate about the classics that we discussed in Chapter 1. At one end of the spectrum there are Harold Bloom and George Steiner, for whom the role of the critic and teacher is to open great books to the reader untouched by the dead hand of inferior commentary; at the other one finds those writing in the style of Lucien Goldman, for whom we cannot comprehend even Pascal's writings without investigating the context of their emergence. Within departments of literature the defenders of the first position are still able to hold their own, but within cultural studies and sociology adherents of the Steiner/Bloom position are in a small minority. It is true that students of Raymond Williams, inspired by isolated comments in Marx to the effect that art and literature cannot be made sense of with the tools of political economy alone, have sought to find a space between these extremes, but it is also true that few have managed to avoid giving the impression of tending towards the second (Milner, 1996).

Perhaps the most distinctive characteristic of cynicism as an approach to inquiry is that it tends towards functionalism, in that certain ways of talking or thinking or certain kinds of cultural activity are held to serve some broader social purpose, in such a way that the talk or the thought, the idea or the value, is treated not as a work to be encountered – looked at, listened to, read – because it has a claim to make on us, but as a cultural artefact which is to have something else read into or off it. We will see later that the work of Pierre Bourdieu, with its eager matching up of cultural activity and social class, is an example of contemporary cynicism, in which neither the content nor the form of works of art or literature themselves warrant sustained attention as possible sources of world orientation or evaluative inspiration. But if for 'social class' we substitute 'race', 'gender', 'sexual orientation' and so on, we can find similar procedures being adopted across the human sciences.

Another notable feature of modern academic cynicism is, as Peter Sloterdijk has pointed out, humourlessness. The ancient cynic as he is presented by Simmel may have been a 'wise person' with a definite ideal in life, but for Sloterdijk he was best exemplified by Diogenes in his tub, the holy fool who uses his naked body – often actively! – to puncture social pretension and social hierarchy. While he discusses such masturbatory or scatological gestures of refusal solely for contrast effect, Sloterdijk also does so in order to point to what he thinks 'social criticism' has become in the modern world, namely a form of cynicism in which the exuberances of the untamed body have been left behind in favour of the forensic and analytic procedures of science, where the aim is not to puncture or oppose so much as to get behind and reveal what is beneath. The versions of modern social critique that have come closest to the spirit of ancient cynicism – what Sloterdijk calls *kynicism* – have been satirical. But for two centuries or more satire has been fighting a losing battle with the spirit of science. Nowhere has this led to more leaden forms of writing and theorising than in the critique of ideology:

> philosophical ideology critique is truly the heir of a great satirical tradition, in which the motif of unmasking, exposing, baring has served for aeons now as a weapon. But modern ideology critique – according to our thesis – has ominously cut itself off from the powerful traditions of laughter in satirical knowledge, which have their roots in ancient *kynicism*. Recent ideology critique already appears in respectable garb, and in Marxism and especially in psychoanalysis it has even put on suit and tie so as to completely assume an air of bourgeois respectability. (Sloterdijk, 1987: 16)

Sloterdijk's observations are well taken, but they were also part of an internal debate within German critical theory, and for all the apparent freshness of his insight it shared some of that theory's blindnesses. Nowhere are these more glaring than in the claim that the problem with ideology critique lay in its 'unmasking' attitude, a particular enlightenment attitude which had become so widespread that any number of groups and parties could claim for themselves the mantle of science, with the result that intellectual opponents confronted one another not as parties to a social dialogue but as unmaskers of each other's ideologies, telling each other: 'I can explain you but you can't explain me'. Although Sloterdijk presented it as news in 1983, it had already been said by Clifford Geertz in 1966 and by Karl Mannheim ... at the end of the 1920s (Mannheim, 1936; Geertz, 1973).

In *Ideology and Utopia* Mannheim tried to develop a theory of ideology that would avoid the crude science/ideology distinction and the attendant problem of mutual unmasking yet still allow the sociologist to relate ideas to their social origin or context. This involved him in some impressive theoretical contortions and the eventual conclusion that the best hope for a 'reality–oriented thinking' that was free from prejudice lay with a free-floating intelligentsia, of which he happened to be a member. This solution has never been considered satisfactory even if it has a certain logic to it. Nevertheless, Mannheim's work from the 1920s is still worth reading because he sets down the issues facing a sociology of culture with incomparable clarity and foresight. In order to see why, we can turn to another work, *Structures of Thinking*.

There Mannheim distinguishes between the 'immanent and sociological consideration of cultural phenomena'. As well as being a science of society, sociology is the study of 'the embeddedness of cultural formations within social life' (Mannheim, 1982: 55). But this embeddedness can conceal an important distinction:

> ... it is quite a different matter to investigate the part that 'social-historical reality' plays in the emergence of cultural formations, how deeply it enters into their inner constitution, than it is to ask what sort of cultivation these formations signify for social life, once they are in being, how far they prove themselves ... to be socialising factors. (Mannheim, 1982: 55)

'Society' and 'culture' for Mannheim are what he calls 'fundamental phenomena', and each of them has a corresponding fundamental science whose task is to work out the concepts which define that area of inquiry. Sociology is the fundamental science of society, and philosophy the fundamental science of culture. Now, whether or not we accept this association of philosophy with culture, the key point for Mannheim is that 'as a science of society, sociology is a fundamental science; as cultural sociology it is a method, a point of view for considering, up to a point, a phenomenon which lies outside of its domain proper' (Mannheim, 1982: 56). By this analytical distinction Mannheim does not mean that there is something improper about the sociological study of cultural phenomena, but rather that it does involve a consideration of such phenomena on a different conceptual level from that on which it is considered 'immanently', by the fundamental science proper to it. Nor does he mean that we cannot distinguish between disciplines according to their degree of fitness for considering, non-immanently, cultural phenomena which lie outside them: 'it makes sense to pursue sociology and psychology of art and culture; but there is no meaningful prospect of pursuing chemistry or physics of art. At most, one could investigate the canvas of the artwork or its marble' (Mannheim, 1982: 57).

Sociologists and students of cultural studies would doubtless concur. But Mannheim's point is that, while in a chemistry or physics of art the work itself would 'completely fade from consideration', there is also an 'inadequacy' built into other approaches. Even the phenomenological description of it by its fundamental science approaches it from a distance, a distance which is all the greater in the consideration of it by a non-immanent method, which inevitably neglects certain parts of the whole in 'bringing a foreign conceptual level to bear' (Mannheim, 1982: 63). This is because cultural phenomena are capable of being directly present to us, are accessible to an intuitive response which precedes the constructions-at-a-distance both of their fundamental sciences and of non-immanent sciences such as sociology.

> An artwork denies its genesis in time and its functionality by presenting itself to us in its quality of being objectified and thoroughly wrought. In so far as expressive elements, messages, and confessions are contained in it, they ask to be regarded as parts of this work, detached from all functionality, and not as functions of some individual life ... 'I have forgotten my own grounds' every formation seems to say to us, in so far as it finds us in the original attitude. (Mannheim, 1982: 65)

Now this 'original attitude' is not the only one possible, for if it were, cultural sociology would not be possible. 'There is an attitude attuned to the functionality of every single spiritual formation, in relation to individual as well as to collective life. This attunement to functionality is a pre-theoretical attitude, not a theoretical one' (Mannheim, 1982: 65). Sociology as a discipline corresponds to this 'pre-theoretical' attunement, and Mannheim has no hesitation in defining sociology as the capacity to see objective intellectual contents as functions of conditions and contexts, and as the capacity to grasp functionality in relation to communal rather than individual experience. But he is clear that, as such, the sociological consideration of cultural formations is 'a mere extension and consistent sustaining of an attitude which belongs to the everyday experience of life' (Mannheim, 1982: 75), and that this attitude, say to the functionality of music, in no way calls into question the validity of the findings of a specialist musical science.

Mannheim is often regarded as a sociologist of culture who distinguished between the natural sciences and, say, art or music, by implying that, while the validity of natural scientific knowledge was not to be questioned by a sociology of science, that of art or music was affected by a sociology of culture. In fact, he maintained the distinction between origin and validity for any phenomenon which was treated with a functionalising attitude. The sociologist of culture, precisely because he performs a genetic rather than an immanent analysis, leaves aside the question of validity:

> ... sociology can comprehend only as much of the formation to be interpreted as has gone into it in the form of a result. What one arrives at in an immanent approach, the meaning-contents and their validity ... does not enter into the sociological view and thus can be neither confirmed nor doubted. This also means, however, that sociological or genetic explanation can neither confirm nor refute the truth or falsity of a proposition or of the entire theoretical sphere. How something came to be, what functionality it may possess in other contexts, is entirely irrelevant to its immanent character of validity. This implies that it will never be possible to construct a sociological critique of knowledge or, as has been recently asserted, a sociological critique of human reason. (Mannheim, 1982: 82)

Nevertheless, the functionalising attitude refuses openly to acknowledge the claim to validity which is prescriptive for a phenomenon considered immanently: to the artist or the religious believer, the functionalising sociologist's indifference to such claims is as repugnant as an atheist or philistine's direct attack on them. Indeed, the sociologist's agnosticism may be the more repugnant. According to one view, the difference between atheism and agnosticism is that while atheism takes religious belief and belief in general seriously, agnosticism does not. Max Weber tried to convince religious believers that they could accept his historical explanations of the origins of their beliefs without undermining the strength of them. It was simply a matter of switching levels. Weber's own 'religiously unmusical' attitude is nowhere more apparent than here, for it ignores the fact that for many religious believers the strength of the belief resides in the fact that it cannot be explained sociologically.

Mannheim writes that the difference between an immanent and genetic consideration of cultural phenomena is made obvious to the sociologist only because he brings them into contact with one another. The sociologist of culture experiences a 'personal union' between them, and knows that attuning oneself solely to the genetically-defined meaning of a cultural content provides for mere comprehension. Here, 'one understands what they mean but they leave one "cold"' (Mannheim, 1982: 84). In other words, the sociologist of culture knows that he is functionalising phenomena the contents of which can make much more direct claims on us. This is not without its consequences.

Now the extent to which a sociological method can be considered reductionist varies with the domain of human activity being studied. The 'sociology of' art and literature or of philosophy or religion is not the same as the sociology of education, work, or law for instance. Although law, with its fundamental science of jurisprudence, is already constituted before sociology approaches it, and although there is a distinction between law as an object of legal reasoning and as an object of sociology, the distinction is a technical one. By contrast, there are areas of human endeavour in which a sociological treatment of them not only introduces criteria which are external to the phenomena but also runs up against the fact that these phenomena − artistic, literary, philosophical, religious − may themselves be sources of world-orientation, of the basic values through which we find our way about, of ideas about how to live, of utopias. What John Milbank says very stridently about the sociology of religion in general, and Roberto Calasso very subtly about the Durkheimian sociology of religion − namely, that it theorises religion out of existence − may also be said, with caution, about the sociology of culture more generally (Milbank, 1990; Calasso, 1994: 156−62). If sociology treats these cultural resources as cultural topics by discovering their social function, or treats a literary work or a painting as a 'social construction', it runs the risk of challenging rather that sitting alongside the work's claim as a work.

Against this suspicion it should be said that in the hands of a sophisticated analyst of culture, a work can be made to appear richer than it would otherwise do to the less educated gaze. Alfred Schutz (of whom more later), for instance, wrote brilliant essays on *Don Quixote* and on Mozart, in which he managed to introduce considerations external to the immanent logic of the work while at the same time drawing out features of it which might otherwise have lain dormant. Bruno Latour's observations about social constructionist approaches to art are well taken:

> The constructivist character is built into the arts in a different way than into a scientific fact. The more I read about the intermediary steps that make up the picture of the *Night Watch*, the more I may like it. Constructivism *adds to the pleasure*, going, so to speak, in the same direction, towards the multiplication of mediators. In some deep sense, constructivism flatters some essential feature of the arts. (Latour, 1998: 423)

However, constructivism, or any externally applied method, may just as well 'go in the opposite direction', dragging the work outside the domain within which it might make a cultural claim on us. The consequence of this unmasking attitude is that whatever else works of art or music or literature or philosophy or films are, they come to be seen as ways of representing a set of social or psychological forces or interests or drives: something else. By contrast, a sceptical approach to such phenomena, even while it situates them historically or socially, would seek to acknowledge them as ways of making sense of and, at the limit, of constituting a world. As such, they are not mute objects awaiting the forensic skills of the social constructionist sociologist or the theorist of social class or colonial desire.

The cynical imagination runs up especially sharply against its own limits when confronted by the modernist work of art or film or text, or any cultural artefact which is self-conscious about the medium in which it operates, about language, about paint, about form, about temporality.[5] A suspicion towards modernism is pervasive in cultural studies and some branches of sociology, where it is often passed over in favour of mainstream television, Hollywood films, teenage magazines, popular music, celebrity, and so on; these are cultural products with few intellectual or aesthetic pretensions of their own but, because they are already produced according to a formula, they are all the more easily explained or contextualised via the formulas employed by the sociologist of culture.

Cynicism, Scepticism and Depth Metaphors

There are several ways in which to describe the intellectual process through which the cynic operates: functionalism and reductionism are two such. But another way of characterising cynicism and scepticism is to draw attention to the way in which they make use of metaphor. We have already seen in Chapter 4 that the use of metaphor is common in sociological theory and that some theorists are more skilled in its use than others. How, then, does the cynic use metaphor? Firstly, the cynic makes repeated use of a depth metaphor, while the sceptic either rejects the appeal to depth or is cautious in his or her use of it. Secondly, the cynic may combine his appeal to depth with a second spatial metaphor, in many cases less obvious than the appeal to depth but one which nevertheless may be legitimately attributed to him. This is the metaphor of centre and periphery. Thirdly, these two moves may be combined with a third, in which what is held to be both deep and at the centre is in turn held to possess causal or generative powers. We can summarise these ideas by saying that many of the grander forms of theory require or appeal to a *central generating mechanism*, by means of which the phenomena under sociological investigation are related not to one another, but to a mechanism which operates somewhere else and gives rise to them.

Depth metaphors have received little explicit attention in books on sociological theory. A sustained discussion is found in the first volume of Roberto Unger's *Politics* (Unger, 1987); the philosopher Richard Rorty popularised the term 'foundationalism', which implies an interest in depth metaphors; Michel Foucault's *Archaeology of Knowledge* (1972) contains a depth metaphor in its title. Foucault, however, was suspicious towards invocations of depth. For while it would be hard to use the term 'archaeology' without invoking layers which lie beneath one another, the whole point of the exercise for Foucault was to avoid attributing causal or generative powers to the layers which lie deeper. They may be older and deeper layers, but they are not foundations for the ones lying above, nor do they 'cause' them. This suspicion towards depth was shared by Unger and Rorty. As Foucault put it:

> Archaeology tries to define not the thoughts, representations, images, themes, preoccupations that are concealed or revealed in discourses; but those discourses themselves, those discourses as practices obeying certain rules. It does not treat discourse as document, as a sign of something else, as an element that ought to be

transparent, but whose unfortunate opacity must often be pierced if one is to reach at last the depth of the essential in the place in which it is held in reserve; it is concerned with discourse in its own volume, as a monument. It is not an interpretative discipline; it does not seek another, better-hidden discourse. It refuses to be 'allegorical'. (Foucault, 1972: 138–9)

There are ways of appealing to depth without proclaiming a deeper truth. The historian Fernand Braudel's depth metaphor is the old one of time as a river, with fast-moving events – politics for example – on or near the surface, economic or geopolitical structures lower down at the level of more slowly-moving currents, and the constraints of geography or nature occupying the famous *longue durée* in which change is barely perceptible. Braudel does not want to tell you that the phenomena located lower down are more important or that they generate phenomena above. The *longue durée* is merely a dimension of historical continuity upon which Braudel happens to focus. His work does not imply that the only way to make sense of, say, political events is to embed them in something deeper, more profound or slow moving. The division into levels is simply a heuristic device for the historian who happens to have an interest in a particular dimension of time and who, as Erving Goffman once said of his own work, must be allowed to pick his level.

A more robust distinction between depth and surface is made by Robert Merton who, borrowing from the language of Freud, distinguished between the manifest and the latent functions of social institutions. Whatever the overt or ostensible point of a social institution might be, it will fulfil some other, unacknowledged and socially important function. In fact, something that is dysfunctional may be interpreted as having what functionalists called a eufunction. Conflict, instead of being a threat to social order, 'really' contributes to it by releasing tensions that if not released might otherwise manifest themselves in more dangerous forms of disorder; the university may exist ostensibly in order to convey knowledge to students but it may also once have fulfilled the function of a marriage bureau, providing a milieu in which people could meet their future spouses; the manifest function of the medical practitioner may be overtly to cure people but, as we saw in Chapter 3, his or her latent function will be broader and deeper, namely to reinforce the values of the professional pattern of occupations characteristic of advanced industrial societies. Now, saying that a social institution has certain consequences which go beyond its ostensible function is not quite the same thing as saying that there is something underneath, a hidden or driving force or a ghost in the machine or a foundation. But as we saw in the discussion of Parsons, it is almost impossible to perform a functionalist analysis without invoking a conceptual hierarchy, and it is not uncommon for that conceptual hierarchy to be interpreted by those who use it as implying a hierarchy of social objects, such that some aspects of social life are seen to be more important, more basic, than others. In Parsons' case, this meant that the pattern maintenance function was more important than the adaptation function, or values were more important than interests. This is a good illustration of a process in which a conceptually rich account of empirical social processes may have available to it a default explanatory move.

Finally, the most uncompromising versions of the depth/surface distinction can be found in the Marxian and Freudian traditions. Marx's distinction between base and superstructure and Freud's distinction between layers of the psyche have themselves been the basis for much of the debate which has sustained the Marxian and Freudian traditions, and it may be suggested that the shared commitment to a distinction between depth and surface has caused so many functionalist and Marxist arguments to resemble one another. This is certainly the view of Roberto Unger. Unger observes that this is 'an approach that no theorist has ever fully accepted but that many theorists have implicitly treated as the bedrock of generalization about society and history' (Unger, 1987: 89). That they have done so has much to do with the fact that, if we wish to avoid simply collecting masses of data and classifying them, we need an approach which makes some sort of distinction between the regularities of observable social life – its routines – and the larger organising frameworks within which those routines are played out. Nevertheless, according to Unger, Marxian versions of deep structure arguments make three moves: i) they distinguish between frameworks and routines (the mode of production would be the framework, while the routines would include the 'daily forms of production and exchange' but also 'even the most intimate and intangible aspects of life'); ii) they treat a particular framework as an example of a repeatable and indivisible type of social organisation (e.g. capitalism for Marxism is not an 'aspect of social structure' as it would be for Weber, but must be treated as a whole, so that if it is attacked it either recovers or collapses, giving way to an alternative framework); and iii) they appeal to the idea of a closed list of possible frameworks the sequence of which is defined by a developmental law (primitive communism, slavery, the Asiatic mode of production, feudalism, capitalism, communism). Unger's belief is that the first move is productive, but that the second and third are unnecessarily restrictive, so that when deep structure argument makes use of them it 'sacrifices to its scientistic apparatus much of its vision of social order as made and imagined rather than as given' (Unger, 1987: 93). Unger thinks that progressive or 'visionary' thought requires a more open sense of the possibilities of structural diversity. Indeed:

> Deep structure social theory disorients political strategy and impoverishes programmatic thought by making both of them subsidiary to a ready-made list of social orders. Nowhere are these perils clearer than in the reliance of leftist movements, the major bearers of the radical project, on Marxism, the most developed version of deep-structure social theory. (Unger, 1987: 93)

We are not interested here in the fate of 'programmatic thought' or in the explicitly political consequences of deep structure social theory. Nevertheless, Unger's warning is instructive: deep structure thought in its Marxist variant has to appeal to the idea that history happens according to a script which establishes in advance 'a list of possible social worlds' (Unger, 1987: 136). Another way of saying this is that it gives us a short–cut to significance. But for the cultural beings that, as Weber says, we are, significance, perceiving it and constructing it and maintaining it, is central to the art of having a world.

One of the ways in which we can have a world is through art, literature and philosophy, and it is instructive that writers in the Marxian tradition have approached them by means of some sort of depth/surface distinction. Here is a passage from Lucien Goldmann, the French philosopher who was once seen as having taken the Marxian analysis of culture beyond a crude base and superstructure distinction onto a new level of sophistication:

> man transforms the world around him in order to achieve a better balance between himself (as subject) and the world. One writes a book, makes a road or builds a house to change the world. Now, all human behaviour is meaningful and makes sense. (Goldmann, 1981: 40)

While we might quibble with the idea that the achievement of a better balance with the world exhausts the possible motives for writing a book, the idea that human behaviour is meaningful is one with which we can agree. But the passage continues: '... whether the subject is within a situation or related to another subject, his action is functional ... this functionality, this meaning, is not necessarily conscious' (Goldmann, 1981: 40). This passage encapsulates perfectly the problems faced by the sociologist of culture who sees it almost as part of his professional identity not to allow cultural artefacts to be taken at face value but who also wishes to acknowledge the basic striving for meaning which may be said to lie at the heart of the greatest cultural works. The result is that functionality and meaning are taken to be interchangeable. Here is a passage in which one sentence promises to do justice to the ideas a work contains, only for the next sentence to refuse to keep it:

> Cultural works are great to the extent that they express a global image of man and the universe. In studying such important works one should investigate privileged groups and the global structure of society. (Goldmann, 1981: 41)

What the one hand giveth the other taketh away. Even writers apparently more open to the 'variousness' and nuance of culture have been tempted into this sort of approach. Edward Said, for instance, was so talented a pianist that he might have made a career as a performer. Yet here is a passage from his book, *Musical Elaborations*:

> A work like the B Minor mass is an astonishing demonstration of piety and invention, but for all the intensity and skill of its various parts ... it must also be read as an extended act of homage to the Elector of Saxony, to whom Bach wrote the most fawning letters imaginable. Music therefore quite literally fills a social space, and it does so by elaborating the ideas of authority and social hierarchy directly connected to a dominant establishment imagined as actually presiding over the work. (Said, 1991: 64)

This is characteristic of a style of writing to be found throughout cultural studies and sociology of culture. The point is not to explore the movement of the music, nor to open us to the variety and nuance which an exposure to different ways of seeing can provide, or to encourage us to see the world in new and different ways, but rather to see different things *in* that world, to notice the 'something else' – imperialism, patriarchy, capitalism – that the music or the play or the book itself does not and cannot point to.

If for Marxism and neo–Marxism depth is to be found in the forces and relations of production or in imperialism or social hierarchy, for Freud it is to be found in the unconscious: 'As the architectural principle of the psychic apparatus, we may conjecture a certain stratification or structure of instances deposited in strata' (Freud, 2002: 24). Freud's conjecture was based upon years of empirical research and clinical practice. Nevertheless, the strata hardened into the well-known schema of conscious, pre-conscious and unconscious, with the unconscious being the deepest and taking on a status which went beyond mere conjecture. As Philip Rieff put it, the unconscious refers to:

> ... any mental process the existence of which we are obliged to assume – because, for instance, we infer it in some way from its effects – but of which we are not directly aware ... the unconscious functions for Freud as a 'god-term', to use Kenneth Burke's suggestive epithet: it is Freud's conceptual ultimate, a first cause, to be believed in precisely because it is both fundamental to and inaccessible to experience. (Rieff, 1959: 34)

> Psychoanalysis is the triumph in ethical form of the modern scientific idea. It is characteristic of modern science that nature, the object of knowledge, is seen as withdrawn and definitively unlike the way we experience it ... Not only is the external nature examined by the physical sciences basically deceptive, but even more so ... our inner nature – the ultimate subject studied by the moral sciences – lies hidden. (Rieff, 1959: 69)

If Freud has a god term, so do many sociological theorists. This might be something at the apex of a conceptual hierarchy or a ghost in the machine or simply the most basic and/or all-encompassing concept; think of Bourdieu's 'habitus', Elias's 'figuration', Giddens' 'structuration', Runciman's 'systacts'.

The reason that Freud belongs with the cynics is that the appeal to depth, combined with the belief in a god term, is almost certain to rob surface phenomena of their significance. Freud constructed a universe of apparently tortuous complexity in which the sort of details of everyday life which we might normally disregard are given the sort of intellectual attention they would not normally receive from social scientists. Yet the appeal to depth meant that surface details in all their variety would often be traced back to the same source. Rieff says that 'even while focused upon the cluttered detail in the symptomatic text, the Freudian argument seeks an invariant – even stereotyped – meaning beneath' (Rieff, 1959: 143).

Admittedly Freud's search is more persistent in some areas than others. In *The Interpretation of Dreams*, for instance, although he is at pains to identify the basic rationale for and mechanism of dreaming, the analysis of most dreams depends upon the account of it given by the dreamer, an account that extends into their waking thoughts as well. These must be expressed in language, and because of this there is, potentially, considerable scope for variation in the meaning of any one dream. Here, Freud was a painstaking and careful listener and interpreter. But in his accounts of art and literature the search for stereotyped meanings asserts itself:

Nothing more clearly overrides the autonomy of the aesthetic imagination than Freud's attempt to rationalise it ... Nothing in his long essay on the obscure *Gradiva*, or the fragment of analysis of *The Brothers Karamazov*, leads the reader to think of these in their artistic individuality, as novels. (Rieff, 1959: 143)

Indeed, *The Brothers Karamazov* is one of the richest and most multi-faceted novels ever written, containing a wealth of theorising, particularly theological reflection, the force of which emerges in the course of the protagonists' discussions and arguments with one another. None of this appears in Freud, who is interested in one topic alone – parricide. Even here, there is little detailed reference to the text, to how it is dealt with by this particular medium of expression, the novel (Steiner, 1959; Williams, 2008).

Why should such short cuts to significance be attractive? One reason is that depth metaphors, particularly for those with less intellectual ability or with less time – free time? – than those who invented them, appear to offer either explanatory power or a last explanatory resort. The fate of the thought of Marx and Freud is again instructive. Regardless of the degree of economic determinism to be found in Marx, regardless of the extent to which Freud made much of human social life depend upon drives and instincts at the expense of other sources of human motivation, these were conclusions arrived at after years of empirical inquiry. Marx came to a conclusion about the centrality of class struggle after immersing himself in world history. Freud came to a conclusion about the structure of the psyche on the basis of years of clinical work. Many of their followers, however, took on board the depth metaphors without going through the process that produced them. In this respect they reflect a culture pervaded by respect for the achievements of the natural sciences, central to which has been the institutionalisation of scientific method, a method which is supposed to be transmissible from one generation to another and across different scientific communities. The adherents of some of sociological theory's most well known depth metaphors seem to buy in on the basic principle of modern scientific culture, namely that in order to be a scientist you do not need to rediscover the basic principles of your discipline for yourself because there is an established corpus of shared knowledge which those doing normal science can subscribe to. The idea of such a corpus has hovered over sociology since its beginning. What, after all, could be more comforting to sociologists than the thought that they are pursuing Thomas Kuhn's normal science, that although they don't have a laboratory to go to every day, there is a body of knowledge sufficiently well-established to provide them with a sense of intellectual security (Martins, 1972).

But the fact that they do not have a laboratory means that sociology is not an experimental science, and one of the costs of this is that it is exceptionally difficult for sociologists to make anything resembling discoveries. This leaves them with a choice: they can either accept this situation and treat theorising as a process in which they apply their depth metaphors and attendant formulae willy-nilly, knowing the result in advance; or they can theorise in such a way that the results of their inquiries are at least provisional and open to further scholarly debate. Most sociologists in the 20th century have preferred the first move, so that 'base and superstructure', 'commodity fetishism', 'surplus value', 'the unconscious', 'repression', 'sublimation', 'hegemony', 'habitus', 'function', 'patriarchy' and a welter of other terms, while initially providing those who devised them with a feeling of cognitive power, turned into magic words, written on the little pieces of paper that lesser thinkers could stick on to the world. What they could never become was what Imre Lakatos called a progressive scientific research programme (Lakatos, 1978; Elster, 1986).

Pierre Bourdieu and the Cynical Imagination

The most important example of the cynical approach in contemporary sociology is the work of Pierre Bourdieu. Notwithstanding the apparent sophistication and complexity of the concepts by means of which he seeks to connect social structure with culture, or economic capital and cultural capital, or the social positions of individuals and their mental or other dispositions, there is at the heart of his enterprise a simple model. The fact that, as Bourdieu himself might say, this has been 'misrecognised' by his many admirers has much to do with modern sociology's residual belief in the scientific community and in its attendant magic words. For many, the work of Bourdieu seems to provide the warm embrace of an intellectual home as well as a working method.

Bourdieu's approach to cultural analysis is displayed in each of his books, and so only two of them (Bourdieu, 1996, 1997) will be referred to here. They display a number of the features we have discussed in previous chapters. They are the work of a classic author, they make distinctive contributions to sociology's inventory of descriptive possibilities, they use diagrams, they address questions of social classification, and they invoke the image of depth. Here is the first sentence of *The State Nobility*:

> In keeping with the usual view, the goal of sociology is to uncover the most deeply buried structures of the different social worlds that make up the social universe, as well as the 'mechanisms' that tend to ensure their reproduction or transformation. (Bourdieu, 1997: 1)

The object of the book is mechanisms and procedures through which France's educational, political and economic elites reproduce themselves, and its data are drawn from a number of sources: the results of a survey of prizewinners of France's *Councours General*, which is a national essay competition embracing several subjects for secondary school students; reports of the examining committee for entrance examinations to the Ecole Normale Superieure and for the *agregation*, an examination allowing students to become secondary school teachers; reports by teachers preparing students for the entrance examination to the ENS. Bourdieu wishes to show that there is a connection between the categories of evaluation deployed by the examining committee and the categories of self-evaluation deployed by the prizewinners; between the hierarchies of intellectual qualities internal to the evaluations and the hierarchies of disciplines represented by the examinations and essays; and between the hierarchies of intellectual qualities and the social backgrounds of those to whom these qualities are attributed. In order to do so he employs a considerable range of empirical material, yet repeatedly stresses, in his summaries of findings, the close fit between social structures and mental structures.

> The language used by the humanities prizewinners to explain why their work was singled out is a perfect illustration of the correspondence that obtains between objective positions in the hierarchy of disciplines and self-image, an image inseparable from the representation of the qualities socially associated with the different disciplines. (Bourdieu, 1997: 16)

Some students will be described as precocious, brilliant, talented, elegant and so on, while others will be described as hardworking, solid, or methodical. And what is true of students is true of disciplines, so that French or philosophy or mathematics will attract the first set of descriptors, while history or geography will attract the second. Now Bourdieu's claim is that, where educational institutions and students themselves associate certain students and certain subjects with qualities such as 'ease' or 'talent' or 'effortlessness', reference to these qualities is a way of speaking which itself enables students of certain backgrounds and milieu to seek and pursue a career associated with that milieu. In other words, these taxonomies of qualities, far from being the product of objective judgements about the quality of work or of the individual student, are classifications with a social origin.

> ... when, in the indefinable nuances that define 'ease' or 'natural' talent, we think we recognize behaviour or ways of speaking considered authentically 'cultured' because they bear no mark of the effort and no trace of the work that goes into their acquisition, we are really referring to a particular mode of acquisition: what we will call ease is the privilege of those who, having imperceptibly acquired their culture through a gradual familiarization in the bosom of the family, have academic culture as their native culture and can maintain a familiar rapport with it that implies the unconsciousness of its acquisition. (Bourdieu, 1997: 21)

Now, while we may feel that there is a measure of truth to this, Bourdieu is making much larger claims. Just how large can be appreciated when we realise that the analysis draws upon Durkheim and Mauss's *Primitive Classification*. Bourdieu says that a careful survey of the acts of judgement – the comments and the marks – performed on the work of students by teachers preparing them for the Ecole Normale entrance examination:

> should enable us to grasp the academic forms of classification that, like the 'primitive forms of classification' discussed by Emile Durkheim and Marcel Mauss, are the product of the incorporation of social structures, specifically those which organize the educational institution ... and that are homologously related to the structures of social space. (Bourdieu, 1997: 30–2)

This is a remarkable statement because, although Durkheim and Mauss's famous book has as its most famous line 'the classification of things follows the classification of men', the book itself traces a history of social classification in three very different cultures, namely those of aboriginal Australia, China and ancient Greece. In so doing it states explicitly that there is considerable historical variation in the extent to which the classification of men is able to determine the classification of things; indeed, as we saw in Chapter 3, there is a developmental path in which the act of cognition, and with it the forms of classification displayed by a culture, are progressively freed from the constraints and limitations imposed upon the imagination by group belonging. The product, knowledge, is increasingly freed from the process that produced it.

Yet Bourdieu is effectively arguing that the relationship between intellectual classification and social structure in France at the end of the 20th century resembles the relationship between the classification of things and that of men in aboriginal Australia. We saw in our discussion of Adorno that attributions of magical or mythic or other modes of pre-modern thinking to modern people might be a useful rhetorical strategy for dramatizing the conformism of 'bourgeois society'; less shrilly, Mary Douglas demonstrated that certain sorts of symbolic – rather than scientific or technical – classification may well have an important place within the cognitive structures of 20th-century society. But Bourdieu, unlike Adorno and Horkheimer, is not doing speculative culture criticism, and unlike Mary Douglas he is claiming that there are surface phenomena that are dependent on deeper forces. Moreover, he thinks that he is saying something more than that there is a 'simple machine' that translates products hierarchised according to an implicit social classification into products hierarchised according to an explicit academic classification which 'is in reality quite similar to' the initial classification; he writes of a 'strange cognitive machine' the result of whose functioning 'permits the realization of a social classification in guises that allow it to be accomplished invisibly'. Indeed, this mechanism for achieving a homology between inherited capital and academic capital 'can only function if it remains hidden' (Bourdieu, 1997: 36). Bourdieu's work is littered with words like 'misrecognition', 'invisibly', 'denial' and so on, words which suggest that he, Bourdieu, can see what others cannot see, and that it is the task of sociology to lay bare the mechanisms that those who enact them are unable to articulate.

> Agents entrusted with acts of classification can fulfill their social function as social classifiers only because it is carried out in the guise of acts of academic classification. They only do well what they have to do (objectively) because they think that they are doing something other than what they are doing, because they are doing something other than what they think they are doing, and because they believe in what they think they are doing. As fools fooled, they are the primary victims of their own actions. It is because they think they are using a strictly academic or even, more specifically, 'philosophical' (or 'literary') classification, because they think they are awarding certificates of charismatic qualifications in literature, or philosophy ('philosophical mind' etc.) that the system is able to effect a veritable *deviation of the meaning* of their practice, thereby getting them to do what they would not otherwise do for all the money in the world. (Bourdieu, 1997: 39, emphasis in original)

Earlier we referred to Mannheim's distinction between an immanent and a sociological consideration of cultural phenomena. If this is central to the sociological enterprise, then the skill of the sociologist consists in being able to maintain it without reducing it to a difference between surface and depth, appearance and reality, ideology and science, and so on. Or at least, not in the manner in which Bourdieu does so here. If we are to distinguish between the immanent and the sociological consideration of cultural phenomena then the relationship between these may vary depending on the type of cultural phenomenon under consideration; that is to say, there may be arenas of social life which are simply more amenable than others to the deep-structural, functional accounts given by Bourdieu.

It may be that the purpose of education is not only the transmission of knowledge but also social reproduction, and that therefore some correspondence is to be expected between classifications of academic ability and classifications of social origins, though this may vary considerably between societies. But Bourdieu applies the same method, and the same conception of depth and surface, indiscriminately, so that art, literature, photography, whose precise social function is not always easy to discern, are treated as though they are the same as education, there for the purpose of social reproduction. The following passage from Bourdieu's representative on earth, Loïc Wacquant, intended as praise for the master's book *Distinction,* Bourdieu's famous account of the relationship between cultural consumption and class, may be read as a useful summary of his weaknesses:

> First, Bourdieu shows that, far from expressing some unique inner sensibility of the individual, aesthetic judgment is an eminently social faculty, resulting from class upbringing and education. To appreciate a painting, a poem, or a symphony presupposes mastery of the specialized symbolic code of which it is a materialization, which in turn requires possession of the proper kind of cultural capital. Mastery of this code can be acquired by osmosis in one's milieu of origin or by explicit teaching. When it comes through native familiarity (as with the children of cultured upper-class families), this trained capacity is experienced as an individual gift, an innate inclination testifying to spiritual worth. The Kantian theory of 'pure aesthetic', which philosophy presents as universal, is but a stylized – and mystifying – account of this particular experience of the 'love of art' that the bourgeoisie owes to its privileged social position and condition. (Wacquant, 2006: 314)

Once one has made this move, it is difficult to see how the student of culture might be directed towards art and literature or music as sources of world-orientation in themselves, or encouraged to distinguish between those works that do and those that do not transcend the context of their emergence. In the preface to *The Rules of Art*, his account of the work of Flaubert, Bourdieu says that we must reject the idea of the creative literary genius along with the idea that novels or other works of art come from nowhere; we must reject the idea that the only relationship we need to understand is that between author and text. Literary works are 'products of human action' which, like any others, can be subjected to 'the ordinary treatment of ordinary science' (Bourdieu, 1996: xv). Initially, he does say that Flaubert's *Sentimental Education* is more than literature. Indeed, he says, as though this were a compliment, that it is a piece of sociology, an analysis of the 'social field' in which its main protagonist makes his way between the worlds of art/politics and politics/economics. But this appreciation of Flaubert rapidly gives way to sociological imperialism. Flaubert's is a sociological sensibility, but it turns out that he is only able to express it by means of a literary form that both reveals and conceals at the same time:

> ... the literary work can sometimes say more, even about the social realm, than many writings with scientific pretensions ... But it says it only in a mode such that it does not truly say it ... The putting-into-form operated by the writer functions like a generalized euphemism, and the reality de-realized and neutralized by literature that he offers allows him to satisfy a desire for knowledge ready to be satisfied by the sublimation offered him by literary alchemy ... A sociological reading breaks the spell. By interrupting the complicity that unites author and reader expressed by the text, it reveals the truth that the text enunciates but in such a way that it does not say it; moreover, sociological reading *a contrario* brings to light the truth of the text itself, whose specificity is defined precisely by the fact that it does not say what it says in the same way as the sociological reading does. The form in which literary objectification is enunciated is no doubt what permits the emergence of the deepest reality, the best hidden (here, the structure of the field of power and the model of social ageing) because that is the veil which allows the author and reader to dissimulate it and to close their eyes to it. (Bourdieu, 1996: 32–3)

This is cynicism at full throttle: the talk is of depth, of hiding and revealing, of seeing what others cannot see. Above all, the acknowledgement of Flaubert's own sociological imagination is tempered – undermined in fact – with the claim that it requires the sociologist to make this imagination visible, to 'break the spell'.

Bourdieu the sociologist was clearly a fan of Flaubert the novelist. So is the novelist Milan Kundera. But Kundera is also the most eloquent defender of the novel's integrity, both in its relationship with apparently more elevated forms of literary expression such as poetry, and in its relationship to 'society'. One doubts that he has read Bourdieu, but in *The Curtain*, his witty and playful defence of literature, he provides the riposte to the kind of approach that Bourdieu represents, writing that the novel 'refuses to exist as illustration of an historical era, as description of a society, as defense of an ideology, and instead puts itself exclusively at the service of "what only the novel can say"' (Kundera, 2007: 67). His earlier *Testaments Betrayed* repeatedly confirms this, one four-page passage in particular – on an unfortunate American professor's 'kitsch-making' account of Hemingway's short story, 'Hills Like White Elephants' – dismantling in a few pages many of the characteristic assumptions of later 20th-century literary criticism and sociology of culture, in particular their efforts to provide external readings – be they 'sociological' or 'moral' or 'political' – of works of art (Kundera, 1995: 142–3).

The question remains, however: is the novelist's or the artist's or the poet's defence of their art the only response to the functionalising attitude of the cynical sociologist? Do we face a choice between the integrity of the work and the attempt to relate it to 'something else'? By no means. There is a viable sociology of culture that has no need to link taste with social class, the disposition of the artist with his or her social location or to talk of the way in which a work of culture 'reveals but also conceals' social relations.

The Sceptical Imagination and the Sociological Analysis of Culture

What are the virtues of a sceptical sociology of culture? Can it achieve a respect for the work of art or literature or, for that matter, the everyday reasoning of individuals, while maintaining the integrity of the object of its own fundamental science, society? What does a sceptical approach to the study of culture amount to? Who falls under the heading? We can ignore here those sociological studies of culture that bracket out the work entirely, for example, studies of music or art that focus entirely on the art market or the music industry and that therefore do not pretend to be telling us something about the work that its own appropriate fundamental science cannot tell us. The dangers of cynicism are easily avoided if you have no eyes for the work in the first place. Sometimes, in fact, this is one of the virtues of Bourdieu's work. His book on photography, for instance, in saying nothing about the act of looking at a photograph and everything about the class character of photography as a leisure activity, avoids the risk involved in claiming to know what photographs mean (Bourdieu, 1990; for the opposite approach see Barthes, 1981). We might also be grateful that in *The Rules of Art* he does not discuss a single poem of Baudelaire's despite quoting from his letters. But you can get a feel for the price to be paid for this by comparing the long-winded account of Baudelaire's position in the literary 'field of production' with Walter Benjamin's approach.

Benjamin is interested precisely in what he calls, in a memorable phrase, 'the theoretical energy contained in Baudelaire's prose', as well as in his poetry (Benjamin, 1983: 13). To be sure, this means that at times he is tempted to impose on Baudelaire's observations about the *flaneur* or the crowd some formulations derived from Marx's theory of the commodity, in which Baudelaire himself may have had little interest. Nevertheless, the link between the society of Baudelaire's day, changes in the economy, developments in the print media, the architecture of cities, and the words on the page, is conveyed by Benjamin with subtlety and skill, with an economy and suppleness that Bourdieu never achieved, and with a constant respect for the writer as someone whose distinctiveness lies in the particular challenges, ideas, theories that a great writer can present to his readers. In this respect, Benjamin's comparison of the responses of Victor Hugo and Baudelaire to the phenomenon of the urban crowd is exemplary, because he treats them as adult writers mature enough to have sensibilities and judgemental capacities of their own, and dispositions that are irreducible to their class position or their location in Bourdieu's literary 'field'.

The phrase 'theoretical energy of his prose' might also have been used by a very different kind of sociologist, Alfred Schutz, in his account of *Don Quixote*, or by Goffman in his magisterial description – in *Frame Analysis* – of the play within the play in *Hamlet*. The same might be said of Foucault's analysis of the 'theoretical energy' of Magritte's paintings (Foucault, 1983). In all of these cases, while the analysis draws on a distinctive theoretical vocabulary, the point of it is not to enable the theorist to say something more clever or penetrating than the objects of his inquiries could say. And precisely because they abjure the theorist's claim to know better, they succeed in entering into the texture of the work of art or literature more convincingly than does Bourdieu. Their scepticism consists in the fact that they neither seek to unmask the text in the name of a greater good, nor bow down before the greatness of great writers, an approach that in any case often produces thin results (Bloom, 1995, is thin in this respect); the theoretical language is certainly intended to enable us to see with different eyes. But it is there solely as an aid to appreciation of the fact that Magritte or Cervantes or Shakespeare knew full well what they were doing. Mozart too. In 'Mozart and the Philosophers', Schutz castigates three distinguished philosophers for reading into Mozart's music their own philosophical agendas, and then proposes that by 'purely musical means', Mozart 'solved the problems of the philosophers in his own way, thereby proving himself to be the greatest philosopher of them all' (Schutz, 1964: 179).

In 'Don Quixote and the Problem of Reality', Schutz almost says that Cervantes, too, was the greatest philosopher of them all. In fact he argues that Cervantes' novel 'deals systematically with the … problem of multiple realities stated by William James', and that 'the various phases of Don Quixote's adventures are carefully elaborated variations on the main theme, viz. how we experience reality' (Schutz, 1964: 136). The key is the relationship between Don Quixote's 'sub-universe of madness' in which there are giants and armies, and the reality in which 'we Sancho Panzas live our daily lives'. The key to Schutz's analysis of that relationship is a close reading of the novel, in which Cervantes himself sets down the terms of the framework, that is the sub-universe of chivalry, a world that is an entire way of life. Chivalry is the queen of the sciences, embracing theology, physics, herbalism, law, economics and astronomy: a medieval version of inter-disciplinary studies if you like. Cervantes at first demonstrates the various ways in which the protagonists seek to reconcile or preserve differences in the schemes of interpretation peculiar to knight errantry and everyday life. Here Don Quixote has to 'establish a "sub-universe of discourse" with the fellow-men with whom he shares a face-to-face relationship within the world of common sense' (Schutz, 1964: 142). Later, however, when Don Quixote encounters people who have read about his exploits, the reality of play or 'let's pretend' is employed by them in order to maintain rather than resolve conflicts between schemes of interpretation – between the worlds of chivalry, the theatre and everyday reality (in the episode of Master Pedro's puppet show), between the worlds of chivalry, science and common sense (in the episode of the Clavileño, the wooden horse). The novel culminates in the 'personal tragedy' of Don Quixote, who, after countless episodes in which the relationship between fantasy, reality and dream is enacted and then discussed at length with Sancho, is forced to conclude that 'even his private sub-universe, the realm of chivalry, might be just a dream and that its pleasures pass like shadows' (Schutz, 1964: 156).

Schutz's account of the novel is masterful, but what interests us is the fact that he brings to bear the perspective of phenomenological sociology without appearing to impose an external perspective on it. He does not try to see what

Cervantes himself cannot see or to break a spell – Bourdieu's strategy with Flaubert – but to lay bare Cervantes' genius. He does make free use of terminology that is alien to Cervantes himself and taken from later centuries – he compares the episode in the cave of Montesinos with Bergson's account of time in Einstein's theory of relativity, the episode of the enchanters is ascribed to 'a non-Hegelian dialectic', Sancho is a 'neo-positivistic empiricist', and at one point the Duchess is described as 'taking the point of view of the Hegelian "cunning of reason", which makes man an unknowing tool of a higher purpose' (Schutz, 1964: 148). But these references to what Cervantes could not have known are no more than guides and hints for today's reader. At one point, discussing Don Quixote's belief in the reality of Dulcinea, and his willingness to admit that his sense of reality is a matter of his own imagination, Schutz says that 'Don Quixote makes a statement which is at the core of our problem and surpasses in its logical boldness all the paradoxes of Russell's theory of classes' (Schutz, 1964: 146).

The point of Schutz's essay is not to 'do a reading' of Cervantes, say in terms of substantive problems such as 'attitudes' to women or ethnic minorities or violence or class, or to read into the novel what is not there by appealing to something beyond the text; nor is it to stay with the text in order to praise great literature; nor yet to deconstruct it and demonstrate the points at which its attempt to mean something cancels itself. To put all this in the language of Paul Ricoeur, Schutz's approach is not a hermeneutics of suspicion – in which he seeks to get at the world behind the text – but rather a hermeneutics of recovery. Ricoeur says that the aim of the latter is to 'open up a world in front of the text' instead of uncovering a world behind the text (Ricoeur, 1970: 32–5), but we can say that in Schutz's reading, what is opened up in front of Cervantes' text is not so much a world as the problematic of world-orientation itself.

'The Problem of Reality' that appears in the title of Schutz's essay was at the heart of everything that Erving Goffman wrote. His most ambitious theoretical statement was his 1974 book, *Frame Analysis*, which, like Schutz's essay, begins with William James. We saw in Chapter 4 the skill and subtlety with which Goffman deploys metaphor in his early work, and the sense of ironic distance that he displays towards his own theoretical tools, his sense of their limits. *Frame Analysis* – the introduction to which should be required reading for all who think they are doing 'reflexive sociology' – takes this combination of insight and self-distance to new heights, so that a highly elaborate technical vocabulary is deployed, but in such a way as never to swamp the material. Goffman's genius was to find a way of marking theoretically the displays of genius that are a routine feature of everyday life, of celebrating life's little pieties or its gross deceptions without either being pious or cunning himself. The metaphor of 'frame' was a way of accounting not so much for conflicts between sub-universes, as in *Don Quixote*, but for ways in which the same strip of activity can be transformed and retransformed by means of the cognitive devices routinely available to ordinary actors.

The important terms here are primary framework, 'keying' and 'fabrication'. Everything we do requires a basic or primary framework or schema of interpretation, but once we have established this banal fact, we can explore the ways in which activity understood in this way gets transformed to mean something else, and realise that a substantial portion of our social life is lived by means of transformational devices. A strip of activity may occur within a primary framework, but that activity may be keyed, as when it is dramatically scripted, or practised, or rehearsed, or engaged in in a spirit of play or make-believe. And a keyed activity – this is Goffman's point – can then be re-keyed, as when a novel is made into a film, or a piece of pornography is transformed from the dramatic scripting of sexual activity into evidence at an obscenity trial. The words are exactly the same, the sense of reality they depict different. Goffman writes that every time an activity is transformed in this way another layer or 'lamination' is added to the outside of the frame, and that our skill as social actors consists in knowing where the outer layer lies. The point of this analysis is to draw our attention both to the skills of actors and to the vulnerabilities of social experience, the limits of possible transformation being often unclear and a matter for negotiation. We know, for instance, the difference between a real fire and a fire drill, but so much so that the sound of a fire alarm in low rise office buildings may well be met with a groan and a leisurely stroll to the fire drill assembly point rather than with any sense of emergency. In recent years, prominent public figures arrested for viewing child pornography on the internet have routinely claimed that the act of looking at indecent or exploitative images was, in their case, part of what they call 'research', a re-keying of the originally keyed activity, a form of looking that is not looking-for-pleasure and therefore not a matter for the courts. The courts in turn have sought to discredit such strategies by claiming that, effectively, there is one less layer to the frame than the defendant says there is.

Along with keyings there are 'fabrications', transformations in which one individual or group sets out to deceive another about the reality status of what they are witnessing or participating in. The fabricators seek to occupy, so to speak, a layer of the frame outside that of those they seek to deceive. Fabrications can be benign – a surprise birthday party, employees posing as customers to test the skills of trainee salespeople, withholding knowledge of a friend's spouse's infidelities – or exploitative. The latter category includes, very prominently, confidence tricks, the art of which is, incidentally, to make the victim believe that he or she is one of the fabricators, in on the scam.

Armed with this equipment Goffman treats us to a bewildering series of examples, ranging from everyday misunderstandings to murder. On its publication some commentators complained about the verbosity and over-complication of *Frame Analysis*. But Goffman always intended his theoretical tools to be picked up when the need arose and laid down when they would not do the job. Once you get the hang of them you can easily see how all manner of episodes might be formulated in frame terms without our having to worry about questions of 'accuracy'. Take the controversy surrounding Salman Rushdie's *Satanic Verses*: expressed in frame terms, for the Ayatollah Khomeini, the book was not a novel with its own logic, but contained a set of false empirical claims about the life of the prophet; for Rushdie, it contained a playful novelistic re-keying of the story of that life; for many otherwise liberal commentators who opposed Rushdie, the fact that the novel had entered the public domain in which Muslim sensitivities might be offended made it a provocative fabrication, a genuine and negative thesis about Islam presented by the author as an innocent novelistic re-keying. The arguments the book provoked were about where the outer layer of the frame resided; they were, as Goffman would have put it, exercises in which one party sought to 'contain' the other.

We bring this chapter to a close with Goffman's account of the play-within-the play in *Hamlet*, because here he takes a text that is familiar to many members of Western society, says something about it that sounds highly technical, yet never gives the impression of imposing an agenda on it, be it normative, social or political. In this way, he manages to bring something out in the text, using his genius to allow us to appreciate the genius of Shakespeare. And it seems to me that that is what the sceptical study of cultural phenomena is about. It is, perhaps, in keeping with the distinctions we drew in Chapter 2, more attentive to the formal than to the substantive aspects – gender or class or race or ethnicity or religion – of the phenomenon, and is hesitant about the message to be conveyed by the work; it doubts indeed, as any sceptic should, whether there is a single message to be found, and sees this as a way of opening the reader to the variousness and nuance of the work.

The 'play within a play' which Hamlet uses to catch the conscience of the king is, starting from the innermost point, a strip of possible past happening – the murder of Gonzago – and the sort of strip that could be keyed from drama were Hamlet real. So we have a theatrical framing of reality. The staged audience for this inner play, including the King, ought to be able to sustain an open agreement with the performers, the visiting troupe familiar of old to Hamlet, that a 'mere' play is in progress: the staged audience need not know the outcome of the play but need only be willing to give itself over to the unfolding drama as if it could be real, yet do this in such a way that it will withdraw its involvement after the curtain comes down, clearly having seen from moment to moment all along that of course only a play was being presented. However, Hamlet's particular choice of play under the circumstances, and especially his quiet change of some dozen or sixteen lines in the script, transforms the theatrical keying into an exploitative fabrication, into something the king would have denounced were he to have known in advance what he was getting in for. So we have a fabricated theatrical framing. But this, of course, is all in itself part of the play that Shakespeare wrote, a play that persons who are actors stage before persons who are really members of an audience. The actors who play the staged audience and the actors who play the stage actors equally share the information state that the producer possesses. And since the play is Hamlet, no actual audience is likely to be much ignorant of the play's development and outcome. However, the individuals on the stage will be obliged to manage and conceal their knowledge of the play's development and outcome in a different way from the way the real audience manages theirs. So one has, starting from the innermost point, a strip of events which could have actually occurred, transformed for dramatic production, retransformed as a construction to entrap the King, transformed once again, since all this plotting actually happens in a play, not merely by means of a play. And of course, the mountain of literary comment on the play is a keying of all this. (Goffman, 1974: 183–4)

One is tempted to say here that this description lies at the outer limit of formal sociological analysis; indeed, someone has recently attempted to mathematise Goffman's work (Baptista, 2003). It is certainly true that, unlike Schutz's account of *Don Quixote*, which speaks of the problem of reality in order to follow the course of the knight's 'personal tragedy', the problem of reality as Goffman understands it contains nothing of the great Shakespearean themes that one might argue should be sociology's too: Hamlet's character, the relationship between father and son, the human and the supernatural, authority, men and women, the tragedy of human action and responsibility. Indeed, immediately after the account of *Hamlet*, Goffman discusses an obscure B movie, *Love and Larceny*, in precisely the same 'frame' terms. He might well have found a story from *The San Francisco Chronicle* in order to make the same point.

However, it should be remembered that the sceptical sociological account of culture, while it is not cynical in Bourdieu's sense, is not setting out to save the text either; that it is bound to bring a distinctive theoretical perspective to bear on the material and to do so to an extent 'from outside'. Goffman is not telling us about *Hamlet* as something written down on paper but about the structure of the relationship between actors and audience when the play – and in particular the play within the play – is being performed. Performances were the object domain of Goffman's sociology. And I think that it is this, together with the degree of its formalism, that saves the account from the 'art and society' problematic that has dogged the sociology of culture and cultural studies. The sense in which it is saved is different from that in which those studies are saved that say nothing about the play or the music or the film or the painting because it is all about context or the power-political processes of reception that led to their canonisation. The account is formal, but it is hard to say that this takes it closer to or further away from what Shakespeare meant, any more than Schutz can be said to take us closer to or further away from what Cervantes meant. The point in both cases is to lay bare the ways in which the work raises questions about the reality status of social experience, and about the ways in which a sense of reality depends upon the framing skills of social actors – the protagonists in *Don Quixote*, the actors and audience in the play within the play and the actors and the audience in the theatre in *Hamlet*. These skills are there to be celebrated by the theorist, a theorist who – like Schutz or Goffman – has the skills and the equipment to bring them out.

Whether we call these exercises in interpretation 'social constructionist' and oppose them to the 'realist' or positivist or materialist accounts of others does not matter much. What matters is that culture is being treated by the sociologist as there to be read and inhabited rather than as something to be explained away. The reading is an adventure in sense-making, a confrontation between the sociologist and the material, material which the sceptical sociologist, for all his or her theoretical commitments, will acknowledge as itself partaking of the qualities to be expected of good sociology. Sociologists of culture may vary in their perceptions of what range of material does possess those qualities; what Schutz thought was achieved by Cervantes and Mozart, or Benjamin by Victor Hugo, Baudelaire and the obscure playwrights of the German Baroque,

Goffman thought was achieved by newspaper reports, diplomatic memoirs and social psychology articles … as well as Shakespeare. In Calvino's terms, these were his classics, to which he would return because they made more than one point and did so as well as he could. The fact that *Frame Analysis* teems with examples does not make it the kind of positivist work that Adorno criticised in *Introduction to Sociology*, one in which a set of categories is invented out of thin air and then the boxes are filled in with as many illustrations as possible; the 'examples' speak for themselves, it is they that are 'Goffmanesque'; but, if we may put it like this, they are made to do this work by Goffman's genius.

It is also worth remembering, in the light of what we said about the role that scientific pretension plays in cynicism, that the writing of Schutz or Goffman or Mary Douglas or Geertz or Foucault combines adventurism with something else, what we may call a drive for exactitude. Only this is not the 'exactitude in science' we encountered in Chapter 2 in the discussion of Borges' map; it is the product of the belief that the world can be made to appear different, that it can be seen with different eyes, not simply through our willingness to move about in it, but through our having available the right sort of equipment. In the next chapter, we will have more to say about the virtues of adventurism and exactitude, only not as approaches to inquiry but as approaches to the art of living. We will also see that they may form part of a utopian imagination.

7

Sociological Theory and
The Art of Living

Introduction: Sociological Theory and Ethics

I have dwelt at length on sociological theory's attempts to make and comprehend a world and the devices that it has employed in order to do so. In the last chapter I broadened the inquiry to consider two intellectual styles, and in calling them cynicism and scepticism also hinted that they might be thought of as attitudes to life. In this chapter I turn more directly to the question of whether and in what way sociological theory can shed light on the problem of how to live.

Are theory and practice all of a piece, as Marxism and Freudianism wanted them to be, or do we say with Goethe's Mephistopheles that there is the grey of theory and the green of life? Or is there a more complicated relationship between them, as Max Weber implies? In a classic collection of essays, Peter Laslett and W.G. Runciman wrote that:

> ... in social theory we are using concepts to understand beings who define them-
> selves by means of their use of concepts, in some cases the concepts that we are
> using to try to understand them. So to construct a theory and to propagate it is to
> afford people a new means of self-comprehension; to give the theory currency may
> well change the very behaviour which the theory attempts to describe. (Laslett and
> Runciman, 1962: 64)

Although this formulation sounds uncontroversial, there is no simple or direct connection between writing about or formulating or teaching a theory and giving it currency, nor between giving it currency and changing behaviour. A theory may 'gain currency' as a result of being 'propagated' by publishers, self-promoting authors, forceful teachers or even the writers of best-selling textbooks; it may enjoy a more or less spontaneous popularity among an intellectual public craving new ideas and new gurus; or it may be discovered for the first time decades after a theorist's death. In addition, although a theory may well change behaviour, it may be less able to do so than a play or a novel or a poem, so while it would be foolish to dismiss the capacity of a theory to have an effect on the conduct of those who are exposed to it, it would be equally unwise to assume that one knows how strong that effect might be. It may be that years of reading Erving Goffman may make you more reserved and detached, and as interested in the way emotion behaviour gets 'done' as in having those emotions yourself; reading Mary Douglas may mean that you are more interested in the classification of food in a supermarket than in its quality, and more attracted to ritual modes of behaviour, be they sacred or secular; prolonged exposure to Wright Mills may change you from a timid vegetarian into a carnivorous biker who believes that the only house worth living in is one you have built yourself (Mills, 2000); and reading Parsons or Luhmann may make you just more boring than if you read Adorno or Foucault. On the other hand, you might agree with Goffman's analysis yet still cry at your grandmother's funeral, or be convinced by Mary Douglas's theory of dirt as matter out of place and still be as untidy as ever; and reading Foucault might make you just as boring as the fans of Luhmann can be.

'The art of living' refers to the strategies and procedures, the techniques and the tools by which an individual orients his or her conduct, and shapes or directs his or her life. Human beings, said Max Weber, are distinguished from animals by the fact that they can lead a life rather than just let it happen 'as an event in nature', and he thought that the point of sociology was to make sense of the different ways in which lives are led – of *Lebensführung* – in different cultural traditions and in different institutional settings. 'The art of living' will be considered in this chapter as a subcategory of *Lebensführung*, in the sense that it refers not so much to the means that institutionalised social membership makes available for the leading of a life as to conscious and explicit world-making and self-shaping.

Now there is a venerable philosophical tradition of thought about the 'art of living' that stretches from the Greeks and early Christianity to Montaigne, Nietzsche and Foucault, but in his magisterial account of it Alexander Nehamas can find no place for sociological thinkers such as Weber, Simmel, Douglas, Goffman, Elias, Adorno and Schutz (Nehamas, 1998). Nehamas is not alone. General surveys of sociological theory, and certainly introductory textbooks, concentrate for the most part on sociology's knowledge claims or its capacity to discern the direction and dynamic of modern society – and this despite the fact that in the last two decades sociologists who once saw the social world in terms of class, stratification, interest groups, constraint, and social control, and all those factors and forces that 'embedded' the individual fairly firmly within society, have turned increasing attention to the ways in which individuals have become detached from their social moorings, uncertain about their futures, and hence confronted with the question of the right way to live.

This does not mean that 'the art of living' needs to be or could be addressed by sociology in the same way as it is addressed by philosophy or literature; the disciplinary distinctions remain important. For instance, since Kant and Hegel philosophers have been debating the relative merits of 'deontological' ethics – in which the question of how to live can only be answered by means of a basic principle, such as Kant's categorical imperative – and an approach in which human conduct, and whatever principles or precepts might govern it, is incomprehensible apart from our determinate institutional memberships in the family, associations and organisations, and the state. Kantians who believe in universal principles of duty have repeatedly seen this attempt to embed principles in practices as a justification of moral relativism, while Hegelians have continued to claim that what matters to human beings is the texture of their ethical and political experience and not their capacity to understand abstract moral precepts.

A recent contribution that illustrates the somewhat sterile character of these debates is Raymond Geuss's *Outside Ethics*. At one point Geuss writes that:

> ... in our societies serious-minded people continually ask the canonical modern ethical question ('what ought I to do?') in principle about all the situations in which they might be called upon to act, and they expect some kind of enlightenment about the possible answers to this question from an autonomous philosophical ethics established as a discipline devoted to giving such answers in purely secular terms. Getting the right answer to this question is still thought to be one of the most important things in life. (Geuss, 2005: 45–6)

This is an extraordinary claim, and one for which Geuss would be hard pressed to provide evidence. But it allows him to construct a contrast between an autonomous (Kantian) ethics, that apparently dominates the thinking of modern people everywhere, and the views of iconoclastic thinkers who have no need for definitive answers to the question of how to live and who therefore operate 'outside ethics'. One of them, according to Geuss, is Adorno. But his formulation of what Adorno believed demonstrates both why Kantian universalists will never lose heart and why sociology might still have something to say to philosophy:

> ... any attempt on the part of the individual to consider what he or she as an individual ought to do is a completely pointless exercise, and the only possibility remaining to us is to continue to reflect on the infinitely complex and subtle ways in which the falsity of the world as a whole poisons the possibilities of genuinely individual action and individual happiness. (Geuss, 2005: 56)

Even if sociologists concur that answers to the question of how to live are not to be had from 'an autonomous philosophical ethics' of the Kantian sort, they have considerably more to do than reflect on the 'falsity' of a world that 'poisons the possibilities of genuinely individual action and individual happiness', expressions that, incidentally, hardly square with Geuss's claim that the world is 'infinitely complex and subtle'. Whether it is Parsons writing about the doctor-patient encounter as an example of the professional pattern of conduct in industrial societies, Mary Douglas examining pollution behaviour and the classificatory strategies from which it arises or styles of thinking about risk, Simmel delineating the dynamics of interaction in the metropolis, Norbert Elias tracing the development of thresholds of shame and embarrassment or involvement and detachment in the baroque court, Michel Foucault telling the story of the birth of the prison and the legacy of confession within modern therapeutic practice, or Erving Goffman describing the moral career of the mental patient or the dynamics of behaviour associated with stigma, sociologists are laying bare some of the most basic features of the social life in which human beings have to deal with, encounter, and interact with one another. They are, in their way, theorists of ethics.

Nevertheless, they are theorists of ethics more in the Durkheimian sense of sociology as a science of moral phenomena; an inventory or history of *Lebensführung* is not the same as an account of how to live, a matter on which sociology seems less able to instruct us. Weber was insistent that it should not try to, but even Durkheim hesitated to specify in any detail the moral guidelines that sociology might be able to provide as a result of its investigations. The reason has something to do with the belief of social scientists in 'ethical neutrality' and 'disinterestedness', but it is also a product of the fact that, despite the emphasis placed by the entire sociological tradition on the rapidity of change in modern society, on the 'disembedding' effects that this has on the relationship between the individual and society, an enormous effort has gone into demonstrating that modern societies are stratified and hierarchical, and that modern individuals, too, are tied into structures that define who they are and what they can become. The idea that the individual could ever be free enough from social ties to be able to develop an art of living was, for decades, marginal to sociology. And as long as the popularity of writers like Bourdieu persists, it will continue to be.

Sociological Theory and Utopia

When sociology has accepted the idea that answers to the question of how to live might be had from basic principles, it has done so not by acknowledging Kantian ideas about categorical imperatives or systems of morality more generally, but by drawing our attention to the role played by utopias in the modern imagination. Utopias are conventionally thought of as visions of collective wellbeing, and on the face of it there would seem to be an irresolvable tension between the utopian imagination and the one that is oriented to the art of living, which in the philosophical tradition is a matter of how an individual shapes his or her life. The tradition of thought about the art of living that begins with Socrates and ends with Foucault is hostile to utopia because any ideal society appears to render that art superfluous; by the same token, 'the art of living' has often appeared to modern thinkers of a utopian disposition to be a matter for aristocratic aesthetes with time on their hands. Tension there certainly is, but it is not irresolvable, and so in what follows we will explore the idea that there may be individual as well as collective utopias. As we will see, such an idea is not an easy one for sociologists to accept, so much so that we will conclude with an exploration of the idea of individual utopias as it appears in the work of a novelist, Robert Musil.

According to Norbert Elias, the emergence of utopian blueprints for an ideal society occurred when modern states began to consolidate themselves territorially and to develop what Michael Mann calls infrastructural power, those resources that would be required by any state seeking to control, manage and

The Art of Living

169

administer its population (Mann, 1984). The idea that such a thing might be possible is contained in the 18th-century theory and practice of a well-ordered police state and enlightened despotism; and it went hand in hand with a proto-sociology. This sociology achieved its mature form in the 19th century with the emergence of 'the social question' and the belief of Saint-Simon, Comte and Marx that political devices could be used not only for the rational organisation of social affairs, but also for the cause of human freedom. The early modern utopias were non-places, such as Thomas More or James Harrington's islands, or the 'heavenly cities' of the enlightenment. By the 19th century, the utopian imagination had been allied to the idea of history as a science, so that the good society was not so much a non-place but a fully realisable potential contained within the movement of history itself. So we might say that 'sociology', 'socialism', 'progress' and 'utopia' were closely connected.

By the 20th century, however, it became increasingly apparent to many sociologists that precisely when it becomes possible to administer human affairs rationally – in the modern welfare state for example – utopian energies are not so much translated into action as absorbed and robbed of their critical potential. This argument can be extended to the thesis that once any utopia comes close to a concrete realisation, it cancels itself and gives rise to the melancholic reflection that utopia can only survive if it is not realised. The death of utopia has been repeatedly announced in the 20th century, but this may be seen as a series of false reports; if its death keeps having to be announced it must be more persistent and tenacious than the reports imply (Shklar, 1969; Lepenies, 1992; Levitas and Velody, 2003)

When we put the matter like that we see how ambivalent is sociology's relationship with utopia: collective utopias have accompanied sociology throughout its development as visions of a better world, but one of their features is the absence of conflict, the lifeblood of much sociology. Where would Marxist sociology be without class division? Where would Weberian sociology be without conflicting values and interests? Where would Durkheimian sociology be without the conflict between the individual and society, between anomie and fatalism? A sociology that aligned itself with utopia would abolish itself (Dahrendorf, 1968).

At the same time, a sociology that ignored utopia would trivialise itself. This partly explains why the work of at least some of the figures we have studied in this book does contain an implicit normative vision, but one whose utopian dimensions are somewhat cramped. Mary Douglas not only identified social order with shared systems of classification, she also argued that these were best maintained by ritual rather than other types of action, and argued that a decline in the strength of such systems had been brought about by 'the retreat from ritual' in later 20th-century society; but her plea for ritual was not utopian but Catholic. For all the charges of cynicism levelled at him, Erving Goffman was sincere when he described the minutiae of everyday conduct as 'the little pieties' by means of which a bearable social world is maintained; but little pieties are hardly utopia. Georg Simmel's focus on social forms was more than an exercise in formal sociology or a striving for a universal language for sociology and, with its emphasis on the distancing effects of social forms may be seen retrospectively as a rejection of the various cults of immediacy and authenticity that have arisen in Western society throughout the 20th century; but no more than that. Pierre Bourdieu's collectivist egalitarianism pervades much of his writing about social stratification; but the way he theorises it, that stratification is so entrenched that a positive vision of a better future is hard to discern.

Cynicism, Scepticism and Utopia

Now one notable feature of even this short list of names is that the ambivalent relationship between sociology and utopia cuts across the distinction that shaped the previous chapter, between cynicism and scepticism. Even if scepticism does not claim that the highest values are 'really' the expression of something else, it does appear to claim that the attempt to realise them will always fail. Isaiah Berlin was a sceptic in this respect, arguing that the gap between intention and outcome not only cannot but should not be closed; there are lofty ideals – truth, justice, liberty, beauty, equality – and the sceptic can acknowledge them to be objectively identifiable when considered separately; but they are mutually irreconcilable, which means that any political attempt to realise them all simultaneously is utopian, and utopia for Berlin must end in tyranny. For Michael Oakeshott, the politics of scepticism is opposed to the politics of faith; faith is defined by the pursuit of human perfection and human perfection is in turn to be brought about by government pursuing a single defined purpose, while scepticism is defined by the maintenance of that political order, but only that order, necessary for the pursuit of the various forms of felicity to which human beings are open.

On the other hand, another sceptic, Max Weber, managed to combine a sceptical attitude to inquiry with the belief that the utopian urge in human beings deserves respect and perhaps admiration; our own ideals and values clash with those of others 'that are just as dear to them as ours are to us', and because of this the social reality in which we move is one in which utopian striving is perpetually defeated. But the dignified response to this is not the pragmatic abandonment of utopian striving, but holding fast to ultimate values while acknowledging the tragedy of human existence.

Nor is utopia entirely alien to modern cynicism, although here the relationship is more virulent. On the one hand, the cynical reduction of ideas to interests, and the apparent indifference towards values, suggest a disdain for utopian striving. On the other, it is hard to ignore the fact that the kind of cynical procedures outlined in the previous chapter have often been deployed by those who subscribe to a politics of faith, harbour utopian dreams of their own and believe that social inquiry may contribute to their pursuit. This ambivalent attitude is expressed in the title of Engels' famous work, *Socialism: Utopian and Scientific*, which argues that the good society, far from being a utopian dream, is to be found in the movement of history itself, a history that can be known, as Marx once put it, 'with the precision of natural science' (Marx, 1975: 426).

Odo Marquard, one of Helmut Schelsky's sceptical generation in postwar Germany, described this as the 'overtribunalisation' of reality (Marquard, 1989; Schelsky, 1957), meaning that historical social reality is treated both as the source of all evil – including all the ideas one disagrees with – and of the means of judging that evil. To the question 'What shall we do and how shall we live?' the modern cynic answers: 'Study social reality scientifically, get behind appearances, and the answer will reveal itself'. The result is that the relationship between values and reality for the cynic is the reverse of what it is for the sceptic. The sceptic sees values clashing with one another in a world where our human finitude prevents them from being fully realised; the cynic by contrast sees values clashing not with other values but with reality. For the cynic, the problem with opposing values or ideals is really a problem with the social reality from which those ideals arose.

It was Karl Mannheim who, in *Ideology and Utopia*, gave the most comprehensive account of the consequences of combining cynicism backed up by science with a utopian sensibility. The cynic's basic intellectual gesture is, as Simmel says, not simply to relate ideals or ultimate values to something baser, but to reduce them to it. Utopianism appears to be the very opposite of cynicism, keeping alive a belief in such ideals. But when the utopian urge is allied to the belief in science as the highest form of cognition, then utopia, which appears to be opposed to historical and political reality, is seen as immanent to that reality as a potential built into it. The utopian urge is transformed into the belief in the correctness of one's 'analysis', and the conclusion is not that someone else's beliefs are wrong and to be argued against, but that reality is wrong and needs to be transformed.

In fact, Mannheim had considerable respect for the utopian urge in human beings and was suspicious of the way in which that urge was distorted or suppressed when allied to a version of science. In his more optimistic moments he seemed to believe that the increasing democratisation of culture and politics would so detach individuals from inherited group belonging and the contingencies and accidents of birth and social position – Bourdieu followers take note! – that they would discover forms of connection that were less and less social. In the face of the de-distantiation between social groups fostered by cultural democratisation, they would find new ways of distancing themselves from society and achieve increasingly voluntary connections with one another. What had once been an aristocratic principle of social distance would become the fate of everyone (Turner, 2003). The utopian urge in human beings would not be eliminated but would assume new and more individualistic guises.

Mannheim's ideas about the transformation of utopia anticipate by half a century a notable trend in recent sociology, the turn away from the theorisation of social structure and towards questions of ethics. If the theorisation of social structure was accompanied by visions of utopia or at least by its ghostly presence, the theorisation of ethics is accompanied by more or less explicit responses to the challenge of finding the right way to live. It is these that seemed to have gained the upper hand over older style projects for social transformation. A notable index of this is the fact that a writer like Roberto Unger, whose work is a sustained attempt to combine a critique of sociological theory's main assumptions with the preservation of a collectivist utopian vision, a combination he calls, significantly, 'armed scepticism' (Unger, 1987: 150), remains a far less popular figure than Zygmunt Bauman, whose instincts also remain utopian in the 19th-century sense but who has come to accept the difficulties that the realities of the late 20th century present to the sustaining of it.

Zygmunt Bauman: Utopia and Ambivalence

Despite the fact that Bauman's contribution to sociological theory's inventory of tools may be said to be limited, and although earlier on in this book we saw the unfortunate way in which he deploys metaphor, no contemporary sociologist has made a more sustained effort to confront the difficulties and dilemmas facing human beings today. It is not surprising that in the course of this he has had something to say about utopia.

A man who began his career in the 1950s and 1960s in Poland under the period of 'building socialism', and left in 1968 along with many other academic victims of official anti-Semitism, Bauman found that the land of Israel no more lived up to its promise than did socialist Poland, and in 1970 moved to Leeds. Leeds in the 1970s could have shattered the dreams of anyone, yet curiously enough in 1976 he published a short book called *Socialism: the active Utopia* (Bauman, 1976). 'Active utopia' is a fine phrase, referring both to Bauman's one time support for the active attempt to implement socialism in his native country and to a vision that stands in tension with social reality but which accompanies it as the potential for a better world.

It is against this background that the works that made him famous need to be understood. Bauman is sometimes called a postmodern figure, keen to emphasise the contingency and ambivalence of modernity against an enlightenment project at whose centre lies the control and planning of both institutional and private life. But if there is a thread that runs from *Modernity and the Holocaust* in 1988 to *Consuming Life* in 2007 (and beyond) it is egalitarian socialism, the only question being whether it is achievable by means of rational planning/enlightened despotism or through the active efforts of human beings in an increasingly individualised society. In an avalanche of books, Bauman has repeatedly insisted on the failures of enlightenment modernity, its dead ends and disasters; but this is easily misunderstood, because unlike sceptics from Weber to Oakeshott, the rejection of planned or administered progress is a long and painful coming to terms with his own previous commitments. What seems obvious to some liberal thinkers – that the dream of complete rationality, or of human perfection, of the totally administered society, is no more than that – is to Bauman something that must be constantly repeated before one can convince oneself that it might be true. The question that hangs over much of his work (and over that of many of his generation, particularly in France) is: if socialism through rational planning cannot work, what kind of vision remains?

In *Life in Fragments* in 1995 he answered this question, and with it conveyed his own sense of the distinction between an art of living fit for our times and the utopias that our times make available. Here he makes it clear that what he calls postmodern society is not a post-utopian society; on the contrary, it produces its own utopias. He calls these utopias those of the market and of 'the technological fix', and says that they are active in a way that differs from the active utopia that was/is socialism.

> Postmodern utopias are anarchistic ... They envisage a world with rights, without duties, and above all without rulers and a gens d'armes, except such as are needed to guarantee a secure promenade stroll and protect shopping bags against the muggers ... They militate against design and plan, against sacrifice in the name of future benefits, against the delay of gratification – all these rules-of-thumb of yore deemed effective thanks to the belief that the future can be controlled, bound, forced to conform to the likeness painted in advance, and hence what one does now matters for later ... The spontaneity of the world which postmodern utopias conjure up makes nonsense of all concern with the future except the concern with being free from concern with the future ... Postmodern utopias want us ... to celebrate the surrender of (demanding, stretching, vexing) ideals as the final act of emancipation. (Bauman, 1995: 27; 2007: 104)

These are the words not of a postmodernist, but of an old socialist lamenting the individualism and selfishness of the times, times in which an active utopia that could only have been implemented by rational administration and planning within large, modern, centralised organisations that educate citizens in the art of delayed gratification and self-sacrifice, has been replaced with one that depends upon the operation of the free market and upon the actions of individuals ready to live in the present moment. 'It is not at all clear,' he continues, 'how the cause of morality, goodness, justice can be seriously promoted in a world which has seemingly come to terms with its own groundlessness, does not seem to mind it any more and is little perturbed by the absence of agencies charged with the task of keeping chaos at bay' (Bauman, 1995: 27).

Bauman has repeatedly described the slaughters brought about by 20th-century totalitarianism as the logical consequence of modernity's basic organising principles rather than as a regression to irrational or premodern ideas or as political religions. But this strategy also allows him, when lamenting those features of postmodern society that seem to render utopian socialism a thing of the past, to stress the rationality and modernity of socialism. For the other side of the claim that rational planning and control – summed up by what he calls 'the gardening state' – gave rise to the horrors of the 20th century – 'a century of camps' – is the melancholia of one for whom planning in its socialist variant did at least aim to improve the human condition.

Bauman's hostility to the idea of personal or individual utopias is all of a piece with his search for something else, an ethical – rather than a planned or organised – socialism. In *Life in Fragments* he writes:

There would be no interest in the 'quality of life' (the concept itself would hardly have been coined) if not for the widespread, often vague but always acute and unnerving feeling that life as it is 'is not good enough'. Discussion about quality of life is not so much about deciding what a truly good life would be like, as it is about giving that vague, elusive feeling of disaffection some flesh and bone ...

For that reason the 'quality of life' discourse is in its innermost core a critique of daily life. (Bauman, 1995: 47)

Bauman's writings over the last fifteen years are an extension of that critique, but one that sees individual utopias as part of the phenomenon that needs to be criticised. This is because the problems that once generated utopian solutions remain largely the same as during the period of sociology's emergence in the 19th century: 'the great issues of ethics – like human rights, social justice, balance between peaceful cooperation and personal self-assertion, synchronisation of individual conduct and collective welfare – have lost nothing of their topicality. They only need to be seen, and dealt with, in a novel way' (Bauman, 1993: 4). *Postmodern Ethics* is Bauman's most important attempt to deal with them; if the egalitarian collective utopias of the past degenerated into organised repression, the impulse that once motivated them remains and, in an age of disorganised capitalism or de-institutionalisation, can be satisfied not by means of individual utopias but by means of an ethics fit for the times. The uprooting of the self is an opportunity for an ethics that respects human dignity more thoroughly than collective utopias once did, and does so because it does not require that the relationships between individuals be mediated by a communal authority called the state or by the postulated communities – or 'neo-tribes' – that now form a staple of multiculturalism (Bauman, 1993: 141); these stifle the individual's capacity for 'moral discretion' (Bauman, 1993: 46). But Bauman is clear that that capacity is equally stifled when, released from the constraints of society, individuals become the slaves of their passions or desires: 'neither reason ... nor passion ... help the self to be moral' (Bauman, 1993: 132). Nor do individual utopias, an example of what Bauman, ever the socialist moralist, would see as postmodern decadence. In the end, what matters to him is whether, among the different life strategies available to modern men and women, there is scope and potential for an ethical relationship based upon the capacity of individuals to 'take responsibility for the other'. Here, it does not seem to matter whether social science can make a difference to this.

In this respect Bauman differs from the other figures whose work we have addressed in this book, all of whom acquired classic status by combining a deep concern for the fate of humanity with a contribution to sociology's inventory of tools, techniques and theoretical moves. Of course, the combination was different in each case as we implied right at the start of this chapter. It is time to find out what that combination was, and so we turn to two classic reflections, not only on the relationship between the art of living and utopia, but also on the threefold relationship between the art of living, utopia and science.

The Art of Living

Max Weber: Vocation and the Art of Living

'Science as a Vocation' was a lecture given by Weber in 1917 during World War I, in response to a request from students for the great man to tell them how to live. Predictably enough, Weber did not give them what they wanted, but instead offered them his conclusions about the human condition, based on a forty-year career of scholarship. I say 'forty years' here advisedly: since Weber was 53 at the time this would put the beginning of his scholarly career at 13. But that is right: consider the fact that at the age of 15 he gave his parents a Christmas present in the form of an essay written by himself, entitled 'Observations on the Ethnic Character, Development and History of the Indo-European peoples' (Weber, 1975: 46).

The most important point is that science – *Wissenschaft*, or systematic knowledge in general – cannot tell us what to do and how to live. It cannot tell us how to live because, while in the modern world science has been freed from the (mostly religious) fetters that once bound intellectual curiosity, it also has to take its place as one 'source of value' among others. In other words, the forces that once limited science were also its anchorages, so that we can say of modern human beings that never were they so free to take scientific knowledge as far as it can go, but never were they so free to ignore the results of science and choose alterative sources of value and worth. There is no doubt that we live in an increasingly scientific age, perhaps an increasingly secular one. But this means only that there are, in principle, no incalculable forces at work in the world; it does not mean that we should refuse to believe in the existence of such forces when we think about how to live, or that we should see the undoubted technical superiority of science as implying anything for ethics or politics. The scientist has a responsibility to the truth, but the politician has a responsibility to power, while the religious believer has a responsibility to God or the cosmos, and there is no obvious hierarchy between these values, nor any obvious means of choosing one and rejecting the others. Weber's famous last words were 'the true is the truth', but a custodian of the truth is no less humble than a custodian of power or of faith in God.

Does this make science – and here, social science – irrelevant to the business of living? Not at all. Ethical ideals cannot be derived from the truth about society, but since human conduct is the conduct of beings capable of orienting themselves through reference to values, and since it is the job of social science to study the social world from the point of view of value-related action, the social scientist may be of assistance to the actor by providing him or her with a measure of clarity about the conditions and the consequences of the various courses of action that he or she proposes to undertake. But what science cannot do, what lies beyond the limits of its capacity, is provide a rationale or any other foundation for values or ideals.

Now there is something double-edged about the conclusions Weber draws from this. His most famous work had stressed the role played by ascetic Protestantism in the emergence of modern rationalised society. Central to asceticism was the emphasis on consistency of conduct, on ensuring that the different aspects or episodes of a human life fitted into a coherent whole, and one might expect that, given his admiration for the ideal of 'vocation' that played such a role in providing an anchorage for such conduct, he would argue that science as a vocation can encourage consistency of conduct by pointing out the contradictions that can often arise between ideals and actions. There is certainly an element of this but consistency for Weber has nothing to do with the ideal of achieving some sort of balance or harmony between the different demands that different aspects of the social world present to us. He thought that the way to consistency of conduct was to specialise, to make a clear distinction between the values to which you can commit yourself and those that are less important, and to allow those values to define your identity. Weber certainly believed that to see with different eyes you needed to remove your current set of blinkers and appreciate the existence of different points of view; it is the job of social scientists – a job they share with novelists – to foster such an appreciation, but they must also remind people that any worthwhile achievement depends upon putting those blinkers back on again or donning another pair. How this is supposed to happen remains a mystery for Weber. He could not explain why he himself worked with such intensity as a servant of science, nor could he explain – although at times he made some half-hearted efforts to – the sources of, say, religious experience, describing himself famously as 'religiously unmusical'. And so, at the very end of 'Science as a Vocation' he says only that it is possible for you to meet the demands laid down by the complexities of life in the modern world if you 'find the demon that holds the very fibres of your life'.

We can reframe Weber's ideas here by making a distinction between two approaches to the art of living. Following Kierkegaard, we could call them the ethical and aesthetic. To live ethically is to live with consistency, to find a way of connecting the various episodes of your life and making of them a coherent whole; to live aesthetically is to live from one experience to another – 'from hand to mouth' as Weber once said of Catholics. This is another version of the distinction that we mentioned earlier between leading a life and letting it happen. The point here is that although this distinction is central to much of modern ethics, for Weber there are numerous points of view, or ultimate values, by means of which to maintain it. They may be ethical in the narrow sense of the term, but they may be political or religious or aesthetic or even economic, as long as you can find the demon that holds the fibres of your life. Here we see how Weber's statement of the problem faced by human beings is more generous than Bauman's. Bauman seems to believe that we are either capable of behaving ethically, in accordance with principles such as justice, equality and so on, or we succumb to postmodern decadence, even in the pursuit of 'individual utopias'; Weber tells us that there are many different ways to live a worthwhile life, only some of which may involve the pursuit of ethical principles.

Note here that Weber's idea of consistency echoes but remains distinct from the Socratic idea of the examined life. Alexander Nehamas describes that ideal like this:

The Socratic dialogues demand of their audience what Socrates asks of his interlocutors: to examine their beliefs on any subject of importance to them, to determine to what other beliefs they are logically related, to accept only those that are compatible with one another, and to live their lives accordingly. (Nehamas, 1998: 42)

Weber was less interested in consistency between beliefs than in the capacity of individuals to serve something higher than themselves and then to work out the relationship between their beliefs and the actions they proposed to carry out on the basis of them. The examined life in Weber's thought is a life of struggle, because to maintain a sense of what it is you are serving you have to face the fact that there are opposing ideals – and types of ideal – that are 'just as dear to others as ours are to us'.

Moreover, this imperative does not follow in any simple way from Weberian social science. Science, whose goal is the 'pitiless sobriety of judgement' (Hennis, 2000), is a specialised business with no prescriptive power. What we can learn from science is clarity about the conditions and consequences of our actions, along with an appreciation of the exemplary character of those who have devoted themselves to science as a vocation or to anything else as a vocation. They teach us that the only worthwhile achievement is a specialised one, that the only way to lead a life rather than let it happen is to don blinkers, and that the only way to don blinkers is to abandon oneself to a goal greater than oneself. Only in that way will you have what Weber called 'personality'.

Weber has no ideology to promote, no clear agenda for social change, and an attitude to inquiry that encourages us to appreciate the variety of perspectives from which a meaningful life might be led. Indeed, the ultimate object of social scientific inquiry is a world that has been formed by people relating the reality in which they move to the values they hold most dear and trying to reduce the gap between the two. But this means that if there is a pitiless sobriety of judgement at the heart of social science, then there is a pitiless hardness in Weber's vision of what a person can be, exemplified by the scarcely veiled suggestion – made at the end of both 'Science as a Vocation' and 'Politics as Vocation' – that if you cannot 'find your demon' then there is always run-of-the-mill, bureaucratically conducted business to fall back on, or the old churches to be embraced by. Weber here presents us with more than a challenge. He seems to be goading us to show him that we are tough enough, that we are more than naïve idealists or romantics, worthy to live a genuinely led life in a world that offers no instructions as to how it should be done.

But what if history and society are not like that? What if, instead of talking of ideas and ideals and values and beliefs, we conceptualise the relationship between the individual and society along the lines set down by phenomenological sociology, by Simmel or Goffman, or for that matter, Mary Douglas? Although his writing has sometimes been lumped together with Weber's, you don't have to read very far into one of Alfred Schutz's essays to realise that he was a very different thinker from Weber. Schutz is even less concerned than Weber with providing prescriptions for action; his virtue is – as we saw in the last chapter – to have given us some of the most subtle and nuanced accounts of the variety of ways in which we as social actors make and sustain a world. One of his more neglected essays also contains some hints about how to live.

Alfred Schutz: Well-Informed Citizenship and the Art of Living

Schutz's essay on the well-informed citizen was written in the 1950s and is a reflection on the situation of individuals in a modern world increasingly pervaded by the effects of science and technology; it is subtitled: 'an essay on the social distribution of knowledge'. The term 'social distribution' has nothing to do with a concern with inequality or with the difference between those who have access to intellectual resources and those who do not. Rather it revolves around a contrast between three attitudes to reality, three modes of world-orientation. Each is defined by a relationship between what individuals need to know and what they may disregard for the purposes of the activity they are undertaking. Let us say that every individual is surrounded by culture – artefacts, ideas, knowledge – and that this culture is divided into zones of relevance. Let us say further that there are four of these, and let us call them the world within my reach, consisting of the things that I can transform and shape by my actions; the world of the possibly relevant, of things that are not within my immediate reach but which might be brought within it should I need to take them into consideration; the world of the relatively irrelevant, consisting of things that I am unlikely to take seriously though which I may, in an emergency or sudden disruption to my routine; and the world of the absolutely irrelevant.

In addition Schutz says that every action has a motive, but that there is a distinction between what he calls 'in order to' and 'because' motives, motives that are our own and motives that derive from our various forms of social membership.

Armed with this equipment Schutz then says that there are three basic types of attitude to reality within a civilisation like ours; they are those of what he calls the man on the street, the expert, and the well-informed citizen. Schutz calls them types, but it is clear that each of us can become each of these figures during the course of a single day. The man on the street is you or me in so far as we have 'projects', everyday tasks that we have chosen to carry out, and for which all that we require is 'recipe knowledge'. We want to phone or email a friend, but all we need to know is how to use the phone or how to click on the mouse at the right time. We do not need to know how a computer or a telephone works. In principle we could find out, but the successful email or text message does not depend on such knowledge. It does depend on an acquaintance with the keys or buttons, but not much more, something not always appreciated by those young people who seek to mock their elders' efforts to use mobile phones, as though they had mastered something technical. In fact, most of our everyday projects are carried out using equipment that embodies a level of technical sophistication well beyond the knowledge of those who use it. Weber made the same point in less abstract terms: the modern worker knows incomparably less about his tools than the medieval craftsman. In everyday life, then, the boundary between what we need to know and what we can disregard is well-defined.

The expert is a type who possesses a specialised knowledge of a particular discipline or field, and whose motives for action are defined by its rules. Although the expert may have chosen this activity, the fact that he or she submits to the rules of the game means that he or she operates on the basis of what Schutz calls 'because' motives. Moreover, like the man on the street, the expert has to have a clear sense of the boundary between matters that are relevant and those that are irrelevant to the activity. Any one of us is acting as an expert whenever we concentrate on a particular activity in which we possess a definite skill; but the figure Schutz has in mind is the natural scientist who, for instance, may be prepared in principle to take into account the ethical import of what he or she is doing, but whose activity could never get off the ground unless clear decisions had been made – by other people who came before him – about what is and what is not relevant.

Now Schutz contrasts these two types with that of what he calls 'the well-informed citizen', who is a far more reflective individual because of the fact that he or she will 'restrict, as far as possible, the zone of the irrelevant, mindful that what is today relatively irrelevant may be imposed tomorrow as a primary relevance and that the province of the so-called absolutely irrelevant may reveal itself as the home of the anonymous powers which may overtake him' (Schutz, 1964: 131). Schutz believed that this mode of world-orientation is not easily achieved; not least because so much of our knowledge of the social world is socially derived from others, on whom we are, moreover, wont to rely. The sources of such 'socially approved knowledge' may be experts whose authority we have little choice but to respect; they may also be fellow members of the same 'in-group', whose opinions it would be foolish or difficult to ignore. But socially approved knowledge in modern society is increasingly that derived from public opinion; and public opinion is little more than the aggregated opinions of the man on the street. This public opinion is not informed opinion, but it does increasingly 'impose itself as relevant upon the better-informed members of the community' (Schutz, 1964: 134). Meanwhile, on the other flank, so to speak, expert knowledge remains unquestioned as a possible source of socially approved knowledge, and confronts the individual as one of those 'anonymous powers' that threaten to overwhelm him. The essay ends somewhat limply with a plea on behalf of the well-informed citizen; in a democratic society, this figure, the boundary between whose zones of relevance are fluid, must 'make his private opinion prevail over the public opinion of the man on the street' (Schutz, 1964: 131).

It would be too simple to say that prolonged exposure to Weber will lead you to admire the expert or specialist committed to his or her 'vocation', while reading Schutz will generate the sort of open-mindedness and sensitivity to nuance of the well-informed citizen. Weber did say that the only worthwhile achievement today is a specialised achievement, but there is a difference between an expert in Schutz's sense and a specialist who does what he does with passion and commitment, for such a figure – be he scientist, politician or businessman – is admirable, undergoing a fate that is exemplary; Schutz, meanwhile, though he championed the well-informed citizen, the boundary between whose zones of relevance are fluid, was himself a master of the kind of precise, considered, not to say dry sentence that one might expect from an expert like a laboratory technician … or banker. But whatever their positions on what sort of a life is worth living, or on the art of living, both prompt us to ask: by what means do I orient my conduct? In 'Science as a Vocation' Weber said that the social sciences could do more than prompt, that they could force the individual to seek clarity about his or her ultimate values.

Weber's use of the word 'force' hints that he faces a recalcitrant public all too ready to ignore science's demand for clarity and to enter the arms of the old churches or their modern functional equivalents, political mass movements, and the pathos of his view is reinforced by his refusal to set out in any detail how a life appropriate to the times might be led. If his historical sociology is thick description, 'find your demon' is a thin prescription. And despite the suggestiveness of his distinction between three kinds of attitude to reality, Schutz's well-informed citizen, too, is a somewhat sketchy figure for a writer of such cultivation.

Had he lived longer, Weber might have written his planned book about Tolstoy, and told us more about Dostoyevsky; his intention to do so suggests that he thought that ideas about how to live might be more readily had from novels than from social science. In a final section, then, we will take him up on this and turn to Robert Musil. Musil (1880–1940) belonged to the generation between Weber's and Schutz's, and attended Simmel's lectures in Berlin. A trained philosopher and scientist, he thought that there were questions about the human condition and particularly the modern human condition that literature could address in a more sustained way than philosophy or science, including social science, ever could.

The Three Utopias of Robert Musil

For the sociological theorist who is also interested in the art of living *The Man without Qualities* is a rich store of ideas and, in its discussions of 'individual utopias', provides a way of reframing many of the concerns that we have touched on already. A novel that contains some remarkable characterisation, it is also replete with stand-alone disquisitions and incomparable passages of dialogue; it combines the imaginative sympathies typical of 19th-century realism with a modernism that raises questions about the reality status of social experience. How knowledge and experience are possible is as important as what we know and feel.

The central character is Ulrich, who, having been trained as a mathematician and engineer, finds himself, at the age of 32, asking what this training has been for:

If someone had asked him at any point while he was writing treatises on mathematical problems or mathematical logic, or engaged in some scientific project, what it was he hoped to achieve, he would have answered that there was only one question worth thinking about, the question of the right way to live. (Musil, 1995: 275)

The question pervades much of the novel. In his search for an answer Ulrich comes upon a number of distinct approaches to life; three of them are described as utopias, and each one echoes or anticipates the terms in which Schutz describes the three types of human being.

The Utopia of Exact Living

The first utopia is called the ideal of 'exact living', and is mentioned in connection with the difference between the natural and the human sciences: 'all the knowledge that has led our species from wearing animal skins to people flying, complete with its proofs, would fill a handful of reference books, but a bookcase the size of the earth would not suffice to hold all the rest' (Musil, 1995: 264). Since there seems to be no progress at all in matters of morality, 'we carry on our human business in a most irrational manner when we do not use those methods by which the exact sciences have forged ahead' (Musil, 1995: 264). This raises a question: in the lives that all of us have to lead, could there be the equivalent of what he calls the scientist's three small treatises, pieces of work in which, for a time, an individual's capacity for achievement takes on the maximum intensity? Musil's somewhat stark conclusion is that there could be, only that it would involve only speaking when there was something to say, and 'remaining indifferent whenever one has not that ineffable sensation of spreading out one's arms and being borne upward on a wave of creativeness' (Musil, 1995: 265). The consequence of this would be, to put it in the terms in which Schutz expressed it, a more rational distribution of individual self-knowledge, in which one would live morally only when the occasion demanded it and for the rest of one's time attempt to follow the ideal of precision: 'There would be no talent left, only genius' (ibid.: 265). Musil/Ulrich anticipates the objection that this is utopian by admitting that this is precisely what it is and proclaiming that it is none the worse for that. Utopias are, after all, simply possibilities obstructed by current circumstance. Utopias in action are 'experiments in which the possible changing of an element is observed, together with the effects that it would cause in that compound phenomenon we call life' (Musil, 1995: 266). The ideal here is one of exactitude being allowed to expand and develop, not by spreading out across the whole of a man's life – for that would diminish the intensity it was capable of generating – but in such a way that that life becomes a combination of precision and indefiniteness, where precision is more than that of the pedantic orderer of facts or of the man who – like Talcott Parsons or Niklas Luhmann – believes himself to be attached in some way to a higher order which he calls his 'system'.

This ideal of exactitude is thought by Musil/Ulrich to be one that the modern specialist might follow. But it inhabits him, lives within him, only during that part of the day when he is at work. This is paradoxical because, as Schutz would say, it is part of the specialist – or expert – professional's dignity to have 'because motives' rather than in-order-to motives, to have well-defined boundaries between his zones of relevance. Mixing professional conduct with utopian ideas must seem like 'an improper experiment on persons engaged in serious business' (Musil, 1995: 266). Yet Musil's utopian ideal of exactitude implies that the professional would, so to speak, transcend the boundaries of his/her profession simply by applying the standards of exactitude which govern professional activity to an element of life to which it is not normally applied. This would not, again putting it in Schutz's terms, turn him/her from an expert into a well-informed citizen, because for the well-informed citizen the boundaries between what is relevant and what is not have been declared open and fluid, albeit that it is not clear for how long such openness is possible. On the contrary, the ideal of exactitude entails that the professional would display the expert's exactitude in a new, but equally restricted domain. But the very fact that it was not his/her normal domain of expertise would be enough to qualify it as experimental, even if in the rest of his life he remained indifferent and inexact, satisfied with the recipe knowledge of the man in the street.

It is not immediately obvious whether this is a modest proposal or a grandiose one. The British sociologist who extended the ordering activity of the survey researcher into the domestic domain, developing a card index system for his chest of drawers, but continuing to wear the clothes themselves with glorious imprecision, might be said to be 'experimental' in this sense, but one cannot help feeling that this is not what Musil had in mind. Especially when one considers that one non-specialist domain that Musil thought the ideal of exactitude might be extended into was 'matters of the soul'. Indeed, part of the aim of his life's work was to overcome the oppositon between 'precision and soul'. On the other hand, set alongside some of the remarks in Weber's work this too sounds like a modest proposal. In Weber, when the specialist transcends the limits of his activity he does so not in order to throw a pebble into the pond of life and create a few ripples, or to modify the terms in which an activity bordering on his professional vocation is conducted; he does so in order to discover some point of view from which life as a whole might have meaning. The connection between intellect and soul is far more explosive in Weber: whereas Musil's utopia of exactitude takes specialism into other areas, including perhaps matters of the soul, Weber's specialist scientist is incapable of genuine achievement of any sort unless he is driven by a passion, unless he has worked out his relationship with or become open to 'the demon that holds the very fibres of his life'. 'Soul' here is not one of a number of possible objects of intellect, as it is for Musil, but the basis of all intellect. Musil said that there was 'too little intellect in matters of the soul'; for Weber there was too little soul in matters of the intellect.

In the face of his own pleas for precision in matters of the soul Musil seems to have believed that, under the pressures of modern living, the utopia of exactitude readily degenerates, that the one who pursues it is likely to lack the strength to open his arms out and be borne upwards on a wave of creativeness, and so find himself back where he started, in mere specialism. And at this point, the opposite, the 'inaccurate human type', might just as easily assert himself.

> ... there are really two kinds of outlook, which not only conflict with one another but, which is worse, usually coexist side by side in total non-communication except to assure each other that they are both needed, each in its place. The one is satisfied to be precise and stick to the facts, while the other is not, but always looks at the whole picture and derives its insights from so-called great and eternal truths. The first achieves success, the other scope and prestige. (Musil, 1995: 268)

Ulrich thinks that he is living in an age in which 'uncertainty had made its comeback': 'Science had begun to be outdated, and the unfocused type of person that dominates the present had begun to assert itself' (Musil, 1995: 269). While Musil is writing about Europe on the eve of World War I, his remark does seem rather readily applicable to sociology since the 1980s. There, all manner of unfocused types have achieved scope and prestige as the champions of exactitude and precision are marginalised.

The Utopia of Essayism, or Living Hypothetically

The second individual utopia, again one which presupposes the exhaustion of collective utopian energies, and one which receives more sustained attention in *The Man without Qualities*, is that of 'living hypothetically'. The relationship with the ideal of exactitude is largely competitive.

If exactitude is the ideal of the professional's inner person, then living hypothetically is the ideal of the young person who is not yet fully formed, who is not yet able to say that he or she is on the way to becoming a professional; not just any young person, for these figures are never concrete individuals but shorthand terms for a kind of sensibility. Living hypothetically is characteristic for a young person who both desires large terms of reference – who thinks about the big questions – but who for that very reason 'cannot say yes to anything without reservation, cannot believe in anything perfect, while at the same time everything that comes his way behaves as if it were perfect' (Musil, 1995: 269). The present for such a person is 'nothing but a hypothesis one has not yet finished with'. The young person with an eye on the big questions is always seeking an answer, always sees his latest enthusiasm as a possible answer, the best thing, but because of this is always ready to discard in favour of a new one. The young person who wants to live like this fears nothing so much as a vocational education, for 'a character, a profession, a definite mode of existence – for him these are notions through which the skeleton is already peering, the skeleton that is all that will be left of him in the end' (Musil, 1995: 269).

Although this might sound like no more than a refusal to grow up, Musil identifies a 'mature form' of living hypothetically, and he calls it ... 'essayism'! We have already seen that both Simmel and Adorno praised the essay as a form of writing; Musil asks whether it might be something more, whether essayism might be a way of living too. What is the essay? It is:

... not the provisional or incidental expression of a conviction that might on a more favourable occasion be elevated to the status of truth or that might just as easily be recognised as error ... an essay is the unique and unalterable form that a man's inner life takes in a decisive thought. Nothing is more alien to it than that irresponsibility and semi-finishedness of mental images known as subjectivity; but neither are 'true' and 'false', 'wise' and 'unwise', terms that can be applied to such thoughts ... and yet the essay is subject to laws that are no less strict for appearing to be delicate and ineffable. There have been more than a few of such essaysists, masters of the inner hovering life, but there would be no point in naming them. Their domain lies between religion and knowledge, between example and doctrine, between *amor intellectualis* and poetry; they are saints with and without religion, and sometimes they are also simply men on an adventure who have gone astray. (Musil, 1995: 273)

Now going on an adventure and losing one's way doesn't seem like much of a philosophy of life, especially for today's student, burdened with the need to plan a career and make full use of the incoherent combination of specialist and 'transferable' skills that universities now pretend to teach. Yet as Musil says, if there is any category of person for whom the adventure is likely to be attractive it is the young person whose personality is not yet fully formed, the student, the reader ... the reader, for example, of books of and about sociological theory.

The idea of living essayistically, of the adventure, doesn't receive much of an airing in books about classical sociological theory. Except of course in the work of Simmel – who else? – who wrote an essay about it. Simmel begins 'The Adventure' by saying that the different elements of the individual's life process already display a mundane connection with one another, having a relationship with what precedes and succeeds it that cannot be broken. Having thus anticipated and punctured the pretensions of every theorist of narrative in the 20th century, he discusses the adventure as a category of experience; it refers to something discrete, with a beginning and an end that have no obvious connection with those events and elements which form the otherwise coherent biographical whole. The adventure is a foreign body in the midst of our existence, like a work of art or a dream. But it is more than this, for here, something marginal, isolated or accidental acquires an importance it would not otherwise possess, at the extreme turning into something with the character of necessity. The gambler, for instance, is an adventurer who combines openness to the unpredictable with fatalism about the outcome of his actions. The adventure involves the mutual entailment of the accidental and the essential: 'despite its accidental nature, its extra-territoriality with respect to the continuity of life, it nevertheless connects with the character and identity of the bearer of that life' (Simmel, 1997: 224). The adventurer gives priority to the process of life over its contents. It is even possible to see one's whole life as an adventure, for example when we say that it is something impermanent when compared to a metaphysical order set over against it, as in the idea of the transmigration of souls.

Sociologists of the life course may be interested to know that Simmel thinks that the adventure is not possible in old age, because only youth can give priority to process over content, only youth can consider the objective significance of the material of life to be less important than the life which bears this content. The content of our life is, as we have heard Simmel say earlier, in the long run grasped by forms which weave themselves between one another: ethics, religion, art and so on. There is always a relationship between life's contents and its forms such that the two cannot, in the course of our everyday life, be separated. But this is precisely what can happen in the adventure.

> For it consists not in the contents which are gained or lost, in pleasure or pain, this is accessible to us in other forms of life. But the fact that there is here a radicalism with which life is felt as a life's tension, as the *rubato* of the life process, that the quantity of these tensions are great enough to separate life wholly from its contents, that is what makes mere experience into an adventure. (Simmel, 1997: 227)

In old age, by contrast, life is either rigidly centralised, with no possibility of peripheral or marginal interests taking centre stage, or marked by the collapse of the centre and the occupation with everyday trivialities. Or to put it once again in Schutz's terms, in old age a kind of expert – with no interest in anything other than what has already been established – and a kind of man on the street – occupied only with projects that require recipe knowledge – triumph over the well-informed citizen.

Now, given sociology's scientific ambitions and pretensions, it is not obvious that an ideal of life as an adventure can be extracted from it. When the classical theorists did think about these questions they tended to stress the continuity of a life, as witnessed by Weber's Protestant Ethic studies and the concern with asceticism in the sociology of religion, by Durkheim's lament at the biographical discontinuity consequent on anomie in *Suicide*, by Freud's emphasis on the disruptive character of trauma; Goffman's remarks on the 'shameless game' that self-presentation becomes in the unpredictable setting of the mental asylum can be seen as a subtle endorsement of the ideal of biographical stability (Goffman, 1968: 165).

It has been left largely to philosophers or philosophically-inclined social theorists to articulate a vision of how to live without continuity. Richard Rorty is one of those who has embraced the contingency of selfhood (Rorty, 1989), but perhaps the most notable figure here is Michel Foucault, and it is no accident that he, like Musil and Simmel and Adorno, has had something to say about the essay:

> The essay – which should be understood as the assay or test by which, in the game of truth, one undergoes changes, and not as the simplistic appropriation of others for the purpose of communication – is the living substance of philosophy, at least if we assume that philosophy is still what it was in times past, i.e. an 'ascesis', *askesis*, an exercise of oneself in the activity of thought ... The studies that follow ... are the record of a long and tentative exercise that needed to be revised and corrected again and again. It was a philosophical exercise. The object was to learn to what extent the effort to think one's own history can free thought from what it silently thinks, and so enable it to think differently. (Foucault, 1990: 8–9)

So Musil's living essayistically is the mature form of an adventure both intellectual and ethical. Contrary to the Cartesian/Kantian idea that the search for truth entails a subject that knows itself, Foucault championed the idea that the search for truth is inseparable from a form of asceticism, an asceticism that, in contrast to the rigourism of Christian ethics based on a code, entails a constant working on and willingness to change oneself. Foucault sometimes calls this a 'stylisation' of the self, sometimes an 'aesthetics of existence'; sometimes he traces it back to ancient Greece and a non-codified, pre-Christian ethics, sometimes he sees in it an aspect of enlightenment (Osborne, 1998). Either way, it is clear that Foucault seeks to identify a way of living that is based neither on an ideal of scientific exactitude nor on an ethical code. Positioning himself outside ethics but also outside science, he says in a famous interview:

> ... in our society, art has become something which is related only to objects and not to individuals, or to life. That art is something which is specialised or which is done by experts who are artists. But couldn't everyone's life become a work of art? Why should the lamp or the house be an art object, but not our life? ... From the idea that the self is not given to us, I think that there is only one practical consequence: we have to create ourselves as a work of art. (Foucault, 1991: 350–1)

Foucault was, perhaps, less puzzled than he ought to have been by the question of how this is to be achieved. Musil was not: 'a man who is after the truth sets out to be a man of learning; a man who wants to give free play to his subjectivity sets out, perhaps, to be a writer. But what is a man to do who is after something that lies in between?' (Musil, 1995: 274).

The Utopia of Everyday Life

So we have two versions of an individual utopia: exactitude and living hypothetically, the utopia of the established professional versus that of the young student, precision in a domain bordering one's specialist field and the essay/adventure, the expert as he might be if he could be more than an expert and the well-informed citizen as he might be if he could turn the blurring of the boundaries between his zones of relevance into an ideal. And we may say that every time he or she opens a book or hears a lecture, the student of sociology sits caught between these two ideals, being pulled now towards the ideal of sociology as a professional activity – research methods, interview schedules, computer-assisted ethnography, the tyranny of accurate referencing – now towards sociology as something looser, a mode of sympathy, a way of approaching reality that would be ready to accept its own provisionality. And how often does this tension express itself unproductively in the student 'essay', a piece of writing that is neither a striving for exactitude, nor really an 'essay' at all. No wonder Americans call it an 'assignment'.

Later in the novel Musil enters more murky waters, where even the more formal sociological theorist might fear to follow him. Firstly he introduces a third possibility, that 'even ordinary life is of a utopian nature' (Musil, 1995: 394). This idea occurs in the course of one of the frankly unimaginable conversations between Ulrich and his friends Walter and Clarisse. It begins with Ulrich elaborating 'the programme of living the history of ideas instead of the history of the world'. The difference 'would lie, less in what happened than in the significance attached to it, in the intention associated with it, in the system embracing each individual happening. The system at present prevailing was that of reality, and it was like a bad play'. The point of living the history of ideas would be that if we did so we could regard our experiences 'with as much detachment as if they were something painted or as if one were listening to a song' (Musil, 1995: 396). To this Walter counters that when one measures this ideal against reality 'it will turn out to be, at most, literature'.

'If you will permit me', Ulrich conceded, 'to include all the other arts under that heading too, all doctrines of the art of living, all religions and so on, then, certainly, I will make a similar assertion, namely that our existence ought to consist wholly and solely of literature'. (Musil, 1995: 397)

Walter then objects that a life lived solely according to such an ideal would, by making art or literature ubiquitous, make it superfluous. For what would be the point of an art or literature that was not in some way a challenge to, or in our terms a re-description of, reality from the point of view of an ideal? Is Ulrich's romanticism – the world as a book or a painting – not the mirror image of the sociologist of culture's functionalist cynicism, and equally unable to do justice to art or literature's capacity to make a claim on us?

Ulrich counters that that is only true if the point of art is to seek perfection, whereas true music or art or literature cuts itself so free from the words or sounds or images that tie it to reality that it goes floating up like a balloon, a balloon we call 'beauty'. A life lived according to the precepts of art would be 'a ruthless upheaval, far more cruel than any political revolution was'. To this Walter responds that such a maxim would be more exacting than any categorical imperative or religious commandment, since it would demand that the individual be 'the poetic creator of his own life', and the failure to live up to such a standard would have consequences far worse than any moral loosening that follows from a failure to live according to an ethical imperative. The individual who sought to be the poetic creator of his own life but then failed would be reduced to the condition of an animal, prey to 'his urges, his moods and the usual banal passions of humanity, in a word, he would be at the mercy of the most utterly impersonal element in the make-up of a human being, and for as long as the obstruction persisted, he would just have to carry on sturdily letting happen to himself, so to speak, whatever happened to occur to him' (Musil, 1995: 400).

Walter's objection to Ulrich reminds us of Weber's warnings in 'Science as a Vocation', only in Weber what is opposed to letting life happen is not art but 'leading a life', taking life and subordinating it to an ultimate value. It also reminds us of Weber's remark that those who set out to bring their 'personality' into their work end by producing exactly the opposite, a series of standard, typical effects. Just as Walter seeks to preserve the distinction between art and reality, Weber insists upon the distinction between science and reality. Or framed in Schutz's terms, the attempt to saturate reality with literature, or to live the history of ideas rather than the history of the world, though it may look like the antithesis of the attitude of the man in the street, easily reproduces it because it cannot recognise the difference between art and everyday life, or between science and everyday life. It is the same sort of process that Adorno identified for free time and leisure time, enlightenment and myth. By contrast, both the utopia of exactitude and that of essayism, whatever their shortcomings and limitations, respect the distinction between zones of relevance; they maintain the human capacity to see significance by not seeing significance everywhere.

The discussions between Ulrich and Walter invite us to reflect on the fact that in sociology too, the study of everyday life has sometimes been seen as a kind of false utopianism that either celebrates it or simply wallows in it, but either way to the detriment of utopian possibilities. It is sometimes thought, for instance, that the work of Goffman is open to this charge; but it seems to me that the whole point of Goffman's work is not to find significance in life's every detail (we saw that that was a shortcoming of Freud) but rather to explore the work involved in the construction and maintenance of those significances that do sustain a world in common. One of the favours we do each other in everyday life is not noticing things as well as noticing them. To be sure, that work is being done most of the time, the 'little pieties' of interaction ensuring that the work goes smoothly. But just because of this there is no utopian ideal of everyday living. To put it in Marxian terms, Goffman and Schutz did not celebrate the realm of necessity, as Norbert Elias believed (Elias, 1998a), they simply showed how it works. Utopias by contrast – be they those of exactitude or those of essayism – point to the realm of freedom, a freedom that manifests itself not in the little pieties of day-to-day and face-to-face interaction, but in the activity of self-shaping.

The Other Condition

Ulrich is described throughout the novel as a man without qualities but also as a 'man of possibility', someone who began a series of careers – engineer, soldier, mathematician – without ever becoming something determinate, and who now, at the age of 32, has to face up to his future rather than let it happen. This lack of determinateness, of a defined career path, in one whose training and background seem to offer just that, goes a long way to explaining why the first two utopias are those of exactitude and essayism: Ulrich might have become a specialist lawyer, engineer, military man (exactitude), but has become none of these; now, he is also old enough to find the youthful idea of essayism and adventure something that has passed him by. The third possibility, living life as the history of ideas, is easily countered by Walter's claim that this would collapse the meaningful distinction between ideal and reality that all utopias require.

Now in the second half of the novel (if an unfinished novel can have a second half) Ulrich, following his father's death, meets his twin sister Agathe at the family home. He hasn't seen her in years, and is startled by the realization that they resemble one another; when Agathe enters the room Ulrich feels that it is he himself coming through the door. This sense of having a double is made more alarming by the fact that Agathe's face gives no clue to her character; the two of them are similar, then, but not because of any determinate features or because of an identifiable social position or even an explicit set of beliefs; Agathe is a 'woman without qualities' just as he is a man without qualities.

They embark on a series of conversations lasting for days on end, in which they discuss family roles and the distinction between individualism and collectivism (a debate, incidentally, that would later be conducted by philosophers of social science, for decades on end). To Ulrich, people's 'bond with others or the self's bruised recoil from that bond into the illusion of its uniqueness' (Musil, 1995: 778) are both natural impulses of individuals, and 'entangled with the idea of the family', in which nobody can live a full life; under the influence of this idea Agathe decides not to return to her dull husband. At the same time, while attracted by his understanding of morality, Agathe is frustrated by Ulrich, who, ever the trained scientist, is always quick to sum things up in formulas without turning his thoughts into action: 'In the short time we have been together, you have given me such wonderful guidelines for my life, but then you always end up wondering whether they are really true! It seems to me that the truth the way you use it is only a way of mistreating people!' (Musil, 1995: 864).

One is tempted to say here that the idea of providing guidelines for life but then wondering whether they are true is practically a definition of the sceptical sociological theorist's vocation. For Ulrich and Agathe, though, something more is involved; 'the other condition' is not a kind of mysticism or monasticism, since that would in the end involve the exchange of one kind of discipline – of the law, of mathematics or physics, of military strategy – for that of another. Ulrich – and here the echoes of Weber's 'Science as a Vocation' are palpable – sees science and science's opponents as part of the same problem, two sides of the same debased coin. Ulrich believes that 'even religious people are under the influence of the scientific way of thinking, that they do not trust themselves to look into what is burning in their inmost hearts but are always ready to speak of this ardour in medical terms as a mania, even though officially they take a different line' (Musil, 1995: 833–4). Conventional morality splits into intelligence and mysticism, into 'practical improvements and unknown adventure' (Musil, 1995: 837). There may be an alternative to this but it has deeper origins than religion; Ulrich reads religious books, but does so not because he is a religious person but because he is trying to understand the possibility of inner movement and divergence from the ordinary which is characteristic of mysticism. But the way he describes mysticism makes it clear that he does not see it as a solution.

> ... a man has two modes of existence, of consciousness, and of thought, and saves himself from being frightened to death by ghosts – which this prospect would of necessity induce – by regarding one condition as a vacation from the other, an interruption, a rest, or anything else he thinks he can recognize. Mysticism, on the other hand, would be connected with the intention of going on vacation permanently. (Musil, 1995: 827)

The solution, or rather the alternative way of living, 'the other condition', is not love, or a withdrawal from the world, or getting close to God, or returning to feelings in a world which has turned mechanical. It is rather a state of mind, a possibility that can be realised precisely without one being isolated from the outer world:

There is no need to be a saint to experience something of the kind! You could be sitting on a fallen tree or a bench in the mountains, watching a herd of grazing cows, and experience something amounting to being transported into another life! You lose yourself and at the same time suddenly find yourself. (Musil, 1995: 827)

Ulrich wants to believe that people can be both intelligent and mystical and that the existence of one should not exclude the other. Behind his search for the relationship between 'the other condition' and 'normal condition', there is his attempt to bring back the appropriate relationship between precision and soul, an attempt not simply to establish a balance between these two worlds – for that was a feature of the utopia of exactitude – but to experience both at the same time.

Ulrich's most explicit statement of what this means is the passage in which he compares the experience of reality in the other condition with being 'like the ocean':

... you must now imagine this ocean as a state of motionlessness and detachment, filled with everlasting, crystal-clear events. In ages past, people tried to imagine such a life on earth. That is the Millennium, formed in our own image and yet like no world we know. That is how we will live now! We shall cast off all self-seeking; we shall collect neither goods, nor knowledge, nor lovers, nor friends, nor principles, nor even ourselves! Our spirit will open up, dissolving boundaries toward man and beast, spreading open in such a way that we can no longer remain 'us' but will maintain our identities only by merging with all the world! (Musil, 1995: 871)

Ulrich is not sure whether or not it is possible to live in such a world without being isolated from everyday life. Still, when Agathe and Ulrich return to Vienna they try to live 'the other condition' together, on the basis that it can only be realised if their relationship has no determinate purpose or social function. It is this purposefulness without purpose that causes it to fail where, as Kant would have said, the art work might succeed.

At first Ulrich and Agathe are open to living 'in the *fire*' and 'at the threshold'. The problem is that once they settle down in Vienna their circumstances change, they are living in a city where they encounter other people, people who are all adults, all members of determinate social groups, with the associated 'qualities' and the limitations that go with them. As a result, talk of 'the other condition' gradually fades, and Ulrich returns to the scepticism with which he appears in the early parts of the novel. The project of dissolving the distinction between I and Thou within a 'pure relationship' founders against the normal condition that asserts itself in the metropolitan existence of modern Vienna, and by implication in every setting in which a determinate social life has to be carried on.

Conclusion

A special issue of the journal *History of the Human Sciences* from 2003 was entitled 'glimpses of utopia' (Levitas and Velody, 2003). In an age in which collectivist dreams of perfection seem to be a thing of the past and in which Musil's other condition would place demands on individuals for 'pure relationships' (Giddens, 1992) that are either unbearable or 'without purpose', the individual is thrown back on his or her own individual utopian capabilities, such as they are.

In the course of his or her studies today's student might glimpse all three of Musil's utopias: the utopia of exactitude contained in the thoughts of specialised professional advancement; the utopia of essayism in the thoughts of the perpetual unfinishedness and provisionality of social inquiry; but also the utopia of everyday life, not in any encouragement to live the history of ideas or experience everything as though listening to a song, but rather in the encouragement to tell their teachers how 'learning' was for them, what they learned from the process through which they learned how to learn, and to blog their way into the future. If they would read a bit more Marx and Durkheim and Weber, and Douglas and Simmel and Adorno, if they would read a bit more Goffman as well as a bit more Bauman, enjoying the former's metaphors while ignoring the latter's, they might be less inclined to see everyday life as utopian and to consider the first two possibilities. The responsibility of their teachers, especially their teachers of sociological theory, is not so much to point them towards one of these rather than the other, but to hint that such directions exist. Only then, when the student has eyes to see them, different eyes from the ones he or she had before, can these possibilities be glimpsed at all.

Conclusion

Anthony Giddens was once asked in an interview about his current reading; he replied that he and most of his colleagues had little time to read these days because they were too busy writing their own books. Now although calling something a false opposition is a cheap form of criticism, this does sound like one. Some of the figures discussed in this book do seem to have given up reading after the age of 35 and to have spent the rest of their careers writing, and writing too much; but many of them, and many of the best of them, were voracious readers as well as prodigious writers, so much so that, for all the light-hearted way in which I have read one or two of them, one cannot help being awe-struck by the sheer human effort that went into their work, by the bloody-mindedness with which they pursued what is, after all, a chimera: the truth about society.

At the end of a general overview that has consisted largely of readings of sociological theory, one hesitates to make any suggestions about how to write sociological theory. When I used the phrase 'theoretical liberalism' I meant to say that the approaches to inquiry discussed here seem too various and too arbitrarily constructed for any synthesis of them to be meaningful. I still take this to be true, yet at the same time the theorists discussed in this book seem too closely related to one another for us to talk of a fragmented discipline whose tattered remains lie strewn across Borges' deserts: 'Deserts are windy places' (Bauman, 1995: 88). No, whatever their differences they are all engaged in the same enterprise, the attempt to conceptualise the social, and seem beset by similar sorts of difficulty when they make that attempt; maybe in this respect there is a sociological sensibility after all, something that is there in the work of every theorist we have discussed here, there even when they run up rather sharply against the limits of what they can say or when they become lost in endless speech.

Either way, the lesson of their works if not of their lives is that without a striving for the impossible the possible would never happen. That is a defence of the idea of utopia, one worth making even if the utopias we now have available are only individual ones; it also a defence of sociological theory, both as something that a small and heroic band of people have written, and as something that a larger group is faced with the task of trying to understand. That larger group includes both students and their teachers. To them I say: keep reading.

Endnotes

1   The Freud scholar Philip Rieff argued that erudition as a scholarly style was a vice rooted in modern Protestantism. His fiercest criticism of it was directed not at Simmel but at Carl Gustav Jung – 'probably no note was left unused' – and then ... at Weber (Rieff, 1966: 126–8, 2008: 124).

2   The tree diagram I include here bears a superficial resemblance to the one Baldamus draws in order to makes sense of Parsons (Baldamus, 1976: 113). But Baldamus's is far more complicated and, for our purposes, unnecessarily so.

3   I should say here that, while I can understand the moral reasons for wanting to disagree with this, I do not see what is gained intellectually by repeatedly claiming that the validity of an analytical device is rendered worthless by the fact of its having specific cultural origins, be they European, or male, or white, or what is worse, all of them together (see Chapter 6). For the origin of the distinction between origin and validity see Bergner (1982).

4   For a failure to appreciate Goffman's use of metaphor, his sense of his own limits, and indeed his sociology as a whole, see Jameson (1976). Whereas for his admirers Goffman's greatest achievement is the fashioning of a battery of categories and metaphors that draw us towards the nuance and variety of social life, for Jameson he has drawn us towards its trivialities. There is something to be said for this line of argument, but in order to maintain a sense of large-scale significance Jameson's preferred tools of analysis are 'late capitalism', 'consumerism' and 'postmodernism', categories that, set against even Parsons' pattern variables, look rather cumbersome. On nuance see Collini (2004).

5   If this openness to modernism is indeed a distinctive feature of the sceptical style then it must be said that the sceptical style remains undeveloped in sociology but also in the social sciences more generally. For an attempt to employ, in a single account, multiple voices in relation to the same phenomenon, see Latour (1996). James Clifford wrote a famous critique of Clifford Geertz's attempt to establish the sovereign authority of his authorial voice, and flirted with the idea of a multi-voiced ethnography without developing it (see Clifford, 1988).

Bibliography

Adler, J. (2003) 'Im Zickzack', *Merkur* 57. Jahrgang, Heft 648 (April): 319–32.

Adorno, T.W. (1976a) 'Sociology and empirical research', in T.W. Adorno et al. (eds), *The Positivist Dispute in German Sociology*. London: Heinemann.

Adorno, T.W. (1976b) 'Einleitung', in E. Durkheim, *Soziologie und Philosophie*. Frankfurt: Suhrkamp.

Adorno, T.W. (1991a) *The Culture Industry: Selected Essays on Mass Culture*. London: Routledge.

Adorno, T.W. (1991b) 'The essay as form', in *Notes to Literature, Vol. I*. New York: Columbia University Press.

Adorno, T.W. (1998) 'Scientific experiences of a European scholar in America', in *Critical Models: Interventions and Catchwords*. New York: Columbia University Press.

Adorno, T.W. (2000) *Introduction to Sociology*. Cambridge: Polity.

Adorno, T.W. (2002) *The Stars Down to Earth and Other Essays on the Irrational in Culture*. London: Routledge.

Adorno, T.W. et al. (1950) *The Authoritarian Personality*. New York: Harper and Row.

Adorno, T.W. and Horkheimer, M. ([1947] 1973) *Dialectic of Enlightenment*. London: Allen Lane.

Alexander, J. (1987) *Twenty Lectures: Sociological Theory since 1945*. London: Hutchinson Education.

Alexander, J. (1989) 'Sociology and discourse', in *Structure and Meaning: Rethinking Classical Sociology*. New York: Columbia University Press.

Alexander, J. (1995) *Fin-de-Siecle Sociological Theory*. London: Verso.

Allen, N.J. (2000) *Categories and Classifications*. Oxford: Berghahn Books.

Althusser, L. (1969) *For Marx*. London: NLB.

Andreski, S. (1972) *Social Sciences as Sorcery*. London: Deutsch.

Archer, M.S. (1982) 'Morphogenesis versus structuration: on combining structure and action', *The British Journal of Sociology*, 33 (4): 455–83.

Arnheim, R. (1966) 'Perceptual analysis of a symbol of interaction', in *Towards a Psychology of Art*. London: Faber & Faber.

Aristotle (1941) 'Poetics', in R. McKeon (ed.), *The Basic Works of Aristotle*. New York: Random House.

Baehr, P. (2001) 'The "iron cage" and the "shell as hard as steel": Parsons, Weber, and the Stahlhartes Gehäuse metaphor in the Protestant ethic and the spirit of capitalism', *History and Theory*, 40 (2): 153–69.

Baehr, P. (2002) *Founders, Classics, Canons*. New Brunswick, NJ: Transaction Books.

Baehr, P. and O'Brien, M. (1994) 'Founders, classics and the concept of a canon', *Current Sociology*, 42 (1): 1–151.

Baker, N. (1989) *The Mezzanine*. London: Granta.

Baker, N. (1990) *Room Temperature*. London: Granta.

Baldamus, W. (1972) 'The role of discoveries in social science', in T. Shanin (ed.), *The Rules of the Game: Cross-disciplinary Essays on Models in Scholarly Thought*. London: Tavistock Publications.

Baldamus, W. (1976) *The Structure of Sociological Inference*. London: Martin Robertson.

Baldamus, W. (1992) 'Understanding Habermas's methods of reasoning', *History of the Human Sciences,* 5 (2): 97–115.

Baptista, L.C. (2003) 'Framing and cognition', in J. Treviso (ed.), *Goffman's Legacy.* Lanham: Rowman and Littlefield.

Barthes, R. (1981) *Camera Lucida.* London: Cape.

Bauman, Z. (1976) *Socialism: the Active Utopia.* London: Routledge & Kegan Paul.

Bauman, Z. (1978) *Hermeneutics and Social Science.* London: Hutchinson.

Bauman, Z. (1988) *Modernity and the Holocaust.* Cambridge: Polity.

Bauman, Z. (1993) *Postmodern Ethics.* Cambridge: Polity.

Bauman, Z. (1995) *Life in Fragments.* Cambridge: Polity.

Bauman, Z. (2000) *Liquid Modernity.* Cambridge: Polity.

Bauman, Z. (2003) *Liquid Love.* Cambridge: Polity.

Bauman, Z. (2007) *Consuming Life.* Cambridge: Polity.

Benjamin, W. (1983) *Charles Baudelaire.* London: Verso.

Berger, P. (1978) 'The problem of multiple realities: Alfred Schutz and Robert Musil', in T. Luckmann (ed.), *Phenomenology and Sociology.* Harmondsworth: Penguin.

Berger, P. and Luckmann, T. (1966) *The Social Construction of Reality.* Harmondsworth: Penguin.

Bergner, J. (1982) *The Origins of Formalism in Modern Social Science.* Chicago: University of Chicago Press.

Berlin, I. (1997) *The Proper Study of Mankind.* London: Chatto and Windus.

Bernhard, T. (1989) *Old Masters.* Chicago: University of Chicago Press.

Black, M. (1962) *Models and Metaphors: Studies in Language and Philosophy.* Ithaca: Cornell University Press.

Bloom, A. (1987) *The Closing of the American Mind.* New York: Simon and Schuster.

Bloom, H. (1973) *The Anxiety of Influence.* New York: Oxford University Press.

Bloom, H. (1995) *The Western Canon.* London: Papermac.

Blumenberg, H. (1982) *Lebenszeit und Weltzeit.* Frankfurt: Suhrkamp.

Blumenberg, H. (1985) *Work on Myth.* Cambridge, MA: MIT Press.

Blumenberg, H. (2001) *Aesthetische und Metaphorologische Schriften.* Frankfurt: Surkamp.

Borges, J.L. (1964a) 'Pierre Menard, Author of the Quixote', in *Labyrinths.* Harmondsworth: Penguin.

Borges, J.L. (1964b) 'Funes the Memorious', in *Labyrinths.* Harmondsworth: Penguin.

Borges, J.L. (1975) 'Of exactitude in science', in *A Universal History of Infamy.* Harmondsworth: Penguin.

Borges, J.L. and Bioy-Casares, A. (1982) 'An evening with Ramon Bonavena', in *Chronicles of Bustos Domecq.* London: Allen Lane.

Bourdieu, P. (1977) *Outline of a Theory of Practice.* Cambridge: Cambridge University Press.

Bourdieu, P. (1990) *Photography: a Middle-brow Art.* Cambridge: Polity.

Bourdieu, P. (1996) *The Rules of Art: Genesis and Structure of the Literary Field.* Cambridge: Polity.

Bourdieu, P. (1997) *The State Nobility.* Cambridge: Polity.

Brown, R.H. (1977) *A Poetic for Sociology: Toward a Logic of Discovery for the Human Sciences.* Cambridge: Cambridge University Press.

Brown, R.H. (1992) 'Social science and society as discourse', in S. Seidman and D. Wagner (eds), *Postmodernism and Social Theory.* Oxford: Blackwell.

Bryson, N. (1983) *Vision in Painting.* London: Macmillan.

Byrne, D. (1998) *Complexity Theory and the Social Sciences: An Introduction.* London: Routledge.

Calasso, R. (1994) *The Ruin of Kasch*. London: Carcanet.

Calvino, I. (2000) 'Why read the classics?', in *The Literature Machine*. London: Vintage.

Clifford, J. (1988) *The Predicament of Culture*. Cambridge, MA: Harvard University Press.

Collini, S. (2004) 'On variousness; and on persuasion', *New Left Review,* 27, May/June: 65–97.

Collins, R. (1994) *Four Sociological Traditions*. Oxford: Oxford University Press.

Craib, I. (1994) *Modern Social Theory*. Brighton: Wheatsheaf.

Dahrendorf, R. (1968) 'Out of utopia', in *Essays in the Theory of Society*. Stanford: Stanford University Press.

Dawe, A. (1978) 'Two theories of action', in T. Bottomore and R. Nisbet (eds), *A History of Sociological Analysis*. New York: Basic Books.

Derrida, J. (1994) *Spectres of Marx*. London: Routledge.

Derrida, J. ([1967] 1997) *Of Grammatology* (corrected edn). Baltimore: Johns Hopkins University Press.

Douglas, M. (1966) *Purity and Danger*. London: Routledge & Kegan Paul.

Douglas, M. (1975) 'In the nature of things', in *Implicit Meanings*. London: Routledge & Kegan Paul.

Douglas, M. (2003) *Natural Symbols: Explorations in Cosmology*. New York: Routledge.

Durkheim, E. ([1915] 1995) *The Elementary Forms of the Religious Life*. New York: Free Press.

Durkheim, E. (1984) *The Division of Labour in Society*. Basingstoke: Macmillan.

Durkheim, E. ([1897] 1952) *Suicide*. London: Routledge and Kegan Paul.

Durkheim, E. and Mauss, M. ([1903] 1967) *Primitive Classification*. Chicago: University of Chicago Press.

Elias, N. (1978) *What Is Sociology?* London: Hutchinson.

Elias, N. ([1939] 1982) *The Civilising Process*. Oxford: Blackwell.

Elias, N. (1998a) 'The concept of everyday life', in S. Mennell and J. Goudsblom (eds), *The Norbert Elias Reader*. Oxford: Blackwell.

Elias, N. (1998b) 'Game models', in S. Mennell and J. Goudsblom (eds), *Norbert Elias on Civilisation, Power and Knowledge*. Chicago: University of Chicago Press.

Eliot, G. (1994) *Middlemarch*. Harmondsworth: Penguin.

Elster, J. (1986) *Introduction to Karl Marx*. Cambridge: Cambridge University Press.

Engels, F. (1970) *Socialism: Utopian and Scientific*. Moscow: Progress Publisher.

Faulkner, W. (1946) *The Sound and the Fury & As I Lay Dying*. New York: Modern Library.

Feynman, R. (1990) *Q.E.D.: The Strange Theory of Light and Matter*. London: Penguin.

Foucault, M. (1970) *The Order of Things*. London: Tavistock.

Foucault, M. (1972) *The Archaeology of Knowledge*. London: Tavistock.

Foucault, M. (1983) *This Is Not A Pipe*. Berkeley: University of California Press.

Foucault, M. (1990) *The History of Sexuality, Vol. 2: The Use of Pleasure*. Harmondsworth: Penguin.

Foucault, M. (1991) 'On genealogy and ethics: an interview', in *The Foucault Reader*. Harmondsworth: Penguin.

Foucault, M. (1998) *Aesthetics, Method and Epistemology*. London: Allen Lane.

Foucault, M. (2000) *Power*. London: Allen Lane.

Freud, S. (2002) *Psychopathology of Everyday Life*. London: Penguin.

Galison, P. (1997) *Image and Logic*. Chicago: University of Chicago Press.

Garfinkel, H. (1967) *Studies in Ethnomethodology*. Englewood Cliffs, NJ: Prentice-Hall.

Geertz, C. (1973) *The Interpretation of Cultures*. New York: Basic Books.

Geertz, C. (1983) *Local Knowledge*. New York: Basic Books.

Gell, A. (2006) 'Strathernograms, or the Semiotics of Mixed Metaphors', in *The Art of Anthropology: Essays and Diagrams*. Oxford: Berg.

Gellner, E. (1973) 'Concepts and society', in B. Wilson (ed.), *Rationality*. Oxford: Blackwell.

Gellner, E. (1979) *Spectacles & Predicaments: Essays in Social Theory*. Cambridge: Cambridge University Press.

Gellner, E. (1983) *Nations and Nationalism*. Oxford: Blackwell.

Geuss, R. (2005) *Outside Ethics*. Princeton: Princeton University Press.

Giddens, A. (1984) *The Constitution of Society*. Cambridge: Polity Press.

Giddens, A. (1992) *The Transformation of Intimacy*. Cambridge: Polity.

Goffman, E. (1959) *The Presentation of Self in Everyday Life*. Harmondsworth: Penguin.

Goffman, E. (1961) *Encounters*. Indianapolis: Bobbs-Merrill.

Goffman, E. (1968) *Asylums*. Harmondsworth: Penguin.

Goffman, E. (1971) *Relations in Public*. Harmondsworth: Penguin.

Goffman, E. (1974) *Frame Analysis*. Harmondsworth: Penguin.

Goffman, E. (1981) *Forms of Talk*. Philadelphia: University of Pennsylvania Press.

Goldmann, L. (1981) *Method in the Sociology of Literature*. Oxford: Blackwell.

Goldthorpe, J.H., Lockwood, D., Bechhofer, F. and Platt, J. (1969) *The Affluent Worker in the Class Structure*. Cambridge: Cambridge University Press.

Gombrich, E. (1996) 'The visual image: its place in communication', in *The Essential Gombrich: Selected Writings on Art and Culture*. London: Phaidon.

Goodman, N. (1968) *Languages of Art*. Indianapolis: Bobbs-Merrill.

Goodman, N. (1978) *Ways of World Making*. Hassocks: Harvester.

Grossman, D. (2006) *Lion's Honey: the Myth of Samson*. Edinburgh: Canongate.

Gumbrecht, H.-U. (2006) 'Über Niklas Luhmanns intellektuelles Vermächtnis', *Merkur* 8.

Hadot, P. (1995) *Philosophy as a Way of Life*. Oxford: Blackwell.

Heilbron, J. (1995) *The Rise of Social Theory*. Cambridge: Polity.

Hennis, W. (2000) *Max Weber's Science of Man*. Newbury: Threshold.

Hobbes, T. (1991) *Leviathan*. Cambridge: Cambridge University Press.

Horkheimer, M. ([1938] 1995) 'Montaigne and the function of scepticism', in *Between Philosophy and Social Science: Selected Early Writings*. Cambridge, MA: MIT Press.

Jameson, F. (1976) 'On Goffman's *Frame Analysis*', *Theory and Society*, 3 (1): 119–33.

Jarvis, S. (1998) *Adorno: A Critical Introduction*. Cambridge: Polity.

Jung, C.G. ([1948] 1970) 'A psychological approach to the dogma of the trinity', in *Collected Works, Vol. 11*. London: Routledge & Kegan Paul.

Kant, I. ([1784] 1970) 'An answer to the question: What is enlightenment?', in H. Reiss (ed.), *Kant's Political Writings*. Cambridge: Cambridge University Press.

Klee, P. (1978) *Pedagogical Sketchbook*. London: Faber & Faber.

Kuhn, T. (1962) *The Structure of Scientific Revolutions*. Chicago: University of Chicago Press.

Kundera, M. (1995) *Testaments Betrayed*. London: Faber & Faber.

Kundera, M. (2007) *The Curtain*. London: Faber.

Lakatos, I. (1978) *Philosophical Papers I*. Cambridge: Cambridge University Press.

Laslett, P. and Runciman, W.G. (eds) (1962) *Philosophy, Politics and Society, 2nd series*. Oxford: Blackwell.

Latour, B. (1993) *We Have Never Been Modern*. London: Harvester Wheatsheaf.

Latour, B. (1996) *Aramis, or, The Love of Technology*, trans. Catherine Porter. Cambridge, MA: Harvard University Press.

Latour, B. (1998) 'How to be iconophilic in art, science and religion', in P. Galison and C.A. Jones (eds), *Picturing Science, Producing Art*. London: Routledge.

Latour, B. (2005) *Reassembling the Social: an Introduction to Actor-Network Theory*. Oxford: Oxford University Press.

Latour, B. and Weibel, P. (eds) (2005) *Making Things Public: Atmospheres of Democracy*. Cambridge, MA: MIT Press.

Lepenies, W. (1986) *Between Literature and Science: the Rise of Sociology*. Cambridge: Cambridge University Press.

Lepenies, W. (1992) *Melancholy and Society*. London: Harvard University Press.

Lévi-Strauss, C. (1972) *The Savage Mind*. London: Weidenfeld and Nicolson.

Levitas, R. and Velody, I. (eds) (2003) 'Glimpses of utopia', in *History of the Human Sciences*, 16 (1).

Lockwood, D. (1988) 'Social integration and system integration', in *Solidarity and Schism*. Oxford: Clarendon.

Luhmann, N. (1986) *Love as Passion*. Cambridge: Polity.

Lukes, S. (2004) *Power: a Radical View,* 2nd rev. edn. Palgrave: Macmillan.

Lynch, M. (1991) 'Pictures of nothing? Visual construals in social theory', *Sociological Theory,* 9 (1): 1–20.

Mann, M. (1984) 'The autonomous power of the state', *Archive Européens de Sociologie,* 25: 185–213.

Mannheim, K. (1936) *Ideology and Utopia*. London: Routledge & Kegan Paul.

Mannheim, K. (1982) *Structures of Thinking*. London: Routledge & Kegan Paul.

Manning, P. (1989) 'Ritual talk', *Sociology,* 23 (3): 365–85.

Manning, P. (2005) *Freud and American Sociology*. Cambridge: Polity.

Marquard, O. (1989) *Farewell to Matters of Principle*. Oxford: Oxford University Press.

Marshall, B.L. and Witz, A. (eds) (2004) *Engendering the Social: Feminist Encounters with Sociological Theory*. Buckingham: Open University Press.

Martins, H. (1972) 'The Kuhnian "revolution" and its implications for sociology', in T.J. Nossiter, A.H. Hanson and S. Rokkan (eds), *Imagination and Precision in the Social Sciences*. New York: Humanities Press.

Marx, K. (1975) 'Preface to a Contribution to a Critique of Political Economy', in *Early Writings*. Harmondsworth: Penguin.

Marx, K. (1978) 'The Eighteenth Brumaire of Louis Bonaparte', in R. Tucker (ed.), *The Marx-Engels Reader*. New York: Norton.

Mauss, M. (1985) 'The category of the person', in S. Collins, S. Lukes and M. Carrithers (eds), *The Category of the Person*. Cambridge: Cambridge University Press.

Mennell, S. (2006) 'Elias and the counter-ego: personal recollections', *History of the Human Sciences*, 19 (2): 73–91.

Merton, R.K. (1993) *On the Shoulders of Giants: A Shandean Postscript*. Chicago: University of Chicago Press.

Merton, R.K. (1996) 'The ethos of science', in P. Sztompka (ed.), *Robert Merton on Social Structure and Science*. Chicago: University of Chicago Press.

Milbank, J. (1990) *Theology and Social Theory: Beyond Secular Reason*. Oxford: Blackwell.

Milner, A. (1996) *Literature, Culture and Society*. London: Routledge.

Mills, C.W. (1960) *The Sociological Imagination*. Harmondsworth: Penguin.

Mills, C.W. (2000) *Letters and Autobiographical Writings*, ed. Kathryn Mills with Pamela Mills. Berkeley: University of California Press.

Mitchell, W.J.T. (1981) 'Diagrammatology', *Critical Inquiry,* 6: 622–33.

Montesquieu (1989) *The Spirit of the Laws.* Cambridge: Cambridge University Press.

Moore, B. (1977) *Social Origins of Dictatorship and Democracy.* Harmondsworth: Penguin.

Moore, W.E. (1963) *Social Change.* Englewood Cliffs, NJ: Prentice-Hall.

Mouzelis, N. (1995) *Sociological Theory: What Went Wrong?* London: Routledge.

Mouzelis, N. (2008) *Modern and Postmodern Social Theorising: Bridging the Divide.* Cambridge: Cambridge University Press.

Münch, R. (1988) *Understanding Modernity.* London: Routledge.

Musil, R. (1995) *The Man without Qualities.* London: Picador.

Needham, R. (1979) *Symbolic Classification.* Santa Monica: Goodyear Publishing.

Nehamas, A. (1998) *The Art of Living.* Berkeley: University of California Press.

Neurath, O. (1980) *International Picture Language.* Reading: University of Reading.

Nietzsche, F. (1976) 'On truth and lies in an extra-moral sense', in W. Kaufmann (ed.), *The Portable Nietzsche.* London: Penguin.

Nietzsche, F. (1994) *On the Genealogy of Morality.* Cambridge: Cambridge University Press.

Nisbet, R. (1967) *The Sociological Tradition.* London: Heinemann.

Nisbet, R. (1976) *Sociology as an Art Form.* London: Heinemann.

Oakeshott, M. (1991) 'Introduction to Leviathan', in *Rationalism and Politics and Other Essays.* Indianapolis: Liberty Press.

Oakeshott, M. (1996) *The Politics of Faith and the Politics of Scepticism.* London: Yale University Press.

Osborne, T. (1998) *Aspects of Enlightenment.* London: UCL Press.

Outhwaite, W. (2006) *The Future of Society.* Oxford: Blackwell.

Parsons, T. (1937) *The Structure of Social Action.* New York: Free Press.

Parsons, T. (1949) 'Propaganda and social control', in *Essays in Sociological Theory.* Glencoe: Free Press.

Parsons, T. (1951) *The Social System.* Glencoe: Free Press.

Parsons, T. (1960) 'Pattern variables revisited: a reply to Robert Dubin', *American Sociological Review,* 25 (4): 467–83.

Parsons, T. (1968) 'Systems theory', in *International Encyclopaedia of the Social Sciences.* New York: Macmillan and Free Press.

Parsons, T. (1969) *Politics and Social Structure.* New York: Free Press.

Parsons, T. and Smelser, N. (1958) *Economy and Society.* London: Routledge & Kegan Paul.

Peirce, C.S. (1958) *Collected Papers of Charles Sanders Peirce, Vol. IV.* Cambridge, MA: Harvard University Press.

Plessner, H. ([1953] 1978) 'With different eyes', in T. Luckmann (ed.) *Phenomenology and Sociology.* Harmondsworth: Penguin.

Poggi, G. (1972) *Images of Society: Essays on the Sociological Theories of Tocqueville, Marx, and Durkheim.* London: Oxford University Press.

Poggi, G. (1996) '*Lego quia inutile*: an alternative justification for the classics', in S.P. Turner (ed.), *Social Theory and Sociology.* Oxford: Blackwell.

Poggi, G. (2001) *Forms of Power.* Cambridge: Polity.

Rex, J. and Moore, R. (1967) *Race, Community and Conflict: a Study of Sparkbrook.* London: Oxford University Press.

Ricoeur, P. (1970) *Freud and Philosophy: An Essay on Interpretation.* New Haven: Yale University Press.

Ricoeur, P. (1977) *The Rule of Metaphor.* Toronto: University of Toronto Press.

Rieff, P. (1959) *Freud: the Mind of the Moralist.* Chicago: University of Chicago Press.

Rieff, P. (1966) *The Triumph of the Therapeutic*. Chicago: University of Chicago Press.

Rieff, P. (2008) *Charisma: the Gift of Grace and How It Has Been Taken from Us*. New York: Vintage.

Rorty, R. (1982) *Consequences of Pragmatism*. Brighton: Harvester.

Rorty, R. (1989) *Contingency, Irony and Solidarity*. Cambridge: Cambridge University Press.

Rose, G. (1981) *Hegel contra Sociology*. London: Athlone.

Rosenthal, M. (1982) 'The prototypical triangle of Paul Klee', *The Art Bulletin*, 64 (2): 299–310.

Runciman, W.G. (1983) *A Treatise of Social Theory, Vol. I*. Cambridge: Cambridge University Press.

Runciman, W.G. (1998) *The Social Animal*. London: HarperCollins.

Sacks, O. (1985) *The Man Who Mistook His Wife for a Hat*. London: Picador.

Said, E. (1991) *Musical Elaborations*. London: Vintage.

Schelsky, H. (1957) *Die skeptische Generation*. Dusseldorf: Diederichs.

Schutz, A. (1962) 'Common-sense and scientific interpretations of human action', in *Collected Papers, Vol. I: The Problem of Social Reality*. The Hague: Martinus Nijhoff.

Schutz, A. (1964) *Collected Papers, Vol. II: Studies in Social Theory*. The Hague: Martinus Nijhoff.

Scott, J. (1995) *Sociological Theory: Contemporary Debates*. London: Edward Elgar.

Shin, S.-J. (1994) *The Logical Status of Diagrams*. Cambridge: Cambridge University Press.

Shklar, J. (1969) *After Utopia*. Princeton: Princeton University Press.

Simmel, G. (1950) *The Sociology of Georg Simmel*, trans., ed., and with an introduction by Kurt H. Wolff. Glencoe: Free Press.

Simmel, G. (1959) *Essays on Sociology, Philosophy and Aesthetics*, ed. Kurt Wolff. New York: Harper and Row.

Simmel, G. (1968) *The Conflict of Modern Culture and other Essays*, ed. Peter Etzkorn. New York: Teachers College Press.

Simmel, G. (1971) *On Individuality and Social Forms: Selected Writings*. Chicago: University of Chicago Press.

Simmel, G. (1980) *The Philosophy of Money*. London: Routledge & Kegan Paul.

Simmel, G. (1984) *On Women, Sexuality and Love*. London: Yale University Press.

Simmel, G. (1997) 'The adventure', in D. Frisby and M. Featherstone (eds), *Simmel on Culture*. London: Sage.

Skocpol, T. (1979) *States and Social Revolutions*. Cambridge: Cambridge University Press.

Sloterdijk, P. (1987) *Critique of Cynical Reason*. London: Verso.

Sorokin, P. (1956) *Fads and Foibles in Modern Sociology*. Chicago: H. Regnery Co.

Starr, P. (1992) 'Social categories and claims in the liberal state', in M. Douglas and D. Hull (eds), *How Classification Works: Nelson Goodman among the Social Sciences*. Edinburgh: Edinburgh University Press.

Steiner, G. (1959) *Tolstoy and Dostoyevsky: Essays in Contrast*. London: Faber & Faber.

Stern, J.P. (1992) *Heart of Europe: Essays on Literature and Ideology*. Oxford: Blackwell.

Strong P.M. (1979) 'Sociological imperialism and the profession of medicine: a critical examination of the thesis of medical imperialism', *Social Science and Medicine, Part A. Medical Psychology and Medical Sociology*, 13: 199–215.

Tenbruck, F. (1959) 'Formal sociology', in K. Wolff (ed.), *Georg Simmel on Sociology and Philosophy*. New York: Harper and Row.

Tenbruck, F. (1975) 'Der Fortschritt der Wissenschaft als Trivialisierungsprozess' [Scientific Progress as a Process of Trivialization], in N. Stehr and R. König (eds), *Wissenschaftssoziologie*. Opladen: Westdeutscher Verlag. pp. 19–47.

Turner, C. (2003) 'Mannheim's utopia today', *History of the Human Sciences*, 16 (1): 27–47.

Turner, S.P. (1994) *Max Weber: The Lawyer as Social Thinker*. London: Routledge.

Unger, R.M. (1987) *Social Theory: Its Situation and Task*. Cambridge: Cambridge University Press.

Urry, J. (1999) *Sociology Beyond Societies*. London: Routledge.

Urry, J. (2003) *Global Complexity*. Cambridge: Polity

Van Gennep, A. ([1911] 1967) *The Semi-Scholars*. London: Routledge & Kegan Paul.

Velody, I. (1989) 'Socialism as a sociological problem', in P. Lassman (ed.), *Politics and Social Theory*. London: Routledge.

Wacquant, L. (2006) 'Pierre Bourdieu', in R. Stones (ed.), *Key Contemporary Thinkers*. London: Macmillan.

Wagner, P. (1991) 'Science of society lost: on the failure to establish sociology in Europe during the "classical" period', in P. Wagner, B. Wittrock and R. Whitley (eds), *Discourses on Society*. Dordrecht: Kluwer Academic.

Wagner, P. (1999) '"An entirely new object of consciousness, of volition, of thought": the coming into being and (almost) passing away of "society" as a scientific object', in L. Daston (ed.), *Biographies of Scientific Objects*. Chicago: University of Chicago Press.

Weber, M. (1949) 'Objectivity in social science and social policy', in *The Methodology of the Social Sciences*. New York: Free Press,

Weber, M. (1951) *The Religion of China*. New York: Free Press.

Weber, M. (1975) *Max Weber: A Biography*. New York: Wiley.

Weber, M. (1978) *Economy and Society*. Berkeley: University of California Press.

Weber, M. (1989) 'Science as a vocation', in P. Lassman and I. Velody (eds), with H. Martins, *Max Weber's 'Science as a Vocation'*. London: Unwin Hyman.

Weber, M. (1994) 'The profession and vocation of politics', in P. Lassman and R. Speirs (eds), *Political Writings*. Cambridge: Cambridge University Press.

Weber, M. (2002) *The Protestant Ethic and the 'Spirit' of Capitalism and Other Writings*. New York: Penguin Books.

Williams, Robin (1983) 'Sociological tropes: a tribute to Erving Goffman', *Theory, Culture & Society*, 2 (1): 99–102.

Williams, Rowan (2008) *Dostoyevsky: Language, Faith and Fiction*. Waco: Baylor University Press.

Wittgenstein, L. (1994) *Philosophical Investigations*, 3rd edn. Oxford: Blackwell.

Wolin, S. (2004) *Politics and Vision*, expanded edn. Princeton: Princeton University Press.

Yates, F. (1982) *Lull and Bruno*. London: Routledge and Kegan Paul.

Index

Weber, Max *cont.*
   ethical/utopian perspective
      comparison with other theorists 167, 169,
         170, 171, 180–1, 183, 186, 188–9, 190
      vocation and art of living 176–9
   formal and substantive theorising 30, 31, 32, 34–5
   as classical theorist 14–15, 18, 20, 23
   metaphor in 80, 84, 87, 105
   on religion 45, 76–7, 146, 176–7
   and Simmel 43, 45

Wittgenstein, Ludwig, 27, 74–5, 87–8, 138
Wolin, Sheldon 12–13, 18
words and images 84–5

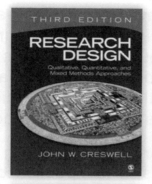

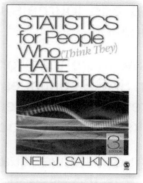

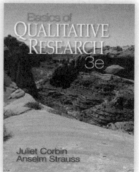